THUMPER

Thumper

The Memoirs of the Honourable
Donald S. Macdonald

DONALD S. MACDONALD
with Rod McQueen

McGill-Queen's University Press
Montreal & Kingston · London · Ithaca

© McGill-Queen's University Press 2014

ISBN 978-0-7735-4469-7 (cloth)
ISBN 978-0-7735-8180-7 (ePDF)
ISBN 978-0-7735-8181-4 (ePUB)

Legal deposit third quarter 2014
Bibliothèque nationale du Québec

Printed in Canada on acid-free paper that is 100% ancient forest free
(100% post-consumer recycled), processed chlorine free

McGill-Queen's University Press acknowledges the support of the Canada
Council for the Arts for our publishing program. We also acknowledge the
financial support of the Government of Canada through the Canada Book
Fund for our publishing activities.

Library and Archives Canada Cataloguing in Publication

Macdonald, Donald S., 1932–, author
    Thumper: the memoirs of the Honourable Donald S. Macdonald /
Donald S. Macdonald; with Rod McQueen.

    Includes bibliographical references and index.
    Issued in print and electronic formats.
    ISBN 978-0-7735-4469-7 (bound). – ISBN 978-0-7735-8180-7 (ePDF). –
ISBN 978-0-7735-8181-4 (ePUB)

    1. Macdonald, Donald S., 1932–. 2. Canada – Politics and government –
1963–1984. 3. Cabinet ministers – Canada – Biography. 4. Politicians –
Canada – Biography. I. McQueen, Rod, 1944–, author II. Title.

FC626.M318A3 2014   971.064'4092   C2014-902918-7
                                                  C2014-902919-5

This book was typeset by Interscript in 11/14 Minion.

For my wife Adrian, always

Contents

Foreword ix

Illustrations follow pages 36 and 136

1 Ancestral Voices 3

2 Setting My Compass 12

3 Band of Brothers 20

4 The Suez and Other Crises 29

5 The Accidental Candidate 53

6 MP for Rosedale 62

7 Pierre and Me 72

8 Tomorrow's Man 82

9 Inside the Cabinet Room 92

10 Herding Cats 105

11 The October Crisis 114

12 Blue-Eyed Sheiks 125

13 Zap, You're Frozen 153

14 Meetings of the Minds 164

15 Heir Rampant 175

16 Private Life, Public Duty   184

17 Leap of Faith   195

18 *Coup de foudre*   205

19 Maggie and the Royals   214

20 Plugged In   223

21 Reflections on a Life   233

Acknowledgments   243

Notes   245

Bibliography   253

Index   257

Foreword

At a certain point in our lives, we are left only with our close relationships and our clear recollections. Any time I want, I can reach into my satchel of memories and pull out an occasion such as the time in 2000 when I met Pierre Elliott Trudeau for lunch in Montreal. As we headed for his favourite spot, I noticed that he was walking with a slight limp. "Oh," he said, with a dismissive wave, "I fell skiing a couple weeks ago at Mont Tremblant." I was not surprised that, at eighty, he was still as physically active as ever.

Lunch was at La Maison du Egg Roll, a Chinese restaurant with a budget buffet, on Rue Notre-Dame near a Dollarama store. The conversation ranged all the way from our time together in 1966 as observers at the United Nations to the recent deaths of friends and colleagues. He must have known that his own demise from prostate cancer was coming ever closer, but he did not mention his condition.

Pierre did, however, have a bone to pick with me about the Royal Commission on the Economic Union and Development Prospects for Canada that he'd asked me to chair in 1982. "I never agreed with your proposal for free trade with the US," he said. "I don't think we should get close to that bunch. We should maintain our distance so as not to be overwhelmed by them."

It was a quiet, but firm, statement that he had not previously shared with me, although I think I knew his views all along. I just nodded. That lunch, alas, was the last time I saw Pierre. Later that same year, he died. His comment about free trade was the perfect finale for our friendship of thirty-five years. Without any rancour, we agreed to disagree about a crucial matter of public policy, just as we had done so many times before.

For all my closeness to Pierre he was always a set of contradictions wrapped in a conundrum. He was a social activist who became a Liberal, a single-combat warrior who grew into a charismatic national leader, and a citizen of the world who worried about getting too close to other countries. He gave us the Canadian Charter of Rights and Freedoms and took away our civil liberties under the War Measures Act. He sought a seat in Parliament, yet said MPs were nobodies fifty yards from the Hill. He was an iconoclast who forced Canadians into a better future whether they wanted to go there or not.

My wife Adrian and I joined hundreds of others at the state funeral for Pierre held in October 2000 at Notre-Dame Basilica in Montreal. His son, Justin, gave an emotional eulogy that, in retrospect, was the launch pad to his leadership of the Liberal Party. Mourners lined the railway tracks to glimpse the train carrying Pierre's remains from Ottawa to Montreal. Thousands more paid their respects as he lay in state in the Hall of Honour on Parliament Hill. Millions across the country and around the world paused and praised his life, each in their own way. He changed us forever. I miss him still. This memoir is as much about the Canada that we helped create together as it is about me.

THUMPER

1

Ancestral Voices

Wars and other international crises have dominated my life since I was a boy. On September 1, 1939, my mother, my sister Janet, and I were preparing to leave Winnipeg after our annual summer vacation with my maternal grandparents. My mother's brothers, Lloyd and Harry, had come to say their goodbyes. The occasion was made sombre by the news that the German blitzkrieg had rolled into Poland. As we all sat in my grandparents' living room, listening to reports on the radio, even as a seven-year-old I understood that the world had just changed for the worse.

We spent the next two nights and a day on the train cut off from any further bulletins. When we arrived at Ottawa's Union Station, we met my father on the platform. Normally, such a family reunion would have been joyous, but he looked grim and preoccupied. My mother's first words to him were, "It's happened, hasn't it?" He just nodded. Britain and France had declared war on Germany. The ride home was quiet; we told no happy tales of our time away. Parliament had been recalled. A week later, Canada joined the war.

The drumbeat of the coming conflict had been audible for some time, even within our own four walls. We listened to Adolf Hitler's tirades on the radio accompanied by simultaneous translations of his menacing message. The war now dominated all broadcasts and every adult conversation. My father, who had flown a bomber and was held prisoner during the First World War, tried to enlist but was turned down because he was nearly fifty. He would spread maps on the dining-room table daily so he could follow the drama of events.

My parents' best friends, Kate and Jim Smart, had a son named Angus, who was ten years older than I. Gus was fascinated by aviation, grew up making model planes, and enlisted in the Royal Canadian Air Force as soon as his age allowed. I saw Gus and his cousin, Paul Howard, resplendent in their handsome uniforms at a family Christmas party in 1941. By the next Christmas, both were dead, killed in action with Bomber Command over Germany. For the first time in my young life, the horrors of war were suddenly very real. I still have one of Gus's planes. Every once in a while, I hold it and think about the hands that made it.

Among the millions of Macdonalds in the world, there must be many thousands of Donald Macdonalds, but likely only one Donald Stovel Macdonald. Stovel was my mother's maiden name, and not a very common name at that. My Macdonald ancestors came from Eigg, a volcanic island off the west coast of Scotland. Eigg (pronounced Eck) is part of the Inner Hebrides that includes five other islands – Canna, Rhum, Muck, Coll, and Tiree – all lying south of the Isle of Skye.

Only the strong survived on Eigg. One of the sites tourists visit today is MacDonalds' Cave, about half a mile from the pier where the ferry berths. In 1577, four hundred members of the MacDonald clan hid in that cave from the marauding MacLeods of Skye. The MacLeods built brushwood fires at the mouth of the cave and suffocated every one of their captives.

After the Jacobite Rising of 1745 came the Highland Clearances, when the landowners drove the tenant farmers away so they could raise sheep on the land. Some on Eigg moved to the Caribbean or the United States, others to Canada. Ships would leave Pictou, Nova Scotia, loaded with white pine logs, bound for Liverpool. Empty vessels would then ply the Scottish coast picking up emigrants for the return trip and a new life in Canada. Family lore says that my forbears took one of those ships to Pictou around 1793. They settled in nearby Arisaig, on the Northumberland Strait, where on a clear day you can see both Prince Edward Island and Cape Breton. We've been looking at far horizons ever since.

My maternal great-great-grandfather carried dispatches for the Duke of Wellington at Waterloo in 1815. Some of my mother's ancestors were printers who hailed from Farnham in Surrey, southwest of London.

One of them started a weekly newspaper in Mount Forest, Ontario, called *The Confederate*, the only paper in the country named after Confederation, so my nationalism has deep taproots.

My father's people were sea captains who sailed the world wherever the cargo took them. My father, Donald Angus Macdonald, was born in 1891 off the coast of Africa aboard a square-rigger bound for the Philippines. Even as a boy, I did not lack for a world view.

My father graduated from the University of New Brunswick, joined the Dominion Forest Service, and then signed up to fight in the First World War. His initial contribution was to supervise the felling of trees on great estates in England for use in building whatever was required to win. But he chafed at the bit, wanting to make a more substantial contribution, so was seconded to the Royal Flying Corps and won his wings with the 99th Squadron.

Assigned to the Royal Air Force in May 1918, he and fellow lieutenant and gunner F.H. Blaxhill flew a DH9 day bomber, a biplane that seated a pilot and rear-facing gunner in separate, open cockpits. These new-design DH9s turned out to be poor performers. They couldn't fly as high as earlier versions so were easy prey for enemy fighters.

On May 27, 1918, Father's plane was shot down during a bombing mission behind enemy lines. A few words from his notebook offer a graphic description: "Left ground at 10 a.m. for raid on Bensdorf. Met 5 Huns. Only 4 in our formation and I was out of luck and out of position. Got out of formation after dropping bombs and had my tail-plane shot off on left side. Loop & spin. Three Huns bit the dust. Landed 1 mile from lines. Oh! What a feeling. For duration now."

Other members of his squadron saw his plane plummet toward earth and presumed the worst. Accounts of Father's demise appeared in the Saint John papers.[1] A few weeks later, a telegram arrived saying that, in fact, he had landed the disabled aircraft safely and was alive. Father spent six months in a prisoner-of-war camp on Rügen, an island in the Baltic Sea near Stralsund, Germany. After the war was over, he met up with some of his comrades in London. They collected their back pay, rented rooms at the Savoy, partied until their money ran out, and then returned home.

I was born on March 1, 1932. My earliest memory is of my father taking me to the barbershop for the first time when I was three years old to have my long curls cut off so I'd be a regular fella. My mother cried when I got home. Now that I'm in my eighties, I'd like to have those curls back.

My father was Dominion Forester in the federal government, a wonderful title for a wonderful man. Because of his secure civil service job, our family didn't suffer during the Great Depression. There was family money, too. Annually, my wealthy maternal grandfather, Chester Stovel, would send train tickets for my mother, Janet, and me to visit Winnipeg for the summer. Father would stay behind to help his minister when Parliament reviewed departmental estimates.

I attended Ottawa Normal Model School on Lisgar Street. In grade two, my classroom overlooked Cartier Square where recent recruits drilled. I'd regularly pretend my pencil broke so I could use the sharpener on the window ledge and watch the troops. At the end of the day, my pencil would be but a stub. The Second World War meant that Canada would never be the same again. Like a steam engine picking up speed, the country began from a standing start to build an army, navy, and air force that eventually encompassed one-tenth of the entire population. In addition, Canada created a manufacturing base for guns, aircraft, ammunition, as well as all the other goods a modern nation needs.

What had been a small, comfortable community began to burst with new arrivals and temporary quarters. Cartier Square was transformed by a series of hastily erected structures that became the headquarters of the Department of National Defence. When I served as minister of national defence from 1970–72, my departmental office was in one of those "temporary" buildings erected thirty years earlier. Someone else sharpened my pencils.

The welter of people coming to Ottawa during the Second World War caused crowding in the public schools. My parents concluded that our education was suffering as a result. They sent my sister Janet to Gloucester Street Convent and me to Ashbury College, the boys' school in Rockcliffe Park. Our separation was regrettable from one particular standpoint. When we attended the same school, I could always count on Janet coming to my rescue if she saw me getting pummelled in the playground. Now, I was on my own.

As a new boy in September 1941, my knowledge of math was abysmal. The teacher asked two of us to add up a column of figures aloud. I'd never done that before, so I fell silent while the other boy rattled off the right answer. My math improved slowly but was never very good, an unfortunate background for a future minister of finance. I had many excellent teachers, including Elsie Hunter for English and Latin, Leonard Sibley for chemistry and physics, and Richard "Tuscar" Wright, who introduced us to American writers such as Damon Runyon, Ernest Hemingway, and Ring Lardner. I distinctly remember him reading to us portions of a piece by John Hersey in the *New Yorker* about the devastating results of dropping the atomic bomb on Hiroshima. In a school where conformity was prized, Tuscar was a significant influence that helped us to begin thinking as individuals.

Ashbury was a tyrannical culture run by the gowned masters, many of whom had nicknames given by the boys. The assistant headmaster, Arthur Donovan Brain, who taught languages and was the disciplinarian, was known as Buggy. At Ashbury, as with most private schools, the cane was an ever-present deterrent. The mere thought of it was enough for me and I was never caned – or maybe I just never got caught.

Before Ashbury, school had been a short walk. Now my destination was more than three miles away. I caught the bus on Elgin Street to Confederation Square – dominated by the Château Laurier hotel and the National War Memorial just completed in 1939 – then rode the Lindenlea streetcar to Rockcliffe. The entire trip could take an hour. During the first week of school, I lost my ticket home. Rather than throw myself on the mercy of the streetcar conductor, or tell someone at Ashbury, I walked all the way. My new school shoes, not yet broken in, pinched so badly that my feet bled.

In winter, there were other rigours. Winnipeggers can talk all they like about the frigid temperatures at Portage and Main, and I've been in the Arctic several times in the years since, but the coldest place in the world is waiting for a streetcar in Confederation Square on a January morning with the winds howling across the Ottawa River from the Gatineau Hills.

After the war, we moved from 68 MacLaren Street in Centretown to 114 Acacia Avenue in Rockcliffe, later called 154 Acacia when the street was renumbered for new construction. This house was contemporary in style, and the rooms were slightly smaller than at the MacLaren location. More importantly for me, Ashbury was mere minutes away on foot.

Rockcliffe attracted interesting denizens and offered fertile soil for the future. Blair Fraser, Ottawa editor of *Maclean's*, lived next door. Down the street was Gratton O'Leary, editor of the *Ottawa Journal*. Half a dozen doors away were John Rae, now a senior executive at Power Corp., and his brother Bob, a future NDP premier of Ontario and interim Liberal leader federally. Across the street was another pair of brothers, Ian and David Scott. Ian became attorney general in the Ontario government of David Peterson; David is a leading Ottawa lawyer. At the end of Acacia lived my best friend, Robin MacNeil, known as Robert when he was co-anchor on the PBS show, *The MacNeil/Lehrer NewsHour*.

Even then, Robin had the debonair manner and dramatic skills that would define his later life. He wrote deft articles for the Ashbury school paper and played the lead in Noel Coward's *Hay Fever*, complete with an ascot at his neck and girls on his arm from Elmwood, our sister school in Rockcliffe. We both read G.A. Henty's historical adventures about courage and leadership in the British Empire, whether it was Clive in India or Wolfe in Canada.

We also devoured the *Swallows and Amazons* series written by British author Arthur Ransome. So beguiled were we that we invented our own special language, one that no one else understood, based on phrases and quotations from the twelve books in the series. Ransome's works featured children living in the Lake District and the Norfolk Broads who, among other outdoor adventures, sailed. We knew nothing about sailing, but one summer Robin and I built a rowboat in my backyard. We found lumber in a nearby construction site and made good progress until we got to the bow. How to bring things to a point?

My father solved our dilemma. The workshop at the Forestry Branch created a prow for our endeavour. We attached the prow, caulked all seams, hauled the finished craft several city blocks in a wagon, and then slid it down a wooded slope to McKay Lake. This pond-sized body of water stood in for Windermere while we punted about and imagined ourselves as plundering pirates in the fictive world of Arthur Ransome.

The student body at Ashbury included fifty boys from Abinger Hill, a preparatory school in England. They'd been sent to Ashbury as boarders in 1940 – complete with headmaster Jim Harrison, teachers, and matrons – to escape the war. Despite the fact that their world was in disarray when they left England, they believed they'd been sent to the middle of nowhere and were living with a bunch of lesser lights. They bullied us as mere colonials and made us feel inferior.

For a while, I endured this without complaint, but eventually learned to stand up for myself. It helped that I just kept growing, until at sixteen I reached my full adult height of 6 feet 5 inches. My unusual size did not, however, produce athletic prowess. I was awkward and, at 150 pounds, did not have the build for football. There were basketball hoops but no one used them.

I played some hockey and soccer, and marched with the cadet corps.[2] However, where I excelled was cricket. A retired R C M P officer taught a group of us the game. We played on the cricket pitch at Government House, then at the local club, and later in the Ottawa League. With my long arms and tall frame, I became a good medium-pace bowler with a deceptive spin.[3]

Alastair Gillespie, who succeeded me as minister of energy, organized one of the last games I bowled when I was in my forties. His son, Ian, was captain of the cricket team at Upper Canada College in Toronto. He and Alastair each put together teams for a match. As bowler, my first ball had such force that it split the centre stump. I still have that stump.

In addition to sports and classes at Ashbury, there were field trips to the great places of Ottawa. In the Parliament Buildings, I was awestruck by the broad hallways, the portraits of prime ministers, and the library with its vaulted ceilings and carved white pine panelling. Then came the sancta sanctorum as we were ushered into the House of Commons visitors' gallery. A guard told us we could return whenever we wanted, and I did, maybe half a dozen times during the next few months. I was fascinated by the ability of the M P s to speak eloquently, think on their feet, and fence with opponents across the floor.

Famous people and politics were part of my everyday life. My father's brother, Hugh – whom everyone called Sam – went to sea at fourteen, was in the British merchant service until the 1930s, then returned to Canada as chief engineer on the Canadian Pacific Railway ferry, ss *Princess Helene*, traversing the Bay of Fundy between Saint John, New Brunswick, and Digby, Nova Scotia. As a teenager, I visited Uncle Sam and saw photos of him with Prime Minister Louis St Laurent and other famous folk. When I asked how Sam came to be in such important company, my father said, "You have to bear in mind that it wasn't easy to get a drink in those days. All the big shots knew, if you were on that ship, that the chief engineer had a cache. They'd all go to Sam's quarters for a drink."

In Ottawa, I'd see Prime Minister Mackenzie King on the streets. When my father took me for lunch in the basement cafeteria of the Château Laurier hotel, he'd point out Jack Pickersgill in the company of half a dozen civil servants from Finance, the Bank of Canada, and other government agencies and departments. Pickersgill started out in External Affairs; became an assistant to King; served his successor, Louis St Laurent; and would become a Cabinet minister in the Pearson government. So powerful was he that the watchword in Ottawa was, "Clear it with Jack." Years later, I told Pickersgill that I used to see him at the Château. "We met there all the time," he said. "There'd be different guys doing trade-offs. We probably did more business there than in the House of Commons."

I was only nine when I saw Winston Churchill. He'd come to deliver a speech in the House of Commons on December 30, 1941. I went to Parliament Hill and joined the throngs standing near the Senate door. That speech, the first ever broadcast from Parliament, became one of the British prime minister's most famous orations of the Second World War. He told his audience that after France fell and Britain declared it would fight alone against Germany, the French generals predicted, "In three weeks England will have her neck wrung like a chicken." Churchill was not only a gifted writer, but also possessed superb timing. He paused and said, "Some chicken!" After the laughter died down, he added, "Some neck!"

Prime Minister Mackenzie King had arranged for Churchill to have a sitting with photographer Yousuf Karsh. Karsh plucked the ever-present cigar from Churchill's lips and captured forever the resulting scowl on the British bulldog that remains the best-known portrait of the wartime leader. Between that image and the oft-quoted speech, that historic visit took on such a lustre for me that I have come to believe I actually saw Churchill being bundled from his car into the Centre Block.

In truth, I cannot be sure. The moment was brief, and as one of the few young people present, I was too short to have a good view amid the jostling crowd. But I look back and think, there I was, aged only nine, going on my own to Parliament Hill in the hopes of catching a glimpse of the great statesman. Even then, I was drawn to the political arena and the people in it.

I was lucky to have lived in the nation's capital. Public policy and political life were the warp and woof of my young world. I was also part of a fortunate generation. By one of those accidents of fate, I grew up in a community undergoing a sea change greater than most other cities in Canada. I was too young to fight, but by 1945, we had not only helped the world win freedom twice but also taken a seat at the global table. Canada was an active participant in drafting the United Nations Charter in San Francisco and in reconstructing the post-war world. Infused by that independence, and influenced by those new directions, I was happily swept along by great events.

2

Setting My Compass

My mother's name was Marjorie, but everybody called her Mar. She was tall and thin and had a high, patrician forehead. She attended Brandon College and met my father after the First World War when he resumed his role with the Dominion Forest Service. He was sent to Riding Mountain National Park, north of Brandon, Manitoba, to conduct air photography and fire protection work. They were married in 1925 at the Stovel family mansion at 6 Ruskin Row in the elegant Winnipeg neighbourhood of Crescentwood. In 1928, my father was promoted to the departmental offices in Ottawa as a fire protection specialist.

Like most mothers of that era, she didn't work outside the home, so had all the time in the world for Janet and me. She was a sport in every sense of the word and loved to bet. If she and my father were discussing something heatedly, and she was sure she was right, she'd say, "I'll bet you two dollars."

During our summer holidays in Winnipeg, mother would bet for real when she took us to the thoroughbred races. I learned how to handicap the horses so a wager stood the best chance of paying off. As the wife of a senior public servant, mother would never go to the races at home. But in Manitoba, far from prying eyes and wagging tongues, there was freedom to enjoy such pursuits. In Ottawa, she played mahjong for pennies, but only with close friends in the privacy of her home where the gossips couldn't gape.

Every week, Mother put on her Sunday best and off we'd go to First Baptist Church, at the corner of Elgin and Laurier. My father, a lapsed

Catholic, would attend twice a year: Mother's Day and Christmas. One of the coming-of-age moments in the life of a young Baptist occurs at twelve when you undergo a full-immersion baptism. I was in swim trunks, and the minister, George Robert Quiggan, wore waders. We stood together in the waist-deep water of the large font that hung on a wall at the front of the church and was accessed by a hidden stair-well. He lowered me ceremoniously backward until I was fully sub-merged. I soon realized he lacked the strength to raise me up again. Assuming the dunking would only last a few seconds, I had taken just a shallow breath. I thought I was going to drown. I grabbed the side of the font and scissor-kicked my legs in a convulsive manner, nearly knocking the minister off his feet as I came up for air. Water splashed everywhere, but like Lazarus, I was alive. My mother was not amused. "What happened?" she asked later, and was not pleased with my explanation.

The congregation at First Baptist included such prominent fig-ures in the King government as James Lorimer Ilsley, the minister of finance, and James Layton Ralston, minister of national defence. I would turn and gawk at them until Mother gave me a sharp nudge and a stern look. At Sunday school, we weren't just told Bible stories by do-gooders using cut-out figures on felt boards. Church members, who were esteemed in their fields, would guide us.

Roy Kellock, just appointed in 1944 to the Supreme Court of Canada, read passages from the Bible with all the drama of the litigation lawyer he'd previously been. That done, he'd turn to the issues of the day. In 1946, Kellock co-chaired the Royal Commission on espionage in Canada that investigated allegations by Igor Gouzenko, a clerk at the Soviet Embassy in Ottawa. Gouzenko defected and claimed that a spy ring of Canadians was feeding secrets to the Soviet Union. To conceal his identity whenever he testified, Gouzenko wore a hood over his head with three holes cut into it: two for his eyes, one for his mouth.

We also heard from John Read, the only Canadian ever named to serve on the International Court of Justice at The Hague. His talks about public international law brought that topic alive for me. I wanted to be a lawyer just like him. Many people helped me along life's path, but it was John Read who opened the door to my future by talking about the law in such a gripping way.

As if seeing Parliament up close and learning about the law weren't enough to propel me forward, I had the best possible role model close at hand: my father. He wore glasses and had a way of looking over the top of them as if he was curious about everything in the world around him, and indeed he was. While most of my friends had no idea what their fathers did, I was fully informed. My parents regularly talked at dinner about his work and the news of the day. I also knew that he held strong views and was not afraid to fight for them.

For example, the Petawawa Forest Experiment Station one hundred miles north of Ottawa, was created in 1918 to conduct forest research. Father's Forestry Branch looked after the trees in the Station (white and red pine, white birch, trembling aspen, and red oak), worked with the pulp and paper industry to improve logging, and conducted research into meteorology, fire management, and silviculture.

Cheek by jowl with the Station (now the Petawawa National Forestry Institute) was the Petawawa Military Reserve (now CFB Petawawa). During the Second World War, the military sought to extend their artillery practice range, which would result in live shells falling into the forest. Father was irate that trees would be damaged unnecessarily. He expressed his disapproval all the way up to the minister of national defence, who scuttled the plan.

I not only knew what he did and how he felt but also accompanied my father into the field. One weekend, to get where he wanted to go, we had to drive through a part of the Petawawa Forest Experiment Station that had been converted into a camp for wartime internees from across Ontario. There were several hundred Germans and Italians, each with a red circle painted on the back of his jumpsuit for easy identification. Never in my young life had I been so frightened and so alert to my surroundings. I don't know how big the camp was, but in my recollection, it took a long time to pass all the grim-faced men. After running that gauntlet, we exited through another gate and plunged into the woods. Relief surged through my body. My pounding heart took a long time to settle.

On another occasion, we drove to a place on the Quebec side of the Ottawa River known as Rapides-des-Joachim. We walked onto an old iron bridge, stopped halfway across, and my father told me that the government planned a power dam to supply electricity for a secret project about which even he was in the dark. Because the dam would flood the surrounding lands, he'd been asked to report on property that ·would have to be expropriated so compensation could be arranged. Only at the end of the war was the nature of the development revealed as the Chalk River Laboratories. By 1945, Canada's first nuclear reactor – and the first in the world outside the US – was operating on that site later occupied by Atomic Energy of Canada.

But if my father showed me his world and who I could be, it was my mother who taught me how to behave. When my father scolded me, the most devastating declaration he could make was, "I don't think your mother would like that." Her rules were simple and straightforward: work hard, be upstanding, don't cause a public ruckus, and treat people with respect. In my memory, neither of them ever seemed to grow old or get grey hair. They weren't afraid to show their love for each other in front of us kids, with hugs and kisses that were far from just perfunctory greetings.

At Ashbury, I went on few dates. Tea dances with Elmwood were heavily chaperoned. Parents attended parties at friends' houses. It was all pretty innocent. For me, getting through school was more important than going out with a girl. In fact, my most memorable nights out were with my father. I was ten or eleven, and I hadn't completed my homework, but he made an exception. Off we went on a weeknight to the Mayfair Theatre to see *The Young Mr Pitt*, a film about William Pitt the Younger, who at twenty-four was the youngest-ever prime minister of Great Britain. Robert Donat played Pitt who was up against Napoleon, played by Herbert Lom, a clear parallel with Adolf Hitler. The movie was one of many propaganda efforts churned out during the war to uplift British citizens under siege by reminding them that they had enjoyed great days in the past and would do so again. I loved the movie so much that when I got a black spaniel I called him Mr Pitt.

In 1943, when Allied victories in Europe began to change the direction of the war, it was decided that the Abinger Hill boys at Ashbury would go home in June 1944. In preparation, the pace of their studies was accelerated so they would be ready to write the entrance exams to attend one of the better schools such as Winchester, Rugby, or Marlborough. About half a dozen Canadian students, including me, proceeded at the same quickened pace. As a result, I skipped grade eleven and did five years of high school in four. I'd also skipped grade four so when I finished grade thirteen in 1948 I was only sixteen.

When my final exam marks arrived by mail that August, I'd done well on everything but trigonometry, which I failed, even with the help of a tutor. Father wanted me to go back and improve my standing in that one subject, even though I'd passed enough courses to go on to university. The phone rang and my father answered. I heard him say, "Well, you better talk to Donald about that." As he handed me the phone, he whispered that the caller was Arthur Brain. As assistant headmaster at Ashbury, Buggy was in charge of organizing classes and assumed, because of my trig results, that I would be returning. He pointed out that I hadn't yet registered and would I kindly do so. I made up my mind on the spot. I'd had more than enough of Ashbury. "Thank you very much, Mr Brain, but I've decided to go to Carleton instead." There I could pursue the pleasures of English, French, history, philosophy, and political science, unhindered by my tribulations with math.[1]

Perhaps there was a bit of my father in my presumptuous response to Buggy. The opening sentence of his August 10, 1910, letter to the Right Reverend Dr H.P. MacPherson, president of the University of St Francis Xavier's College, as it was then known, in Antigonish, Nova Scotia, brimmed with self-confidence. "I have decided to enter your college," he wrote. Father freely admitted his poor academic standing. "Partly through sickness and partly through lack of application I failed to graduate this year from St John High School making an average of 48 while the pass mark is 50 per cent."

The authorities forgave his audacity and overlooked his poor marks. Rev. MacPherson directed him into a drafting course, telling him that with some extra work in mathematics, he would be able to complete the first-year course of study despite his tenuous grounding. In the small-world department, the room in the student residence where my father lived was three doors from the maternal grandfather of Adrian Merchant, my second wife.

After first year, my father switched to the University of New Brunswick in Fredericton. Upon graduation with his Bachelor of

Science in Forestry he joined the Dominion Forest Service. I would follow a similar two-step path. My first choice had been Trinity College at the University of Toronto with which Ashbury had a long-standing connection. Barney Lawrence, a fellow student who had befriended me when he was head boy at Ashbury, had graduated five years ahead of me, went to Trinity, and was now studying law. But Trinity was full, and my failure in math also stood in my way.

Carleton College – as the Ottawa institution was then called – was my second choice. I knew something about the place because my sister Janet was already a student there, as was Ed Fox, the man she would marry. Moreover, my application was accepted by Carleton. The world and I were both in transition. The euphoria of war's end had worn off. The economic boom of the 1950s had not yet begun. Czechoslovakia, freed from the hands of Hitler in 1945, fell in 1948 by *coup d'etat* to the regime of Stalin as the Soviet Union threatened further aggression. Canada, with the United States and other nations, formed the North Atlantic Treaty Organization to counter the Soviet threat. Against this backdrop, I studied grade thirteen trig on my own while at Carleton. In June 1949, I wrote the exam again, and this time got a C. I was on my way to Toronto and Trinity. Carleton's motto was, "Ours the Task Eternal." For me, the task lasted just a year.[2]

The Ashbury uniform might have been retired, but I continued to dress for classes at Carleton and Trinity in a sports coat, flannels, and tie. I had never rebelled as a teenager; I was kept under tight rein. Even when I lived away from home for the first time, in residence at Trinity during my second year at university, I did not abuse my new-found freedom. My parents took a drink in the past, but by the time I was a teenager, they had stopped. They'd serve alcohol to guests, but they were teetotal.

For my part, I drank a few beers, particularly at the fraternity I was drawn to, Delta Kappa Epsilon, where Barney Lawrence was already a brother. My most independent step was to stop attending church. Without my mother's presence, there was no longer any driving force. Later in life, I attended church occasionally with my family, usually at the behest of my erstwhile Presbyterian mother-in-law. These days, I go more regularly with Adrian, who is a Catholic, as was my father's family.

I pledged at Deke, as the fraternity was commonly called, that first term at Trinity. Joining any fraternity usually involves a ceremony that borders on the religious in combination with some sort of a test to see if you have the necessary persistence and self-sufficiency to survive. I was blindfolded and driven outside the city one fall night in October 1949. When we arrived at this mystery location, I was dropped off and told to find my own way back to the fraternity house on the edge of the campus at 80 St George Street. I had no money, no ID, and no idea where I was.

I seemed to be on the main street of some small town. It was about 10:30 p.m. with no one in sight. I'd only walked a few steps when a police cruiser pulled up, and the officer asked, "What are you doing here?" I explained my circumstances, told him I had no money, and had to get back to downtown Toronto. He looked me over, glanced at his watch, and must have decided that he had both the time and inclination to help. "I'll drive you to the main road," he said. "You can hitchhike from there."

I'd been dumped in Markham, which at that time was rather remote. A convict had recently escaped from a nearby penitentiary. My benefactor was sufficiently worried about my safety that he ended up driving me to the northern loop of the Yonge streetcar line, and gave me carfare. I was at the frat house shortly after midnight, the first of the pledges to arrive. I was so speedy they weren't officially set up to register us as we straggled in. I didn't reveal my methods. For all they knew, I flew.

John Hurst, one of the brothers in charge of initiation, was assigned to give every new member a nickname. When he looked at my toothy grin and size 13 shoes, his eyes lit up. "Thumper," he said, thinking about the rabbit that kept thumping his left hind foot in *Bambi*, the Walt Disney animated classic. The name stuck with my fraternity brothers, spread to classmates at Trinity, and followed me to Parliament Hill.

The many explanations over the years about where the name Thumper came from have been as erroneous as they have been numerous, everything from the sound of my feet on the locker-room floor to how I dealt with opponents in Parliament. I've been called Thumper all my adult life, by friend and foe, and that's just fine with me. I can be kind or I can be cold-hearted. As I often said during my political career, "I'll support you or I'll attack you, whichever you find most useful."

I played hockey and football at Trinity. I was not good enough at either for the varsity squads, but our football team made it to the interfaculty finals in 1950. The game against Forestry for the Mulock Cup was played in late November on a snow-covered back campus. Forestry won, 24–14. My forester father never let me forget that result and was forever finding new and more imaginative ways to revive the topic and rub it in. At Trinity, I also participated in debating, followed by moot courts at Osgoode Hall. Both were good training for the House of Commons because they demanded sound research, direct delivery, and fast footwork to rebut an opponent.

When the Korean War broke out in 1950, fellow Deke Bud Whitaker and I decided after a few beers one night to enlist in the Canadian contingent. When I told my father, his response was restrained. I'm sure he didn't want me in harm's way, but when he wrote, he sounded sanguine. "So much depends on this week's Cabinet meetings and the policy to be laid down for defence preparations," he said. "Don't get carried away by any local views on enlistment. Such things need a bit of cogitation." His cool-headed response to my plans for Korea was wise. When he and I next discussed the matter, my romanticism had abated. Just as well. More than 500 Canadians were killed in Korea. I'm glad I wasn't among them.

3

Band of Brothers

Because I had done my first year at Carleton, I needed just two years at Trinity for my three-year pass arts degree. I lived at the Deke house in my final year, where several brothers introduced me to music, an area where my education had been sorely neglected. I had been too young to appreciate the rise of the swing era when it was happening. My life-long devotion to Benny Goodman began with the release in 1950 of the three-LP set recorded live at Carnegie Hall in 1938. Among my favourite songs were "Don't Be That Way," "One O'Clock Jump," and "Sing, Sing, Sing." My tastes then expanded beyond the King of Swing to include pianist Teddy Wilson, vibraphonist Lionel Hampton, and bandleader Artie Shaw.

Later in life, when I was Canadian High Commissioner in Britain, one of the most memorable evenings of that posting in London was spent with Benny Goodman's brother, Harry, who was married to the mother-in-law of my former parliamentary colleague Hugh Faulkner. Harry was quite a musician in his own right and told a story that was typical of the band's shenanigans. The horn player said he needed so much water to keep going one hot summer's night that he put a bucketful beside his chair. At one point, Harry got a little thirsty himself, so he dipped a cup into the bucket and took a drink only to find it was pure gin.

I was treasurer and Deke house manager during the school year 1952–53. For my duties I got free room and board, but the trade-off wasn't worth it. My all-purpose role included being landlord, police chief, and sanitary engineer. You could never please any one of the dozen brothers living at the house for very long. If there were a choice between being house manager and death by firing squad, I'd say, "Shoot me."

There was one occasion, however, when I was grateful for my band of brothers. In March 1951, I began suffering abdominal pain, and took to my bed. In a fraternity house, someone is always sick, often with a hangover, so scant attention was paid. Eventually, a doctor was called, who said it was just the flu, but the next day I was far worse. Sam Toy – later a judge on the B C Court of Appeals – phoned for an ambulance that carried me to Toronto General Hospital. My appendix had ruptured, causing an infection called peritonitis. Without immediate treatment I would have died. Sam's timely call and emergency surgery saved me from certain death.

My recovery from abdominal surgery was slow; exams were imminent and I was incapable of writing them. Trinity gave me what's known as an aegrotat, which meant my final results would be based on my marks during the year. I did, however, have to face one exam, in religious knowledge, a topic that apparently held special significance at this institution founded by the Anglican Church.

I complained bitterly to anyone who would listen about what I saw as an onerous and unnecessary burden until my father finally said, "Do you think maybe, considering what you've just been through, you might want to thank the Good Lord for the opportunity to write this exam?" He was right. I wrote the exam, passed my year, and showed up at Convocation Hall in June ready to graduate with the class of '51.[1]

Wearing cap and gown, I stood in a line arranged in alphabetical order, behind Nona Macdonald (no relation, but a good friend later in life) from Saskatoon. Suddenly, Nona whirled around, waved the program at me, and said, "Your name's not on the list." At first, I wasn't worried, but then she added, "What happens if they don't call your name?" What, indeed? The line was snaking forward. I spotted a door near the steps to the stage. I thought, if my name isn't called after Nona's, I'm fleeing through that exit into oblivion rather than be left standing alone, an obvious reject in an otherwise continuous process of personal success. Fortunately, my name was called. I had my Bachelor of Arts degree and the fresh abdominal scar to prove it. In 2009, sixty years after first entering Trinity College, I attended another convocation, this time to receive the degree of Doctor of Sacred Letters (*honoris causa*). I didn't have to write an exam for that designation, either. Apparently, living a life was enough to receive such a great honour.

For all my seeming success in later life, throughout my early years I had a low opinion of myself. While such angst might not be unusual for a teenager, these problematic feelings followed me into adulthood. My lack of self-confidence infected the career choice I made to go into law. At Osgoode Hall Law School in Toronto, some topics bored me, and I wondered if I wouldn't be better off leading a literary life. It wasn't that I saw myself as a great writer. All I knew was that I would rather read Boswell's *Life of Johnson* than a textbook on the laws of torts. My classmates included Bill Davis, who later became premier of Ontario; Robert Stanbury, who served in Cabinet with me; Sinclair Stevens, who sat in opposition, and his wife Noreen, who was smarter than the rest of us put together and always finished near the top of the class.

I knew the law was excellent preparation for many possible careers, including business or public life. Despite such powerful motivation, I struggled in my first year. I failed torts but rewrote the exam and passed. In second year, I found my sea legs. Even then, studying at the boisterous frat house was difficult. I got an evening job in the great library at Osgoode Hall retrieving books for lawyers researching cases. It wasn't a busy post so I was able to study while sitting at the desk surrounded by silence. It also provided an opportunity to meet practicing lawyers and see how they prepared briefs and arguments.[2]

I spent third year articling with the firm of Gowling, MacTavish, Osborne and Henderson in Ottawa so I could live at home and save money. Some assignments at Gowlings, such as searching real estate titles in the registry office or serving documents on other law firms, were boring. But there were also exciting days. Adrian "Bud" Hewitt did civil litigation and would take me to court as his assistant. I also worked for Duncan MacTavish, one of the senior partners. MacTavish was a long-time adviser to Mackenzie King, served as chairman of the National Liberal Federation, and mentored me on matters both legal and political.

Another role took me further afield. In the spring of 1952, my father said, "We're sending a forestry survey team to Yukon and we put the summer job out to all the forestry schools. We wanted two students but got only one. If I were you, I'd send them a letter, saying, 'I have reason to believe you have a job available.'" He gave me the address and, sure enough, I got the job.

My boss was Louie Nozzolillo, a former prisoner of war. He arrived at Stalag Luft III only a month after "The Great Escape." Second in command was Arnie Berg; both were members of the federal forestry department. Larry Scales, the other student, was taking forestry at U of T. The cook was Ken McGee, who, of course, was called Sam McGee after the Robert Service poem. McGee sardonically referred to me as "the man with a face like a pail of frozen garbage." The money was good, the company hilarious, and it was a relief to escape the law.

We met in Whitehorse during that cold, wet summer and travelled to Dawson City assessing the extensive softwood forests on the Stewart and Pelly rivers, both tributaries of the Yukon River. We would tromp into the bush, mark off twelve-chain plots (a chain is about twenty meters), select several trees, drill them with an increment borer to assess their age, and then estimate their height, density, and growth in the last ten years.[3]

The evenings were spent debating everything from intellectual honesty to social justice. Nozzolillo would regularly browbeat me about my Trinity background, bourgeois upbringing, and my anglophile ways. My arguing skills and mental agility both improved as the summer passed. The trip was my first excursion to northern Canada. It wouldn't be my last. "From the land," said political historian A.R.M. Lower, "must come the soul of Canada."

In fourth year, we were all back at Osgoode for classes. I realized I had to buckle down and could no longer live at the Deke house. I took a room at 276 Inglewood Drive in the Moore Park home of Eileen Urquhart, the widow of a former judge. The quiet surroundings, bereft of frat house temptations, allowed me to finish in the top twelve in my class of two hundred and win the Insurance Law Prize of $100, one of only seven scholarships awarded that year.[4]

I cannot remember any of my fellow students expressing satisfaction, let alone pleasure, about our years at Osgoode. The most positive moment came in June 1955 when we were called to the bar. I purchased my barrister's gown and waistcoat, paying the princely sum of $46.75. At our graduation banquet, there was so much rowdiness and bun tossing that the event was cancelled for a number of years. At successive reunions we awarded a trophy to the class member who most personified rambunctiousness. I'm proud to say that I've never won.

In his speech to the graduating class, John Wellington Pickup, then chief justice of Ontario, told us that the best investment we could make was a continuing education in the law. The more you learn, he said, the more you receive in return. I took him at his word. I had the time for more studies. Because I had finished high school at sixteen, university at nineteen, and was called to the bar at twenty-three, I was at least two years ahead of everyone else.

After interviewing with several Toronto firms, I'd settled on McCarthy & McCarthy, and they said that they would hold my place if I did post-graduate studies. My father asked a friend at Syracuse University where I should go in the United States. There were two choices, came the reply, both in Massachusetts. If I were interested in diplomacy, I should attend The Fletcher School at Tufts; if international law, then Harvard Law School. To me, Harvard was the obvious choice. To double my chances, I applied to both the law school and the school of business administration.

When asked on my application why I wanted to attend Harvard Law, I wrote that my law degree from a place like Osgoode Hall, which was run by the legal profession, "places too strong an emphasis on training in the execution of the ordinary affairs of everyday practice to the exclusion of developing a capacity for original legal thinking in the student. Undoubtedly, with the continuing progress of the business community, new situations will arise for which novel solutions will have to be obtained, and I feel that post-graduate legal study affords the best training for meeting such problems as they arise."

I was accepted by Harvard Law and then worked in the summer of 1955 at Lockhart & Trusler, a law firm in Sarnia, Ontario. After I'd arrived at Harvard, I received a droll letter from Owen Lockhart in which he wrote:

To my dismay I found that immediately upon your departure from Sarnia, our firm was faced with countless law suits resulting from omissions, incorrect advice, very sloppy writing and deficits in the Trust Accounts, mortgages on wrong lots, and finally and most important of all our vault is missing. We were unable to properly reply to any of the above matters so at the present time, I am spending my daytimes avoiding the Sheriff and my night-times avoiding my wife ...

Undoubtedly the vast and considerable amount of experience you obtained while you were privileged to spend your holiday at our office has fitted you for one of the outstanding positions in the present-day struggle to keep ahead of the class, and no doubt you are continually bragging about your close association with myself to your fellow students. I do not mind and you are quite free to use my name from time to time as if you had actually met me in person.

Who says lawyers have no sense of humour?

Harvard was a world away from anywhere I'd ever been. Even walking the grounds of that storied place left me feeling a bit like the proverbial country bumpkin. I lived in Ames, one of five interconnecting dorms with common lounges and shared kitchens and bathrooms. My class-mates were mostly Americans but included a few other Canadians such as Arthur Stone, who became a litigator and later a Federal Court of Appeal judge, and Purdy Crawford, who went on to have a distin-guished career as a securities lawyer and later was chief executive officer of Imasco.

There was a smattering of other foreign students, including Ahmed Zaki Yamani, who I would meet again in the 1970s when I was minis-ter of energy, mines and resources and he was Sheik Yamani, minister of petroleum and mineral resources for Saudi Arabia. At Harvard, he and I would talk at length in our study stalls, which were side by side on the north side of the library stacks. He was suave and courtly, European in his dress and North American in his demeanour, coming as he did from schooling at the University of Exeter and New York University of Law. Usually he wore bespoke suits, but every couple of weeks would show up in full Arab regalia. When I asked why, he said, "I just want the American people to know that it's our oil and they better treat us right." In those days, the source hardly mattered; oil cost a mere $2 a barrel. For years Zaki sent me at Christmas the next year's calendar engraved on a small, silver slab.

I went to Harvard to study public international law but also took courses in corporate and securities law. One of my assignments was a fifty-page treatise for Harold J. Berman on the legal implications of US export controls. Our professors, buttressed occasionally by guest lecturers from the various branches of government in Washington, DC, were an illustrious group. Among the most memorable were Louis Loss on securities, Lon Fuller on contracts, Austin Scott on trusts, and Paul Freund and Archibald Cox on constitutional law. Cox was later special prosecutor on Watergate and the focus of controversy when President Richard Nixon ordered Cox fired. In what became known as the "Saturday Night Massacre" in October 1973, Attorney General Elliot Richardson refused to fire Cox, and resigned. His deputy at Justice, William Ruckelshaus, also refused and resigned, leaving Solicitor General Robert Bork to do the hatchet job.

There were no boring moments at Harvard. All seats were assigned so each prof could call on anyone by name. Many used a method that began by picking out a student and saying, "You gave some thought to the so-and-so case overnight. Now, let me just change the facts a little bit." After describing the new circumstances, the prof would conduct a stiff cross-examination that sometimes turned into a public hanging in front of your peers.

I worked hard and did well, finishing in June 1956 with an A average and my Master of Laws (LL.M.). A fellow student, Frank Francis, encouraged me to attend his alma mater, Cambridge. Francis, who was British with a father living in Switzerland, told me about Trinity Hall where I could study for a Diploma in International Law. Cambridge had already been on my mind. The previous summer I had applied for the Newton W. Rowell Scholarship, a $1,500 award for graduate studies at Cambridge. In April 1956, when I learned that I had won the prize, I decided I would attend.

The scholarship honoured Newton Wesley Rowell, a former leader of the Ontario Liberal Party and a member of Robert Borden's Union government. He was also a lawyer who in the 1920s won the Persons case that made women eligible for appointment to the Senate of Canada. His granddaughter, Nancy Ruth, sits in the Senate today. Her brother, Hal Jackman, would run against me three times – in 1963, 1965, and 1974 – as the Progressive Conservative candidate in the riding of Rosedale.

I'd heard from a fellow student at Harvard about cheap transatlantic passage on a vessel owned by his family, so I set out in July 1956 as the only passenger on the *O.A. Brodin*, a Swedish ore carrier, leaving from Wabana on Bell Island, Newfoundland, to Rotterdam in The Netherlands. From there I took a train to Amsterdam and then a ferry to England. I don't imagine very many of the others heading for Cambridge travelled by so modest a mode of transport.

I finalized arrangements for lodgings with other post-graduate students in a house at 1 Adams Road, across from the cricket field. The rooms were being redecorated and term didn't start until October, so I headed for the continent. In Hamburg I paid the equivalent of $200 for a new motor scooter, a bright blue Victoria "Nicky" Kraftroller, with a top speed of about fifty kilometres per hour. Among my stops on the first motorized device I'd ever owned were Stockholm, Oslo, Copenhagen, and Kronborg, the castle near the Danish town of Helsingor, immortalized as Elsinore in Shakespeare's *Hamlet*.[5]

When my scooter underwent repairs, I took the train to Geneva to visit Frank Francis, my Harvard friend, then travelled by bus to Lugano and St Moritz, Munich and Düsseldorf. As I tripped around, I felt a sense of freedom and wonderment I'd never before enjoyed. I didn't realize just how young and truly vast Canada was until I experienced Europe first-hand with its multiple countries so close together, cobbled streets, and cathedrals dating from the Middle Ages.

When I arrived back in England, my Cambridge digs were still not ready and the rest of my luggage was stuck in customs in Liverpool, so I took off with Don Hill, an Ottawa lawyer who'd been a year ahead of me at Osgoode, for a week of touring in Scotland, the Lake District, and Wales.

Among my many powerful memories was seeing the Scottish National War Memorial in Edinburgh Castle commemorating those who died while serving with Scottish regiments. The Rolls of Honour showed that the Queen's Own Cameron Highlanders alone lost some 500 officers and 10,000 enlisted men. I was overcome with the solemnity of the surroundings, the sorrow of the sacrifices, and a feeling of pride for the people from whom I am sprung.

4

The Suez and Other Crises

If Harvard was brash, Cambridge was bucolic. Trinity Hall was founded in 1350, but even so, it's only the fifth-oldest college comprising the University of Cambridge. While all of the architecture at Cambridge is breathtaking, Trinity Hall has long been admired for both its beauty and riverside site. Said Anglo–American novelist Henry James, "If I were called upon to mention the prettiest corner of the world, I should draw a thoughtful sigh and point the way to the gardens of Trinity Hall."

My room was spacious, fifteen by twenty feet, and had a bay window with a southern exposure, a new rug, continental bed, desk, several arm chairs, sink, gas heater, and a small hotplate for making breakfast. My adviser was Robert Jennings, the Whewell Professor of International Law. Jennings had an illustrious career that included service in the Intelligence Corps during the Second World War. At Cambridge he spent some of his time drafting constitutions for Commonwealth countries emerging from under the protective umbrella of the Empire into the sunshine of statehood. A student noted that one of the countries Jennings had worked with had relapsed back to tribal anarchy. Replied Jennings, "Well, it was one of my early constitutions; I was finding my way." Jennings and I had no set schedule. If I wanted to see him, I did. If he came across an article he wanted to share with me, he'd stop where I was seated at lunch in the great hall and suggest I come to his office.

When I first arrived at Cambridge, the Suez Crisis riveted the world. Egypt was growing closer to the Soviet Union. In response, in July 1956, the United States and Britain withdrew their offer of financial support for the building of the Aswan Dam. A week later, Egyptian president Gamal Abdel Nasser responded by nationalizing the Suez Canal. Britain appealed to Canada for support in what appeared to be a plan to put the canal under international control, by force if necessary. Canada usually followed Britain's lead when it came to such international matters, but not this time. Israel, Britain, and France planned and conducted a secret attack against Egypt on October 29.

The US urged Britain to withdraw, a view that did not sit well with some Brits who wanted control of the canal and Nasser ousted. In the spirited debate that followed, others thought British prime minister Anthony Eden should resign. "For Britain the experience of Suez was a traumatic one, and in retrospect appears to mark the final transition from the imperial mentality to however you may describe the present one," I said in an address (known as The Toast) to the Cambridge University Dinner held in Toronto on April 1, 1967. "For a Canadian, at Cambridge, it was also a significant experience. No doubt we as a country had had disagreements with Britain over public questions before; but surely none had the same imprint on the public consciousness as did the sharp dissent of the Canadian government from the action of the Eden administration."[1]

Some Britons were also among the dissenters. While I was in London conducting research at Whitehall, I walked to 10 Downing Street to watch the protesters. The crowds were dense, chanting slogans and carrying signs saying "Law Not War" and "Eden Must Go." Police on horses charged the crowd several times, resulting in injuries. Fights among the protesters as well as firecrackers that frightened the horses further exacerbated an already electric atmosphere.

Upon hearing my accent, strangers would automatically assume I was American. They were not mollified to learn I was Canadian. In Britain, Canada was seen to be siding with the US and therefore acting in a manner insufficiently supportive of the Mother Country. Cambridge lectures on other topics often turned into heated debates about the Suez Crisis. Secretary of State for External Affairs Lester Pearson, as head of the Canadian delegation to the United Nations, in November proposed a ceasefire and a UN police force to restore peace while a settlement was achieved. For creating the first of many such UN peacekeeping missions, Pearson won the Nobel Peace Prize.

Even such a high-profile Canadian solution did not improve British feelings toward us. The Brits could not stomach a Canadian telling them what to do – especially when it was for the best. At pubs or parties, when my Canadian accent was noticed, there would always be arguments about Pearson's actions. After one such occasion, I commented to a British friend that I appreciated how well I was treated in the feisty circumstances. "It was the fact that you were 6-foot-5," he said. "Nobody was in a hurry to get into a fight with you on a matter of international law."

Apart from my size, the outcome was a sign to me that Canadians in general, and Lester Pearson in particular, could be able players on the international stage. The Suez Crisis marked the beginning of the end of the British Empire. No longer could Britain send in troops to occupy land not rightfully theirs. Instead they had to heed an international organization.

Not everyone at Cambridge denigrated Canadians. Some students wanted to hear more about Canada and how they might emigrate. Roy MacLaren, who later became a member of Canada's foreign service and won a seat in the House of Commons in 1979, was reading English at St Catharine's College. As secretary of the Canada Club, he took it upon himself to distribute material to those who were interested in a new life in Canada and helped facilitate their emigration.

In addition to such vigorous discussions, there were many enjoyable aspects to Cambridge: tea in the nearby village of Grantchester, pushing other people out of punts, lunch at the Eagle, and a pint of ale at the Fountain Inn. Sports were my best connector to other students. I was a member of the rowing crew in an eight-man shell on the River Cam, and played some cricket, much to the surprise of the British. I did not bowl as well as some chaps who had grown up in the bosom of the game, but I was able to help out my side.

I also played defence for the Cambridge hockey team in our red shirts and blue pants. We managed to do decently in the annual grudge match in February against Oxford. Oxford usually had a more talented team because of the many Canadians who attended Oxford on Rhodes scholarships. Two years earlier, for example, Cambridge had been humiliated 29–0. The year I played, Cambridge put on a better show; about three-quarters of our team was Canadian. We were down only 3–2 with ninety seconds to go. In desperation, we pulled our goalie, but the strategy backfired when Oxford scored twice into the empty net to win 5–2. I had an assist. *Light Blue*, the Cambridge sports magazine, reported that "the Captain, Fred Meredith, rose from his sick bed to play an heroic game in goal. The most outstanding player was Don Macdonald, who, unfortunately, was only here for one year, but who was a great defenceman."[2]

At Christmas, rather than go home, I was invited to join a combined Oxford–Cambridge hockey squad that travelled on the continent. We played a string of games in France at Chamonix and Megève at the foot of Mont Blanc, Kitzbühel in Austria, Garmisch-Partenkirchen in Bavaria, Kresnice in Yugoslavia, Bolzano in Italy, Gstaad in Switzerland, and then Paris for our last game. During the twenty-day trip, we won four games and lost seven against the various European teams that were by then beginning to improve. Between the hockey tour and my own travels, I visited about a dozen countries during my time at Cambridge.

My diploma required no course work, but I was able to audit any lecture. Among the classes I attended were Kurt Lipstein's on private international law. A fellow at Clare College, Lipstein had emigrated from Germany before the Second World War, earned his doctorate at Cambridge, spent time in an internment camp during the hostilities, then later became a professor.

When I first attended Lipstein's class, I sat at the back and kept quiet. He must have made inquiries about me because after a couple of classes, he called on me during a discussion on the conflicts of laws and asked, "What would Dr Falconbridge say on that question?" I knew John Delatre Falconbridge had been dean of Osgoode Hall from the 1920s to the 1940s but I was not sufficiently familiar with his work to be able to respond. I took the honest route and replied that I did not know but would consult his lectures after class, a response that evoked mirth all round.

Students of international law, such as myself, would also gather monthly at the feet of the established masters to hear a paper then discuss the question. Distinguished participants such as Lord McNair, who had just retired from the International Court of Justice, his successor Sir Hersch Lauterpacht, and Sir Gerald Fitzmaurice, then legal advisor to the Foreign Office, would often join us.

Much of my time was spent in more lonely pursuits – studying in my room or ferreting out research material from the library. My thesis topic involved the relationship between public international law and national attempts to control foreign trade by legal measures. My focus was on the particular impact of the General Agreement on Tariffs and Trade (GATT), first negotiated in 1947 during a United Nations conference on trade and employment. Canada was one of the original signatories. Even that earliest treaty lowered thousands of tariffs and affected billions of dollars in global trade. By the time I began my studies, GATT had been renegotiated in three more sessions by a growing numbers of countries.

Over the years, GATT expanded beyond tariff reductions to include labour standards, investment practices, and patents. GATT governed international trade until the 1990s when it was replaced by the World Trade Organization. Thousands of bureaucrats, trade lawyers, and other experts devoted their careers to negotiating, interpreting, or fighting GATT. In 1956, however, there were very few interested academics. I wanted to see if the body of practice being created by GATT was hardening into the imperatives of law. As one of the pioneers studying the topic, I set my own pace and my own path. When I consulted F.A. Mann, a top British solicitor, he was very supportive of my thesis work. "Few lawyers have written about this," he said. "It's all economists."

I conducted research in three libraries at Cambridge – the Squire Law Library, University Library, and the Marshall Library of Economics – as well as at the British Museum, the London School of Economics, and the University of London. When I was in London, I also met with trade attachés, lawyers, UN officials, public servants, and others. During the Easter vacation, I travelled to Geneva where I visited the GATT secretariat, discussed my paper with officials, and made contacts for follow-up advice and information.

My time in Cambridge also opened my eyes to a level of integrity and sophistication that previously I could never imagine. When it came to the arts and intellectual life, Britain set a high standard. I was further impressed by the degree of tolerance and co-operation among governments and agencies in Europe. This all struck me as proof that such co-operation was not only possible on an international basis but also practicable. I resolved to do what I could to raise the consciousness of Canadians on a wide variety of fronts.

The sun rose early on the morning of May 6, 1957, so I had been awake for a while, but was just having breakfast, when there was a light knock on my door. It was the hall porter, Mr Eames. His mien was sombre. "With great sorrow," he said, "I have a bad telegram for you."

The telegram read: "Very sorry Don your father passed away this evening of a heart attack suggest you fly home if possible." It was signed by Ed Fox, Janet's husband. At first, the words had no impact, and I wandered aimlessly in my room, my mind a blank. Mrs Eames came to see me, and when I told her my news, I broke down and wept for the man who had meant so much to me and set the compass for the life I would lead.

I hadn't seen my father since leaving home the previous summer. I was aware that he'd suffered a heart attack a few weeks earlier, but my parents downplayed his situation, telling friends he just had the flu and needed rest. They did not want me to worry, either. In his letters, Father continued to call me "old top" and constantly expressed confidence I'd do well with whatever issue I happened to be struggling with at the time. Right to the end, my father sacrificed his pleasure for my pursuits. At the time of his death, he was only sixty-five.

As a civil servant for forty-four years, he'd never been one of those bureaucrats who stayed tethered to a desk. He was enthusiastic about the forests and good public policy, and I was the beneficiary of his passionate, broad-brush approach to life. In his final years, he joined other public servants who were representing Canada abroad. In the 1940s, he attended the Third World Forestry Congress in Finland, the Fourth Congress in India, as well as meetings of the Food and Agriculture Organization of the United Nations held in Oslo and Rome. Among his achievements was the Canada Forestry Act of 1949 that provided federal aid for reforestation. By the time of his retirement six months before his death, 58 million trees had been planted on Crown land as a result of his vision.[3]

This sudden end to my father's life was all that much harder to bear because I felt I had never adequately shown him my gratitude. I rallied into action and sold my motorbike to raise money. My adviser loaned me the rest of the airfare, and I was on a flight home from Heathrow later that same day. Friends said they would pack up my things and ship them later. My time in Cambridge was cut short, but only by a few weeks. Since I was not expected to sit exams as part of my diploma, I was able to return to Canada where I could complete the thesis required for my diploma on my own.

It was a time of tumultuous change for Quebec, for Canada, and for me. My father's minister in the Department of Northern Affairs and National Resources had been Jean Lesage, who would in 1960 become premier of Quebec and the father of the Quiet Revolution. A month after my father died, an electoral Prairie fire in the form of John Diefenbaker swept Louis St Laurent out of office, thus ending twenty-two years of Liberal government.

After my father's funeral, I stayed with my mother for the summer to help tidy up his estate. Since choosing McCarthy & McCarthy in 1955, I had kept in touch with the firm; they had told me whenever my graduate studies were concluded, I had a role with them in Toronto. As I left Ottawa to begin my new life in commercial law, Stanley Clark, our family lawyer, gave me a copy of a letter written by Harold Fisher, a lawyer, mayor of Ottawa, member of the Ontario Legislature, and founder of Ottawa Civic Hospital where I was born. Fisher's letter, written in 1925 to a young lawyer, John O. Trepanier, contained excellent advice that I tried to follow.

What you want to do is give the people of your locality the idea that you are reliable and able to do your work, and the best way to accomplish that is to be reliable and be able to do your work. You have to do anything that comes to hand, no matter how small. At the same time you should be prepared for anything no matter how big. That means you should keep on studying. Something always depends on the way a man starts. You should dress and live as well as you can and should endeavour to mix with the substantial people of the community. Keep away from the wrong kind of people and keep them away from you. They can do you more harm than anything else. When you have a job to do always do the best you know how. That helps you in two ways. It helps you to do better work and before long people will come to know that you can be relied on.[4]

Standing behind their children, Hugh and Bill, are my grandfather, Angus Macdonald, and his wife, Minnie, aboard the *Canara*. My grandmother was pregnant with my father, who was born at sea in 1891.

My father, Donald Angus Macdonald, second from left, as a young pilot at the
Reading Flying School in England in 1917. He was later shot down and spent
six months as a prisoner of war.

My mother Marjorie, sister Janet, and me, aged about four, at 6 Ruskin Row, my maternal grandparents' house in Winnipeg where we summered.

Prize-winning graduates from Osgoode Hall Law School in 1955. From left:
William DesLauriers, Henry Kerr, Reginald Haney, Harvey Daiter, and me.

Rowing on the River Cam while I studied world trade at Cambridge, 1956–57. I'm the third rower from the coxswain urging us on.

A jubilant Pierre Trudeau after winning the Liberal leadership in 1968. As the first MP from Ontario to support him, I'm close by, just to the right.

An enjoyable moment with a proud Walter Gordon, Canadian nationalist, minister in the Lester Pearson government, and a wonderful mentor to me.

Riding in a military jeep on the base of the Royal 22nd Regiment (Van Doos) during the October Crisis of 1970.

As minister of national defence, I visited troops across the country, in Europe, and on the high seas, as attested by this jackstay transfer from navy supply ship to destroyer.

When President Nixon addressed the House of Commons in 1972, he noticed that we pounded our desks rather than applaud, so joined in by using my desk.

Inspecting the troops in Germany with my minister of defence counterpart,
Helmut Schmidt, who later became chancellor.

Indira Gandhi, prime minister of India, was one of the most serene yet toughest leaders I was honoured to meet.

Chou En-lai was both visionary and practical in 1973 when he told me what China's priorities would be for the next twenty-five years.

During the energy crisis in 1974, I visited the Shah of Iran (left) in the hopes of selling them a CANDU nuclear reactor.

"Our Problem is how to keep the price of oil at Eight Dollars a Barrel, Right?"

MAR. 3, 1976

Editorial cartoonist Duncan Macpherson takes a lighter look at my efforts as minister of energy to keep oil prices low in Canada. (*The Toronto Star*)

5

The Accidental Candidate

Two senior partners, Beverley Matthews and Salter Hayden, ran McCarthy & McCarthy. During the Second World War, Matthews attained the rank of brigadier in the 48th Highlanders and received the Order of the British Empire. He was active in the Progressive Conservative Party. Hayden ran as a Liberal in the Toronto riding of St Paul's in the 1935 election, and was defeated, but was appointed to the Senate in 1940. Thus, the firm had close connections with both parties. Such political links mattered when it came to landing new business or putting clients in touch with the right Cabinet minister.

Founded in 1855, McCarthys had two of the major chartered banks as clients, an unusual arrangement, since one bank client per law firm was more normal. Matthews had been on the board of The Dominion Bank since the late 1940s; Hayden became a director of the Bank of Nova Scotia in 1955. I was a long way down the ladder. My starting salary was only $4,500. It took three years before I could afford to buy my first car, a used Chev.

Law firms today are behemoths with several hundred lawyers. When I joined McCarthys, there were about two dozen lawyers. As was typical of all law firms in those days, McCarthys was an old boys' club. There were no female lawyers; women were assigned to minor matters. The first Jewish associate wasn't hired until 1971. The culture was formal; no first names, please. Our offices were in the Canada Life Building across University Avenue from Osgoode Hall's heritage courtrooms.

Canada Life was the firm's biggest client. Other corporate clients included Union Carbide Corporation, Atlantic Sugar Refineries, and

TransCanada PipeLines. The firm had some of the finest lawyers in a variety of fields. Among them was Harold Fox, author of a book on patents and former owner of Lightning Fastener Company, of St Catharines, Ontario, for years the exclusive holder of the zipper patent in North America. Another distinguished partner was John J. Robinette, Canada's highest profile litigator, with multiple victories in both civil and criminal cases.

Most lawyers joined firms because they had a family connection. I had no such pull; I got the job on my own. John Clarry, who became my political mentor, used to say it was as though I had been catapulted in from outer space. In my first month, I appeared gowned before a High Court judge representing a client in an estate matter and served as a scrutineer at a meeting involving Great Sweet Grass Oils Ltd.

In the months that followed, my workload included corporate and commercial law. I did research, often on an overnight basis, on a range of topics, including the Combines Investigation Act, rights of minority shareholders, provincial succession duties, and mining claims. I also served as a junior to Senator Hayden on an inquiry by the Restrictive Trade Practices Commission.

My guide in corporate law was James Walker. An Oxford graduate, he spoke German, joined McCarthys in 1931, was an intelligence officer during the war, and was discharged with the rank of lieutenant colonel. I also worked with John B. McDonald, a tax lawyer, who published articles in the *Financial Post* under the *nom de plume* Robert Tresilian. The name was an inside joke. The historical Robert Tresilian was a corrupt chief justice in England who was hanged in 1388. To give the modern-day "author" extra heft, Tresilian carried the designation QC – Queen's Counsel – as part of his byline. In addition to writing articles himself, McDonald also corralled colleagues. In 1960–61, I wrote numerous contributions, each of which filled half a page in the broadsheet newspaper, on topics as diverse as the state of Canadian combines law and conflicts of interest in the boardroom. For each published article, I received $50, grocery money for the month.[1]

In my spare time, I played cricket all over the city, including once with the national team against Pakistan in Varsity Stadium. When I bowled in the Docklands, near the city incinerator, dark ash in the air turned our natty whites a tattle-tale grey. I also worked on my Cambridge thesis and, in August 1958, submitted my eighty-nine-page work entitled, *Legal Controls of Foreign Trade and International Law: With Special Reference to the GATT.* "When states espouse true collaboration of policies as opposed to resorting to individual means in the solution of their economic difficulties, then the rule of law can expect to play a more dominant role," I concluded. "Until such an event occurs, legal rules are most advisably confined to the flexibility and informality of systems like the General Agreement."[2]

My adviser at Cambridge, Robert Jennings, wrote on October 16, 1958, saying, "I think it is a jolly good piece of work. In particular, I think it is very well written. You should be hearing shortly about the diploma. I cannot think that there would be any doubt in the matter. I like your treatment of the subject. Your comments are shrewd and I learned quite a lot by reading it." In due course, my diploma in international law arrived. Elegant though the diploma looked, framed and hanging on the wall, I was prouder of the compliments by Jennings written in his own hand. In 1984 he was knighted and appointed a judge at the International Court of Justice. From 1991 to 1994 he served as president.

The same trade issues are still playing out today. Every country wants international rules to favour their exports while at the same time reining in imports from other nations seeking an advantage to promote their own goods. Canada–US relations have been dominated for decades by such debates, dilemmas, and disputes. The Royal Commission I chaired in the 1980s became seized with this very topic of regularizing trade between our two nations. I'm not putting myself forward as somehow prescient for becoming engaged in this subject at a young age, but it was a topic that intrigued me, and a matter that has dominated my life as well as world politics. In this, as with many other elements of my life, I have succeeded more by good luck than good management.

After my father died, my sister Janet and her husband, Ed Fox, an economist with Canada Mortgage and Housing Corp., moved into 154 Acacia with our mother so that their three boys – David, Bob, and Jim – could attend Rockcliffe Public School, where classes were smaller than elsewhere in Ottawa. After a time, my mother moved to Toronto and lived with me in my first apartment at 39 Leacrest Road in Leaside, and later at 10 Lamport Avenue in Rosedale. She suffered from angina, became a semi-invalid, and died of a heart attack in Ottawa on March 6, 1960, while visiting Janet and the grandchildren. She was sixty-one. Both my parents had been taken by heart attacks, three years apart. I was only twenty-eight.

I now had my Bachelor of Arts from Trinity, my law degree from Osgoode Hall, a master's from Harvard, and a diploma from Cambridge. I was well schooled and well launched, but I did not yet have that most important relationship – someone with whom to share my life. I had dated a number of women but nothing serious. There's an old saying that life is what happens to you when you're making plans. You can cause a certain number of things to come about by hard work and making the right choices, but serendipity also plays a major role.

One morning, at the Rosedale subway station, there was just such a moment. I ran into Ruth Hutchison, who had been raised in Ottawa where her father, George, was a dentist. Her mother, Lillian, one of the first women to graduate from McGill University, ran a dairy business owned by her father. I was in kindergarten with Ruth's older sister, Barbara, and had dated Bobbie – as she was called – a few times and Ruth once.

It was only much later, after Ruth and I became reacquainted, that I learned the truth about that date. Bobbie had paid her younger sister to take her place and go out with me. Worse, when Ruth arrived home that night, and her mother asked about the evening, Ruth said, "Nice guy, but a little ..." and drew the shape of a square with her fingers.

I knew nothing of that when I saw Ruth again in Toronto. If Ruth remembered, she kindly gave no indication. Ruth was fair-skinned, blue-eyed, blonde, striking, and tall, about 5 feet 8 inches. We rode downtown together on the subway and got caught up. In high school, she'd been a boarder at Bishop Strachan School in Toronto. On occasion, she and some friends would make a rope from the veils they wore on their heads at the private school's morning chapel and use it to escape out a window. Once free, they'd head for Fran's Restaurant at Yonge and St Clair for cocktails.

At the University of Western Ontario, Ruth was a member of the varsity golf team, participated in other sports, and was elected vice-president of student council. After graduating in 1957 in English and economics, Ruth obtained her certificate in a business administration program at Radcliffe College jointly sponsored by Harvard Business School.

At first, Ruth's application had been rejected. Her parents had given her a new car as a graduation gift from Western, so she drove the 600 miles by herself and talked officials into admitting her to the program. Next, she did economic research at the Bank of Commerce; when I met her she was a bond trader at a brokerage firm. I admired her pluck and was impressed by her style. We skied and played tennis together; it didn't take long for me to realize that Ruth was a better athlete than I. Ruth could also be outspoken. I liked that, too. You always knew where you stood with Ruth. After dating for less than a year, we were married on March 4, 1961.

Since my father was a civil servant in a company town, my parents had always been careful to hide any partisan views, although I was well aware that they voted Liberal. Their low-profile behaviour coloured my activities to the point where I did not join any political clubs while at university. At McCarthys, John Clarry encouraged my political involvement. During the Second World War, Clarry served in France and Germany and rose to the rank of major with the Royal Canadian Army Corps. He graduated with the silver medal from Osgoode Hall law school in 1950, just five years ahead of me. But because the war had interrupted his career path, he was thirteen years older.

As president of the Rosedale Liberal Association, Clarry asked me if I'd like to become involved in helping Thomas O'Neill, the candidate in the 1958 election. O'Neill, who was known as "Windy," had played defence for the Toronto Maple Leafs when they beat Montreal for the Stanley Cup in 1945. I agreed to help, began to attend meetings, and served as a poll captain in the Moore Park area. I discovered that I enjoyed going door-to-door as well as helping to get out the election-day vote.

The 1958 election result was a rout. John Diefenbaker won 208 out of the 265 seats, the largest majority in Canadian history. In 1957,

Progressive Conservative candidate David Walker had won in Rosedale over the incumbent, Liberal Charles Henry, by about 5,000 votes when Diefenbaker formed a minority government. In 1958, Walker beat O'Neill by more than 9,000 votes. Although the other side was victorious, I was hooked on politics. I loved the direct involvement with voters; working in common cause with others was stimulating. Lifelong friendships could be formed in the crucible of an election campaign.

When Clarry asked me to join the executive of the Rosedale Liberal Association, I immediately agreed and became secretary-treasurer. There seemed to be no way for the beleaguered Liberals to go but up. Whatever I did had to be helpful. Moreover, the Liberal Party was the only place for me. The Co-operative Commonwealth Federation (CCF), which would merge with the Canadian Labour Congress in 1961 to form the New Democratic Party, was too socialistic. As for the Progressive Conservative Party, their previous leader, George Drew, seemed like a decent enough fellow until I heard him speak. I thought he was a gasbag.

With the exception of Sir John A. Macdonald, as far as I was concerned, Canada's most accomplished political leaders were all Liberal. Sir Wilfrid Laurier forged an alliance between French- and English-speaking Canadians to create the national Liberal Party. Mackenzie King made a modern, independent nation from what had been a British colony. Louis St Laurent helped create a Canada with a dynamic private sector and vigorous Crown corporations. By contrast, Diefenbaker's desire to maintain strong ties with Britain smacked of days gone by. I preferred the international vision of Lester Pearson, who had just been elected Liberal leader in 1958. I was a progressive, a centre-left Liberal. I believed in a guaranteed annual income for single mothers and disabled individuals.

After Diefenbaker's 1958 election victory, the Rosedale Liberal Association had only seven paid-up members. John Clarry and I were two of them. The third was Denton McMurtry, who had a small engineering practice. McMurtry took over from Clarry as president, and we'd meet in McMurtry's second-floor office at Bloor and Sherbourne streets. David Walker seemed firmly ensconced as MP. Not only was he made minister of public works in 1959, but he was also a Diefenbaker confidant. Voters like their MPs to be powerful, and Walker certainly was. We got busy and tried to attract people to our cause, but you almost had to sign them up at gunpoint, there was so little interest.

To help rebuild the Liberal Party in Rosedale, we opened a constituency office south of Bloor to deal with local problems. A search committee, headed by Clarry, sought a candidate for the next election, expected in 1962. As likely possibilities rejected our approaches, we kept returning to the same name: Walter Gordon, who lived in the riding and was a pillar of the Toronto business community. Keith Davey, a former sales manager at Toronto radio station CKFH, who was by then national director of the Liberal Party, put a stop to that idea. "Nothing doing," the word came back. "Dave Walker is a pretty effective guy, and he's likely to win. Get somebody else." Davey's view was that Walter would do better west of Yonge Street in a riding like Davenport. In those days, and for some years to come, everyone listened to Keith Davey. He was a brilliant strategist, indefatigable, and an eternal optimist. Editorial cartoonists routinely ridiculed his bushy sideburns and pinstripe suits.

One night in June 1961, the Rosedale riding executive met yet again in Denton McMurtry's office. We discussed more names of possible candidates, but none of them sounded right. After a while, the list was exhausted and so were we. The room fell silent. Finally, Clarry turned to me and said, "Why don't you become the candidate?"

Astounded at the idea, I blurted, "What will the firm say?"

"You leave that to me," said Clarry.

Clarry later told me that the idea for my candidacy began with Thomas O'Neill. At some meeting, I had apparently spoken extemporaneously and with some passion about what we needed to do to win. After my remarks, O'Neill leaned over and whispered to Clarry, "That's the guy who should be our candidate."

The two senior partners at the firm, Bev Matthews and Senator Salter Hayden, gave their blessing. Matthews told me that he'd tried for the nomination himself in Rosedale in the 1930s but was unsuccessful. He also said that I was unlikely to win. But, he added, "Go run a good campaign, and there will be a place for you in the firm afterwards."

While I was encouraged by everyone's faith in me, I realized that I was little more than a sacrificial lamb being led to the election slaughter. Rosedale had voted Tory for most of the twentieth century; Charlie Henry's two victories in 1949 and 1953 were more of an aberration that anything else. I didn't even live in the riding. Ruth and I were renting at 37 Madison Avenue, west of Yonge, near Bloor and Spadina.

For the nominating meeting held at the Club Harmonie on September 27, 1961, Jack Pickersgill, by then the MP from Bonavista–Twillingate in Newfoundland, flew in from Ottawa to deliver one of his stemwinders charging the Diefenbaker government with "colossal and impudent interference" by offering advice to Britain about the Commonwealth. Walter Gordon got out of his sick bed to chair the meeting and gave me a glowing introduction.

My own speech covered a range of topics from increased trade with Europe to the failure of the Diefenbaker government to provide adequate public housing in the riding. "No more than a few hundred yards from where we meet are some of the most appalling living conditions in Toronto," I said. "Low-cost housing requires no further justification than that it is a humane act. Mr Walker has witnessed the conditions at first-hand and has carelessly dismissed any responsibility for his constituents and fellow human beings. I would look forward to an opportunity to meet Mr Walker on a public platform and to hear him attempt to defend his abysmal record on the question."[3]

I won the nomination by default: nobody else wanted the job. My beginnings were inauspicious. A story in the *Toronto Star* the next day wrongly identified my riding as Parkdale, a few miles to the west. The *Telegram* took pains to point out that I was *not* Donald C. MacDonald, leader of the Ontario CCF.[4] The only good news was a modest groundswell in the number of memberships. By the time of my nomination, they'd risen from an anemic seven to a more robust one hundred and sixty.

Once I was nominated, I called on Walter Gordon in the limestone building at 15 Wellington Street West where Clarkson, Gordon was located. (The facade of that building has since been preserved and moved, stone by stone, a short distance south to the Allen Lambert Galleria in Brookfield Place.) Clarkson, Gordon was the bluest of Canada's blue-chip accounting firms. Walter joined as a student in

1927 and was made partner in 1935. Unlike some accountants who are content to sift through the entrails of financial statements, as a nationalist, he tried to put his creed into his deed through investments in Canadian firms via his own company, Canadian Corporate Management.

Walter, who was in his mid-fifties, couldn't have been more helpful. He was warm, direct, and witty. His confidence in me was both fatherly and far-reaching. Moreover, I admired his nationalist views even though they were not popular in the party. For decades, the Liberal Party had been continentalist, always looking for stronger ties with the United States. The foreign leader most frequently visiting the Franklin Delano Roosevelt White House was Canada's Mackenzie King. I left Walter's office feeling as if, with his help, I could conquer the world. He was as good as his word about helping me and, in April 1962, with an election in the offing, was the guest speaker for a meeting of the riding association held at Rosedale Public School.

I even had a client who brought me some favourable publicity. Some dissident members of the Toronto Flying Club were upset at what they saw as high-handed self-dealing by their board of directors. Members paid annual dues and then were charged on an hourly basis to go flying at Malton, a much smaller airport than Pearson International is today. The directors, however, were flying for free. A sense of entitlement had crept into their behaviour. The other members obviously felt this was unfair and so did I. I was delighted to represent them in a matter that was so blatantly wrong. We obtained an injunction to prevent the re-election of the incumbents. After the chairman called the annual meeting to order, I presented the injunction. After some debate, the chairman asked me, "What if I don't obey this injunction?" "You will go to jail," I said. The meeting adjourned, the old board stood aside, and a new board was elected.[5]

Newspaper reports about my performance gave me a boost going into an election campaign where everybody knew the incumbent and few had ever heard of his challenger. Even under such difficult circumstances, I was not unhappy to set aside the law to run for public office. Although I had grown up wanting to be a lawyer, the reality of the profession was turning out differently than I had expected. All too often, the work was tedious. I now had higher hopes and sought wider horizons.

6

MP for Rosedale

Rosedale was a sprawling riding that stretched from Yonge Street on the west to the Don River on the east, Mount Pleasant Cemetery in the north all the way south to Lake Ontario, including the Toronto Islands. Within that area, the spread of annual income was huge – from high-paid bank executives living on Binscarth Road to the public housing of Regent Park.

When the election was called in April for June 18, 1962, other Liberal candidates running in Toronto appeared to stand a far better chance than I. In addition to Walter Gordon in Davenport, there was Mitchell Sharp, a former deputy minister of trade and commerce, running against Finance Minister Donald Fleming in Eglinton, as well as Leonard Patrick "Red" Kelly, who played for the Toronto Maple Leafs, running in York West.

Thomas O'Neill, our 1958 candidate in Rosedale, gave me a good idea for campaigning that he'd seen used by Roland Michener when he was the Progressive Conservative candidate in St Paul's. Michener made a life-sized photographic cut-out of himself that drew attention as he greeted voters at subway stations and streetcar stops. As a result, on my first morning of campaigning in April 1962, both O'Neill and my life-sized image accompanied me when I met voters on their way to work. For the rest of the campaign, I rarely went anywhere without the cut-out that became known as "The Thin Man."

Among my other key volunteers in 1962 was a fraternity brother, Steve Goudge, a lawyer who later became a judge on the Ontario Court of Appeal. He could charm the most harried commuter into a conversation or convince them to wait a minute to meet me. People seemed to be impressed by the simple fact that I was out on the streets at the same time as they were heading for work. Politics was like articling for a law career. You learn on the job and get better as time passes. I soon realized that voters in all parts of the riding preferred to meet their candidate face to face and make their own personal assessment rather than listen to speeches or read policy papers. Retail politics was all-important.[1]

Public life today is littered with the debris left by strafing your opponent with negative advertising. I much prefer the friendliness of individual encounters that allow people to see who you are and hear where you stand, not what or whom you're against. A firm handshake, a friendly grin, and an unpretentious manner can go a long way. People remember their moment with you long after the noise from a nasty attack has died down or the campaign literature has been tossed aside.

A malaise had set in on the Diefenbaker government. Unemployment was rising. To fight a recession and boost exports and tourism, the Canadian dollar had been fixed at US$0.925, far below the US$1.05 value of only two years earlier. Cartoon-style Diefenbucks papered the land, mocking the government's role in the economic mess.

My campaign was mainly an infantry effort with the national battle in the background. I'd meet commuters in the morning, canvas door to door during the day, and in the evening attend living-room gatherings where neighbours were invited. Among the most contentious issues was whether or not the federal government would bring in medicare. My position, which seemed to resonate well, was that any plan had to be established with the full co-operation of the provinces and the profession. Doctors would continue to choose the type of practice they wanted and patients would be free to choose their doctors, who would be paid on a fee-for-service basis that had been negotiated with the profession. Universal health care took a few more years, until a Liberal government in 1966, and Canadians have been well served since.

Our first child, Barbara Leigh Macdonald, was born on May 19, 1962, a month before the vote. Her picture was featured on the front page of our next campaign newspaper. For days after, everyone I met asked, "How's your baby?" By comparison, the articles on my personal activities and policy views were of far less interest.[2]

Nor was Leigh's fortuitous birth our last such well-timed pregnancy. Ruth was pregnant during three of the next four elections. Our second daughter, Nikki, was born November 26, 1963 so Ruth was about six weeks pregnant on election day, April 8, 1963. Althea was born April 3, 1966, with Ruth four months pregnant when the 1965 election was held on November 8. For the 1968 Trudeaumania election, there were no new additions to the family. Our fourth daughter, Sonja, arrived on December 11, 1972, about six weeks after that year's election.

On election night in 1962, after the polls had been closed for an hour, we started to hear from our scrutineers that I was doing surprisingly well. But as we watched the televised results roll in from across Canada, there was no mention of Rosedale. It seemed like a conspiracy among members of the media, who were afraid of David Walker and didn't want to announce he'd lost in case he ended up winning and visited retribution upon them later. Finally, well after midnight, the CBC declared that I had beaten Walker by about 600 votes. (The final margin was 594 out of 23,806 ballots cast.) I had been elected to the 25th Parliament of Canada.[3]

I heard later that when Lester Pearson arrived at party headquarters, he asked first about Rosedale. He was delighted I'd beaten David Walker, whose barbs in the House of Commons got under his skin. (In the end, losing worked out well for Walker. Diefenbaker appointed him to the Senate in 1963 so he was around Ottawa and the party for years.) Of the eighteen seats in what had been Tory Toronto, we Liberals won twelve.

Other first-time Liberal candidates who won that night included Edgar Benson in Kingston; Lucien Lamoureux in Cornwall; and Herb Gray and Eugene Whelan in Windsor. In Montreal, we won twenty of the twenty-one seats. First-timers included Walter Gordon's brother-in-law C.M. "Bud" Drury and John Turner, who was briefly at Ashbury ahead of me before transferring to St Patrick's. I was just thirty years old, one of the youngest in the enlarged Liberal caucus.

Diefenbaker, however, remained in power, as the leader of a minority government with a seat total reduced from 208 in 1958 to 116 in

1962. Fully seventy-nine per cent of eligible voters went to the polls, a far cry from the sixty-one per cent today. The Liberals won ninety-nine seats, more than double our forty-eight seats after the 1958 election. The Social Credit Party held thirty seats and the New Democratic Party, nineteen. No one expected the new minority government of John Diefenbaker to last very long.

Journalists soon took note of my arrival in Ottawa. In the September 28 issue of *Time*, an article described the 25th Parliament "one of the brightest in Canadian parliamentary history." It featured profiles and photos of eight freshmen MPs: the NDP's David Lewis, Tom Berger, and Andrew Brewin; and the Liberals' John Turner, Edgar Benson, John Stewart, Jack Davis, and me. I was "young, athletic, and in awe of no one. A meticulous organizer, he listened as much as he talked during his campaign to unseat Tory Works Minister David Walker, and against all odds did." The article quoted an unnamed friend as saying, "He is the sort of man who runs against the trend and succeeds."[4]

In October 1962, Ruth and I moved into the riding, taking an apartment at 16 Summerhill Gardens. My salary as an MP was $8,000 a year plus $4,000 tax-free for expenses. That was less than the $15,000 I'd made as a lawyer, so I watched my spending. After all, I had to be true to my Scottish roots. I kept a careful tally in a lined notebook of all expenses, from Bell telephone bills to birthday gifts, gasoline to groceries.

In order to save money, when in Ottawa, I lived with Ruth's parents on Richmond Road. The price was right, but George Hutchison was so enamoured with politics that no matter how late at night I arrived, he would be waiting for me, armed with a bottle of Scotch, eager to hear every detail of that day's debates. After a while, I could take the confabs no longer and moved to a furnished apartment on The Driveway, a fifteen-minute walk from Parliament Hill.

Since 1949, when I'd left Ottawa for Trinity College, the city had awakened. There'd been a welcome boom in downtown office-tower construction. Residential development now extended far beyond the city limits. Parliament Hill, however, was as breathtakingly the same as ever. The Gothic architecture always looked to me like frozen music. As a boy, I had sat riveted in the visitor's gallery. Now this was my place of employ and my inspiration. I was happy to have been elected, not a little humble, and ready to work for change.

My seatmate was another freshman, Bryce Mackasey, an Irish Catholic from the Montreal riding of Verdun who was filled with blarney and bluster. Our seats were the last two in the back row on the opposition side. To see us, the Speaker had to turn his head ninety degrees to the left. Said Mackasey, "We only just made it. Two more yards and we'd be out in the hall."

In the early going, I had the temerity to rise in my place during Question Period and ask the prime minister about the relationship between trade negotiations with the United States and a round of talks with the United Nations. Diefenbaker absolutely flattened me in three sentences. "Mr Speaker, if the honourable gentleman will study both he will see there is a vast difference. The President of the United States realized there was a difference when he accepted the suggestion of the Canadian government," said Diefenbaker, underlining how little I knew. "I would ask the honourable gentleman to make an examination, and I believe when he does he will understand what the government is proposing." Diefenbaker shot me a triumphant look, tossed his head as if to say, "Take that," and resumed his seat, almost cackling with delight.

I thought I'd been scarred for life, but I was wrong. I later ran into Amédée Gaudreault, the parliamentary correspondent for *Le Soleil de Québec*, who said, "You've made your mark."

"How so?" I asked.

"You made an impression on the prime minister. He probably already knew who you were because you defeated one of his best friends, David Walker, but he paid you the compliment of a spirited riposte rather than give you a brush-off answer," he said. "Secondly, everybody in the press gallery now knows who you are, too. During the exchange, we all stood up and leaned over the balcony to see who it was that Mr Diefenbaker had selected for special attention with his thunderbolt. I'm going to refer to you in my story as the man who brought the members of the press gallery to their feet!"

So, my first lesson in Ottawa was this: don't assume things are what they seem. My second lesson was that you don't always know who are your enemies and who are your friends. A few days after my exchange with the prime minister, I was waiting for the elevator when the doors opened, and there inside was Diefenbaker, who said, "Well, Mac, how are you?" We chatted amiably as we rode up together. Ever after, we enjoyed a cordial relationship that was nothing at all like he had with most Liberals, or even some members of his own party who later vilified him as their leader. I could only assume that he'd checked me out, learned of my First Baptist upbringing, and decided that as a fellow Baptist I was all right in the eyes of God and him. And not necessarily in that order.

Undaunted by that first smackdown, I tried to raise my profile through more questions as well as by sponsoring a private member's bill aimed at reducing interest rates for consumer loans.[5] While the Tories were our major opponents, we also had to worry about the NDP attracting Liberal supporters. I didn't expect to win over the hard-left NDPers, but I wasn't prepared to cede any votes, either. In a letter to the *Toronto Star* on October 18, 1962, I described the difference between the Liberals and NDP as follows:

> While the Liberal party advocates the setting of national economic objectives to which federal economic measures will conform, the NDP proposes a rigid economic framework in which business must either conform or be punished. The Liberal measures will constitute incentives to businessmen by tax, loan and other measures to pursue their private activities in conformity with the objectives of the national plan. The NDP proposes to issue commands to businessmen in the manner in which they must make investments and hence on how, ultimately, they must carry on business. If he fails to take advantage of the opportunities provided by the Liberal measures, the businessman's loss will only be of an opportunity to increase profits. If he fails to obey the orders of the NDP Investment Board, however, the businessman would be faced with the prospect of jail. In simplest terms, Liberals provide a carrot – to persuade; the NDP prefer to beat with a stick – to command.[6]

In my maiden speech to the House of Commons on December 14, 1962, I did not follow the rookie MP's usual path and simply extoll the virtues of my riding. Because of my post-graduate education in the US and England, as well as my extensive travels in Europe, I knew something of the world and Canada's place within it.

As a result, my speech was about international trade. I attacked the Ontario government for its "Buy Canada" policy because I believed it was no more than a boycott that befouled relations with our trading partners. Far better, I argued, to work with Britain and the United States to expand foreign trade during the multilateral trade negotiations set to begin in 1964. "For the first time in a generation the log jam of structural arrangements in the international economy is being broken," I said. "We will have an opportunity to make for ourselves trade arrangements which could assure the Canadian manufacturing industry and other Canadian producers effective participation in world trade."[7]

Those years of minority governments were fractious. A bitter rancour developed between the two party leaders, Lester Pearson and John Diefenbaker. Of the many topics where the two men diverged, the debate about nuclear weapons provided the best litmus test. Initially, Diefenbaker had agreed to deploy the Bomarc missiles but then changed his mind, a decision that split the Diefenbaker Cabinet. Pearson argued that Canada should live up to its commitments to collective and continental defence. For him, such a pledge meant allowing tactical nuclear warheads on Canadian soil. The Cold War was on and keeping the Soviet Union at bay using the Bomarc surface-to-air missile demanded no less. In a speech in Scarborough, Ontario, in February 1963, Pearson said, "As a Canadian, I am ashamed if we accept commitments and then refuse to discharge them." Fulfilling the commitments was "the only honourable course for any government representing the Canadian people."[8]

In the last week of the 1963 election campaign, Pearson was clearly ahead. After a speech in Vancouver, even members of the media were applauding along with the crowd. On April 8, Pearson won a minority government with 128 seats to 95 for the Conservatives. In Rosedale, I defeated Progressive Conservative Hal Jackman by more than 6,000 votes. As part of a new government, I was named parliamentary secretary to the minister of justice. Justice was the perfect place for me. The department acted as the government's lawyer, offering opinions, drafting legislation, defending lawsuits, and buying and selling land, all of which was familiar ground.

Once I had been re-elected, Ruth and I decided we could enjoy more family time together if we lived in Ottawa. We sublet our apartment on Summerhill Gardens to a young journalist from the *Vancouver Sun* with a wife and baby. He'd won a Southam Fellowship to study at the University of Toronto for nine months. The journalist was Allan Fotheringham, who would go on to fame as the back-page columnist at *Maclean's*. His first month's cheque bounced.[9]

During my first two elections, there were no all-candidates meetings. By the time of the 1965 vote, the local churches were sponsoring such gatherings. The most politically conscious congregations in my riding were St Luke's United, St Peter's Anglican, and Sacre Coeur, the Roman Catholic church.

While the churches might serve their communities on an even-handed basis, in politics their partisanship was obvious. Clark MacDonald, the minister at St Luke's, chaired an event at his church, and gave an effusive introduction to NDP candidate Harding Bishop. PC candidate Hal Jackman and I, on the other hand, were denounced as devils incarnate. A few days later, at St Peter's Anglican, Jackman received a warm introduction and the minister was equally polite to me (after all, I was a Trinity grad). He couldn't remember the NDP candidate's name even though you'd think "Bishop" might have rung a church bell in his head.

The last event, at Sacre Coeur, was held on a Saturday night at 7 p.m. I thought the timing was a bit odd, but showed up, only to find the church hall full of bingo tables. Thinking I was the first to arrive, I asked about my opponents. "The other candidates? Oh no, we wouldn't invite *them* here," the priest replied. My special status evaporated when he told me that my remarks would have to wait until after the first game of bingo, that I was to speak for no longer than ten minutes, and that I then had to leave immediately.

Letters from constituents were equally full of surprises. One began by saying, "Whether I like it or not, you are my representative in Parliament." Another asked for help obtaining a buffalo skin for a coat lining. UFO sightings were regularly reported.[10] At times I took umbrage. One such case occurred when I received a letter praising an article in *Maclean's* by historian Donald Creighton and asking me to help "keep the Prime Minister from bringing about the ruination of the Canadian way of life which is cherished by English-speaking Canadians." I replied, saying, "I read Professor Creighton's article with disdain but not surprise. He was as narrow-minded, particularly in respect of French-speaking Canada, when I listened to his lectures as he is today. I have never been able to reconcile Professor Creighton's inability to comprehend how Canada functions with his admiration for Sir John A. Macdonald who was obviously much wiser on these questions."

I held regular constituency meetings so that interested citizens could tell me their views. One such event at Rosedale Public School in the 1970s attracted the radical Western Guard, an ultra right-wing group known for its noisy demonstrations and anti-Semitic views. Throughout the evening, the members of the Western Guard glowered at me from the front row and kept interrupting the proceedings.

Try as I might, I could not identify another group of men, who were very attentive but spoke not a word. When 10 p.m. at last arrived, I closed the meeting, and made to leave. Suddenly, this group of mystery men leapt from their seats and closed ranks around me. Worried this was another bully-boy brigade, I said, with a tinge of fear in my voice, "Hey, what's going on?" "It's all right, Mr Macdonald," came the reply, "I'm Corporal Jones with the RCMP." A flying squad hustled me outside to a waiting taxi and sent me safely on my way before I could come to any harm.

After my first time elected to office on a shoestring, subsequent campaigns were better financed. A group of lawyers, all of whom attended Our Lady of Perpetual Help, a Roman Catholic church, formed a fundraising committee, and I was never faced with paying off debt after an election. More importantly, never during my time in office did a donor come to me and say, "I gave, you owe me." If there had been any such a plea, I would have given it short shrift.

The minority Pearson governments in which I served shaped the Canada of today. We brought in medicare, the Canada Pension Plan, the Auto Pact, the Order of Canada, and the Canadian flag. As a leader, Pearson understood Canada and always knew the right course in difficult situations. In diplomacy, and then in domestic politics, Pearson had the gift of being able to persuade others to follow courses of action that they would not necessarily choose.

Pearson also stood up to the United States in a manner unlike any previous prime minister. In a speech delivered at Philadelphia's Temple University on April 2, 1965, Pearson declared that he supported the purposes of the US in Vietnam but he suggested a pause in the US bombing of North Vietnam as the only possible way toward a peaceful resolution. President Lyndon Johnson was irate. At a Camp David meeting the next day, Johnson told Pearson, "Don't you come into my living room and piss on my rug." Pearson stood his ground, wet or otherwise. I was proud to be a member of his government.

7

Pierre and Me

Among the many pleasures of being a Member of Parliament was the opportunity for foreign travel. In July 1965, I joined an all-party delegation to Czechoslovakia and the Soviet Union. On the trip were several senators, including David Croll, the first Jewish senator; four Liberal members of the House of Commons; three Progressive Conservatives, including Michael Starr, minister of labour in the Diefenbaker government; NDP leader Tommy Douglas; Réal Caouette, leader of the Ralliement des Créditistes; and Bud Olson, a Social Credit MP who later crossed the floor to the Liberals, supported Pierre Trudeau for leader, and became a Cabinet minister.[1]

Few foreigners were permitted into the Soviet Union at the time. We were the first parliamentary delegation to visit the USSR. Trade between our two countries was modest. The major Canadian export to the Soviet Union was wheat, usually due to their poor harvests. In the midst of the Cold War, we were warned to be careful what we said and did.

Our first stop in Moscow was the Kremlin, where I was fascinated by the difference between the grandeur of the magnificent palaces dating from csarist times and Lenin's humble quarters. We attended cultural events, including the opera *Ruslan and Ludmila*, *Spartacus* by the Kirov Ballet, and a circus starring Popov the clown. We toured the university and rode the subway system with its museum-quality design promoting the Communist Party. Some of the stations had massive columns, marble walls, high ceilings, and huge chandeliers.

At my request, I was able to meet a deputy chairman of the Supreme Court and see a People's Court in action.

What propaganda we were fed was mild, little different from speeches you might hear praising democracy at a service club lunch in Canada. At one banquet, I sat beside a Second World War air ace who twice received the Order of Lenin for downing thirty-eight German planes in defence of Leningrad. The only sour note was a news conference where Soviet journalists peppered us with questions about Vietnam, a country with which Canada had little involvement. They seemed ill informed; some of the good will dissipated.

People on the crowded streets appeared healthy enough but not very well dressed. The liveliest visible groups were the military, who exuded a certain muscular bravado. Suburban architecture was brutal in design; all multi-storey apartment buildings were covered in the same rust-yellow wash. Trees struggled to survive; landscaping was unkempt.

Our group, accompanied by a member of the Supreme Soviet, also visited Sochi, a resort city on the Black Sea, and Leningrad, where we saw the renowned art collection of the State Hermitage Museum. Everywhere, there were official lunches and receptions, visits to local factories and farms, concerts, and more propaganda. For all toasts and most meals, we needed a speaker. If everyone else begged off, we could always call on Réal Caouette, a former car dealer, to hold forth at any length on a moment's notice. His oratory and timing never failed to draw applause and laughter with simple stories told at a pace that translators could easily follow.

The differences between the Soviet Union and Czechoslovakia, our final stop, were remarkable. The Czech countryside was fertile and cultivated; in Prague, the stores were well lit and fully stocked. The people looked better off, the hotels were superior, and the architecture more attractive. By comparison, the Soviet Union was a failed experiment. But life in Czechoslovakia was not fully normal, either. At the end of the official trip, I took the train to Vienna on my own and rode in a car along with one other person – a well-dressed and watchful man. At the border, guards searched under the train and scoured all cars except mine. With the investigation complete, my shadow stood, looked at me, and in perfect English, wished me a pleasant trip. Obviously, he had been assigned to make sure I left the country safely and as planned.[2]

At home, the Liberal Party was undergoing a necessary renewal. Fresh policies can have an impact, but new people are the best way to bring about organizational change. The three who would revolutionize politics and revitalize the country like no others who had gone before were Jean Marchand, Gérard Pelletier, and Pierre Elliott Trudeau.

While the Union Nationale government of Maurice Duplessis was debating jurisdictional matters with Ottawa, some young Quebecers preferred full independence. As they became more strident, Gérard Pelletier found himself increasingly at odds with the separatist view. As editor of *La Presse*, he wanted change, too, but he believed change could be achieved by a Quebec within Confederation. In response to his views, separatists burned Pelletier in effigy. After a bitter strike at the newspaper, he was fired as editor in 1964.

At the same time, Jean Marchand, president of the Confederation of National Trade Unions, was also worried about increased tensions between Quebec and Ottawa. In Marchand's opinion, francophone leadership in Quebec was becoming less effective. He began to consider running for Parliament.

Marchand, Pelletier, and Trudeau had forged a friendship during the violent Asbestos Strike in 1949 by standing together against provincial police sent in by Premier Duplessis. Over a bottle of Scotch, Marchand and Pelletier convinced Trudeau to join them in running for Parliament. In 1970, Pierre told a group of us during lunch at 24 Sussex Drive, "It was the only occasion in my life when I became tight on Scotch." Marchand took the occasion to admit that he drank ginger ale, the first time Pierre learned that his friend stayed sober to make the case.

All three were elected in November 1965. In Quebec, they were known as *Les Trois Colombes* (The Three Doves), and in English Canada, The Three Wise Men. Jean was appointed to the Cabinet as minister of citizenship and immigration, while Gérard, Pierre, and I were named parliamentary secretaries.

After the election, Doug Fisher did some Cabinet making in one of his Toronto *Telegram* columns. Among his choices were Pierre, who he described as "a literate, well-spoken Canadian nationalist," and me, saying I was "aggressive and bright." Writing in *Maclean's*, Fisher further declared I was among the six most effective M P s, calling me "superbly prepared" and a young man "with a wide range of interests."

Two writers at the *Montreal Star* also cited me as an up-and-comer. Leslie Roberts predicted I would either be minister of justice or president of the Privy Council. After suggesting several candidates for prime minister, James Stewart wrote, "Below these men is a layer of young, talented and modern politicians who must be given at least an outside chance at the leadership." I was on that list, too.

In fact, I was three years away from Cabinet, but Gérard and I were both parliamentary secretaries to the secretary of state for external affairs, Paul Martin Sr. It was unusual for a minister to have two parliamentary secretaries. Gérard was designated to look after francophone relations while I was responsible for the balance of the departmental duties.

Paul was twenty-nine years older than I and treated me like a son. We'd both been born in Ottawa and had travelled the same academic path: University of Toronto, Osgoode Hall, Harvard, and Cambridge. In the fall of 1966, Paul took me to New York as part of the Canadian delegation to the United Nations. On the first morning, he phoned my hotel room at 6:30 a.m. and asked, "Well, what's happening?" Fortunately, I'm a morning person and was up and around, but I remember thinking, "Well, what *could* be happening at this hour?"

As the early-morning calls continued, I realized that Paul just liked to talk about all sorts of topics all the time. Little wonder. He knew everyone in the diplomatic community, had been involved in all the important international meetings since the founding of the United Nations in 1945, and always had a thoughtful opinion on events of the day.

I gave several speeches at the U N on numerous subjects, including marine resources, sovereignty over natural resources, and trade and economic development. "The international community has grasped more clearly than ever before that development is a co-operative endeavour. Translated to the aid field this means that donor countries must make greater and more determined efforts to expand the volume and improve the terms of assistance they extend. But it also means that recipient countries must do more to ensure that those limited human and financial resources are used with maximum effectiveness," I said on October 7. "From industrialized nations there should come initiatives designed to enhance the capacity of developing countries to take full advantage of expanding world trade." I urged improved access for exports from developing countries, supplementary financing, stable markets through international agreements on commodities such as sugar and cocoa, and technical assistance to accelerate industrialization.[3]

That New York posting brought me closer to another member of the Canadian delegation, Pierre Trudeau. As parliamentary secretary to the prime minister, he was rarely in Ottawa, travelling instead at Pearson's behest to Paris, Africa, and the Middle East as part of his education in global affairs. Our time together in New York was an opportunity for me to get to know Pierre, to understand Quebec better, and to see the special qualities that he brought to public life. In return, I was able to instruct him, following my four years in Ottawa, about how the House of Commons did and did not work. Or he'd ask, for example, about the need to go to Ottawa for a meeting, and I'd tell him, no, that's just a regular caucus meeting, we can remain in New York.

Pierre was perfectly bilingual, a man of broad dimensions who had been educated at the best institutions: Harvard, the London School of Economics, and the University of Paris. He had travelled widely, fought corruption in Quebec, and supported reform as editor of *Cité Libre*, an influential political journal.

In broadcaster Gordon Donaldson's memorable phrase, Pierre hit Ottawa "like a stone through a stained glass window." In private, however, he was shy. Pierre had a dramatic impact on me, a boy who had grown up parroting British books. His world view, captivating manner, and fertile brain reached inside me to trigger capabilities I never knew I had.

Pierre had a photographic memory. His Jesuitical training gave him clarity of thought. His nimble demeanour, ageless appearance, and glittering light-blue eyes combined to create a quixotic nature that meant he could rise to whatever station in life he chose. But, most of all, he had a set of beliefs and a core of forged iron against which he could test proposals and people. If he found you or your arguments wanting, he was not afraid to say so. He was not one of those politicians who would rather be loved than be able to lead. You either followed him or you fell behind. I knew I could follow; I hoped I could help.

And yet, Pierre was not initially seen as a potential party leader. Because of his success with disparate labour leaders, Jean Marchand was supposed to succeed Pearson. By comparison, Pierre's background as a law professor and the son of a wealthy businessman did not appear to be proper preparation for high office. Nor did Pierre show any interest in the role. As he wrote in his memoirs, "The idea of running for the leadership myself never crossed my mind, not even for a split second."[4]

At the UN, one of the issues on which Pierre and I worked together was recognition of what was then called Mainland China. He and I agreed that Mainland China should be a member of the UN at a time when the US puppet regime of Taiwan was officially recognized. Paul Martin responded cautiously to our continual prodding, but he did propose to the UN that both Mainland China and Taiwan be seated in the General Assembly with Mainland China taking a seat on the Security Council. When the vote was held, Canada's initiative was defeated.

Because of our time together in New York, I got to know Pierre better than any other anglophone in the Liberal caucus. That's not to say I understood him fully; he always held something back, perhaps even from himself. But during my years in politics, and in the time since, I can honestly say no one has ever come close to him in terms of charisma and character or leadership and legacy. A look from Pierre could wilt a woman, flummox an opponent, or convert a doubter.

In 1966, Ruth and I decided to live permanently in Ottawa as a family. We had leased – and later bought – 15 Westward Way, in Rockcliffe

Park. Our home was across the street from Gordon Robertson, then clerk of the Privy Council and secretary to the Cabinet for Lester Pearson and Pierre. It was just a short stroll from McKay Lake, site of my boyhood boating days with Robin MacNeil.

That fall, at the Liberal Policy Conference held at the Château Laurier in Ottawa, I was one of Walter Gordon's few supporters in his nationalistic stance against American takeovers of Canadian businesses. Walter had just published a book, *A Choice for Canada: Independence or Colonial Status*, and I concurred with his thesis that the long-run objective should be Canadian control of Canadian enterprises.

In advance of the floor debate, I tried to line up backers, but found few. Walter told the delegates that foreign acquisitions had reached such proportions that there should be legislation to control foreign investment as well as tax incentives to encourage Canadian investment in Canadian companies. Half of the oil and gas sector as well as manufacturing were foreign-owned. When the proposal eventually reached a vote, it passed, but in a watered-down form.

Walter had already suffered as a result of his nationalist views. Appointed minister of finance in April 1963, his first budget took the position that foreign capital was welcome but only if it created new businesses with Canadian partners. He presented numerous galvanizing ideas, such as a thirty per cent tax on the takeover of Canadian firms by non-residents, but his proposals got lost in a sideshow about hiring outside consultants as advisers for budget preparations.

During the attacks on Walter, I was the most senior person in government to remain loyal. It was not the last time I saw Cabinet members distance themselves from a wounded colleague. Walter was campaign chair in the 1965 election that produced another Liberal minority, missing out on a majority by only two seats. Since he had pledged to resign if the Liberals didn't win a majority, Walter stepped down as finance minister and rejected Pearson's offer of another post.

I wrote Walter a commiserating letter; his reply focused more on my future than on his own loss. He said he was sorry he wasn't continuing in Finance because he had been looking forward to having me steer the banking and tax legislation through the House. Such assistance, he said, would have given me good experience and allowed him more time to think about broader themes. "I have a high regard for your abilities quite apart from your strength of character, and hope it will not be very long before you are given a real chance to show what you can do," he wrote to me on December 20, 1965. "One can never tell about anything in politics, and I think it is foolish for anybody in the business to become overly preoccupied with personal ambitions. Having said this, it is clear that you are one of those who, given the necessary luck and opportunity, and breaks on timing, might easily become the leader of the party at some time in the future."[5]

Despite Walter's resignation, Pearson continued to keep him in favour. In December 1966, Walter's prospects improved again. He was headed back into Cabinet. When Walter called to tell me the news, he said, "I'm sorry for you this is happening. Another minister from Toronto spoils your chances for Cabinet." I replied, "I'm happy for you. I'll help however I can."

But his appointment as minister without portfolio did have an impact. There were already three Toronto MPs in Cabinet: Paul Hellyer, Mitchell Sharp, and Robert Winters. Hellyer had first been elected in 1949 and served in both the St Laurent and Pearson cabinets. Sharp's background as a public servant and businessman gave him credibility in both worlds. Before holding public office, Winters was a mining company president.

With Gordon as the fourth Toronto minister, the likelihood of my being summoned to Cabinet was slim to zero. A number of my contemporaries were already ministers: Edgar Benson, Judy LaMarsh, John Turner, Larry Pennell, Bryce Mackasey, and Jean Chrétien. I was beginning to wonder if the prime minister was sending me a message.

In September 1967, the Progressive Conservative Party chose as its new leader Robert Stanfield, premier of Nova Scotia. As a result of the publicity generated by their convention, the Tories rose in the opinion polls. It was clear to me there would be an election soon – perhaps not at a time of our party's choosing – and we might not fare well. I told my riding executive to begin looking for a new candidate. I was thirty-five, with three children under six, and no apparent Cabinet prospects.

Assuming an election in 1968, I would by then have been away from the law for six years. Any longer, and it might be too late to go back. The world has a tendency to move on and leave behind those who are otherwise engaged. The constituency executive refused to listen, and urged me to continue as MP, but I was not convinced.

In late November, I met with the prime minister, shared with him my disappointment at not being in Cabinet, and told him I might not run again. "Don't be in any hurry to leave," Pearson said. "I'm not going to be here forever. There might be an entirely new scene. Just keep thinking about what you want to do. This is not a time to return to private life."

Two weeks later, on December 14, 1967, the prime minister announced he was retiring. A leadership convention was set for April 1968. My world suddenly shifted, just as he had predicted. I decided to postpone my decision about standing for re-election until after the convention. I sent word to the prime minister about my change of heart and Prime Minister Pearson wrote from Florida on December 31 to say he was pleased. "Perhaps the result of that convention will, as the members of your constituency executive hope – and I share that hope – cause you to change your mind."[6]

By then, the prime minister had met with Jean Marchand and Pierre Trudeau to urge that one of them become a candidate to replace him. While Marchand was the Quebecer that Prime Minister Pearson had originally sought, Pierre had overtaken him in popularity. Named minister of justice earlier that year, Pierre introduced an omnibus bill amending the Criminal Code on divorce, abortion, and homosexuality. I supported him even though some members of our party did not. Pierre persisted, and his opponents finally said, in effect, if you want to destroy your career, go ahead.

Pierre wasn't just a life force; he had an alluring style. He wore an ascot and sandals to the House. Pierre was also quotable. "The state has no place in the bedrooms of the nation," he famously said when speaking about his omnibus bill. When asked by the media about his Mercedes, he responded, "Do you mean the car or the girl?" He then answered his own question by saying, "No matter, I'm keeping both." Journalists fawned; Canadians became fans.

Even members of my own family were drawn into his orbit. One evening, when I returned to the House after dinner, I brought along my daughter Nikki, who was then about eleven. Pierre was wearing a safari suit; Diefenbaker twitted him about coming to work in his pajamas. Amidst the joviality, Pierre noticed Nikki and her blonde pigtails, sitting in the gallery, and summoned a page to take her the red rose from his lapel.

Pierre's face seemed made for television, the "perfect mask" as it was described by communications guru Marshall McLuhan. Expo 67, the very successful World's Fair in Montreal, created new-found pride among all Canadians. After far too many years of fractious standoffs in minority Parliaments, Canada seemed ready to head full tilt into the future. Pierre was just the man we needed to take us there.

Amidst such seismic change, I had to position myself properly. I concluded I could not in good conscience continue in my role as parliamentary secretary to Paul Martin. First elected to Parliament in 1935, Paul had served his country and his party well. I assumed Paul would be a candidate for leader, but he was sixty-four, only a year younger than Lester Pearson when he first took office as prime minister. I deeply respected Paul and his accomplishments, but it was time for the next generation. Since I could not support Paul, I did not feel it was appropriate to continue working for him. With some trepidation, I met with him and laid out my dilemma. He could not have been more gracious.

Released from my role, I visited the prime minister, told him I wanted a change and why. Pearson understood immediately, and with his approval, on January 7, 1968, I became parliamentary secretary to Industry Minister Bud Drury, who was unlikely to run for leader. I now had no conflict of interest and could support whomever I wanted. What followed would set my sails for the next ten years.

8

Tomorrow's Man

I first met Ethel Teitelbaum when she was a volunteer canvasser in my riding during the 1965 election. Ethel went on to work in our constituency office, became riding president in 1970–71, and then a political assistant in Ottawa when I was in Cabinet. She knew everybody and kept in touch with them all. As Ethel used to say, "Alexander Graham Bell invented the telephone for me."

Her knowledge and advice were never more important than on January 3, 1968. I was in my constituency office at 541 Parliament Street when Ethel called to ask, "Who are you supporting for leader now that Mr Pearson is standing down? I haven't seen your name in support of any candidate."

"My candidate would be Pierre Trudeau," I replied, "but he's refused to put his name forward until he's completed his legislative program."

Ethel grew up in Montreal and continued to have good friends and contacts there. She told me about a group headed by Marc Lalonde that was organizing for Trudeau, with or without his consent. Lalonde had worked for Davie Fulton, a minister in the Diefenbaker government, and was an adviser in the prime minister's office. "You get on the telephone and tell Marc you're with Trudeau and are ready to start working for him right now!"

Ethel, her artist husband Mashel, and historian Ramsay Cook – who had known Pierre from academic circles – had already launched a "Draft Trudeau" petition. Cook was signing up academics; the Teitelbaums were seeking support from the cultural community.

Among the signatories were the CBC's Peter Gzowski and Barbara Frum as well as writers June Callwood, Trent Frayne, and Pierre Berton.

You don't say no to Ethel, so I called Marc Lalonde. We met the following Monday on one of those classic winter days in Ottawa that I remembered from my youth. It was sunny, with a high blue sky, and the temperature well below zero. I had done some soundings in Toronto and told him that enthusiasm for Pierre was strong and growing. He said that Pierre had the support of eighty per cent of the party membership in Quebec and a solid backing in BC as well.

I was the first Ontario MP – and probably the first outside Quebec – to champion Pierre Elliott Trudeau for leader of the Liberal Party of Canada. To my mind, he was the first politician since Sir Wilfrid Laurier with a vision for the country. Yet he was not well known and not seen by many in the Liberal Party outside Quebec as a likely leader. Support was stronger for Paul Hellyer, Robert Winters, and Paul Martin Sr.

As part of my efforts to help, I flew to Charlottetown later that month for a meeting in the Confederation Centre with the University Liberal Club. In my speech entitled "Some Reflections on Choosing a New Leader," I promoted Pierre even though he had not yet announced. Most of the attendees remained uncommitted, waiting for all the candidates to declare.

Meanwhile, I was also trying to improve my oral French by auditing a class in Quebec Civil Law at the University of Ottawa. I had begun attending in September and found that my language skills were getting better as a result. My fellow students were very interested in politics, particularly articles about Quebec's separation written by René Lévesque, who would form the Parti Québécois the following year.

I continued working on my French during my entire time in Ottawa, even spending part of one summer with Ruth and the family in a French immersion program in Quebec. Eventually, I was able to read and write French capably; I was never pleased with my oral fluency, although it was good enough to give media interviews in French. Caucus and Cabinet meetings were conducted mostly in English.

In late January, I met with two dozen Trudeau supporters, including former MP Maurice Moreau and current MPs Robert Stanbury and Russell Honey. Honey, the member for Northumberland–Durham, was named chairman of our group, the Ontario for Trudeau Committee, as we set out to find others to join our cause. These few months were crucial for me. Either I was going to stand down and not run in the next election, or I was going to help Pierre become leader and hope to join his Cabinet.

Pierre's other key supporters included Quebec MP Jean-Pierre Goyer; Gordon Gibson, a British Columbia businessman who had worked for Arthur Laing at Northern Affairs; Pierre Lavasseur, an MBA graduate and former public servant in Quebec; and Jim Davey, an Oxford-trained management consultant who was with Canadian National Railways and lived in Montreal. We were nothing if not confident. Our convention planning report, a confidential document circulated to key officials, declared: "We intend to go into the convention in the lead and never to lose it."[1]

For the longest time, Pierre remained above the fray, neither acknowledging efforts on his behalf nor showing any interest in the leadership. Instead, he travelled the country girding for a February meeting with the premiers on constitutional matters. His profile as minister of justice meant that he was very much in the public eye. His proposal for a Charter of Rights seemed just the sort of forward-thinking policy Canadians craved. But I worried about his sometimes-flippant comments. Although they could be captivating, they could also sound gratuitous. What we needed was a sensible balance without giving up any of his Gallic charm.

Pierre's devotion to Canada, however, was never in any doubt. His book, *Federalism and the French Canadians*, sold 80,000 copies in French. The English translation was published in time for the convention. "The die is cast in Canada: there are two main ethnic and linguistic groups; each is too strong and too deeply rooted in the past, too firmly bound to a mother-culture, to be able to engulf the other," wrote Pierre. "But if the two will collaborate at the hub of a truly pluralistic state, Canada could become the envied seat of a form of federalism that belongs to tomorrow's world."[2]

Pearson had already begun the collaborative process. He'd appointed more francophones to his Cabinet than any other prime minister. Moreover, he had set out to make the federal civil service bilingual.

Canada's long-term unity was well served, as John English points out in his two-volume biography of Pearson. "Under Pearson, French and English began to work – and quarrel – in the same forum. The propinquity bred some fears, occasional contempt, and much anger; but by the mid-1960s, French and English Canada could no longer lead separate lives together in the same party or the same country. The Liberals learned that lesson then, with much pain; for the Tories, the realization and the pain came later," wrote English.[3]

At the constitutional conference in early February 1968, Pearson put Pierre on display in the chair beside him. When Quebec premier Daniel Johnson referred dismissively to Pierre as the "député de Mont-Royal," Pierre returned the favour by calling Johnson the "député de Bagot." Johnson pressed for more provincial powers, saying, "We all know that Canada is made up of two nations." Pierre tartly replied that if there were two nations in Canada, there should also be two nations in Quebec. "I believe that it is not a particular status in Confederation for the Government of Quebec but an equal status for all French-speaking Canadians in all of Canada that will bring enduring unity to our country,"[4] he said.

Robert Stanfield, by comparison, was hamstrung by his party's "deux nations" policy that appeared to permit special status for Quebec. Pierre had differentiated himself from his eventual rival even though he had yet to declare any interest in the leadership. Little did we know then that constitutional issues would outlast an entire generation of politicians.

The Ontario wing of the Liberal Party was scheduled to meet at the Royal York Hotel in Toronto the weekend following the constitutional conference. Declared candidates had been invited to participate, but Pierre had not yet announced so had no official status. As a result, the Ontario for Trudeau group had to find ways for him to greet potential supporters in a race he hadn't entered at a meeting he shouldn't be attending, at least according to the other candidates.

We decided that Pierre could meet delegates informally, outside the convention framework. I arranged a standard hotel room, thinking delegates could talk to him in small groups. As the numbers expressing an interest grew, I cancelled the room and reserved a suite.

Excitement continued to build, so I booked one of the meeting rooms on the mezzanine floor that could comfortably hold seventy-five people.

By the Friday of the weekend meeting, the list wanting to see Pierre was so overwhelming that we asked the hotel to move the furniture out of the room in order to free up space. When the hotel refused, we switched the event to the Ontario Room, one of the hotel's larger ball-rooms. When Pierre arrived, he was mobbed by scores of delegates. We could barely manoeuvre him to the stage even with Tim Reid, a member of the Ontario Legislature and former football player with the Hamilton Tiger Cats, leading the way.

I introduced Pierre to the clamouring crowd. I had prepared no notes, my remarks were just off the cuff, and I have no recollection of what I said, but others who were there tell me to this day that my performance was passionate and persuasive. Pierre spent the next two hours greeting individuals as best he could, given the maelstrom whirling around him. We were finally able to extract him from the throng by forming a wedge and leading him to a waiting elevator with delegates almost clinging to his clothing.

In a suite on an upper floor, where peace descended, no one – including the non-candidate – could believe what had just happened. Pierre seemed genuinely overcome and surprised by the outpouring. Although he had greeted people graciously and with enthusiasm, there was also a reticence about him, a modesty that I liked. There were those who saw him as intellectually arrogant, and indeed he could be, but he had another very human side that I admired. It was as if he always held something in reserve and did not show his whole face.

That existential capacity meant he could keep himself apart from the adulation he attracted. After such a love-in, most politicians would spend the next few hours stoking their vanity by reliving the crowd's fervour with anyone who would listen. Not Pierre. Instead, he fell into a lengthy discussion with Ramsay Cook, worrying about some of his views and how they would be perceived in Quebec. Cook assured him that he would not be seen as a *vendu*, a sellout. Quebecers, Cook said, had voted for Laurier and St Laurent despite the criticism of nationalists in the province.[5] At that point, Pierre still seemed to be genuinely struggling with his decision. If the Toronto visit had evoked no interest, he probably would not have entered the race. But Trudeaumania combusted spontaneously that weekend, and I was there when it happened.

On February 16, a week after his appearance in Toronto, Pierre declared his candidacy for leader.[6] As he travelled the country in the days that followed, excited crowds gathered everywhere he went delivering his message of two official languages and the equality of all peoples. I took it upon myself to write him a four-page memo, dated March 4, 1968, offering a wide variety of advice that included saying he was better suited to TV appearances than set speeches, but when he did make a speech, he should try to be more forceful. I don't know if or when he read the document, all I know is that he didn't reply for two months. In addition to a brief typed note of thanks, he added a handwritten postscript saying, "Just to show you that I have caught up with my mail!"[7]

The media had long since climbed aboard the bandwagon. "By electing him leader – and thus Prime Minister – the Liberals would serve their country well and their party superbly," wrote Arnold Edinborough, editor of *Saturday Night*, in the March issue of the magazine. "Let us hope they have the foresight, courage and commonsense to do so. If they do, the optimism and swing of the Kennedy regime in Washington might come to Canada." The cover photograph was accompanied by a declaration that was unusually positive for any general interest magazine, "Trudeau: The best possible choice for Canada."[8]

With so much attention focused on the leadership campaign, Parliament was poorly managed. On a Monday night in February, I was there for a vote on a tax matter but too many of my colleagues were absent. We squeaked through by one vote. House leaders had agreed there would be no more votes, but Finance Minister Mitchell Sharp wanted to press on. We lost the next vote 84–82. The House erupted into chaos, with opposition members shouting, "Resign," and indeed, under a strict interpretation of the rules, the government had been defeated and should have resigned.

But the recently elected opposition leader, Robert Stanfield, did not press his advantage. Prime Minister Pearson flew back from his

Jamaican holiday to take charge. Bank of Canada Governor Louis Rasminsky told Stanfield that the Canadian dollar was in peril. The international financial community would lose confidence in Canada if the tax matter was not passed and the government fell, Rasminsky said. A new motion was presented to Parliament and the government won. No snap election was required. Stanfield suffered a mortal blow from which he never recovered.

At the Liberal leadership convention, held at the Ottawa Civic Centre in April, the candidates included Pierre; Paul Hellyer, who had unified the armed forces; Eric Kierans, a brilliant thinker, former provincial Cabinet minister in Quebec, and president of the Montreal Stock Exchange; Joe Greene, a folksy politician with an appealing platform presence; Robert Winters, the candidate from Bay Street; the astute and well-educated Allan MacEachen; Paul Martin Sr, who was first elected in 1935; and John Turner, everyone's idea of the dashing young star.

Endorsements for Pierre poured in. "Pierre is better than medicare," said Newfoundland premier Joey Smallwood. "The lame have only to touch his garments to walk again." I helped prepare Pierre for the policy session and was one of the floor managers for the vote on Saturday, April 6. My height was a great advantage. I was able to spot badges of delegates supporting other candidates – as they fell by the wayside, I would push my way through the crowd to pin on a Trudeau button and collar another vote.

Pierre led from the first ballot. By the fourth ballot, there were three candidates left: Pierre, Robert Winters, and John Turner. There was no way the third-place Turner could win, but he decided to remain on the ballot anyway. If he had dropped out, and thrown his support to Winters, Winters might have won. Turner had nothing to lose; he knew he would be in the Cabinet under either man as leader. In the end, Pierre had more votes than the other two combined. The 195 Club, made up of the diehards who supported Turner on that final ballot, celebrated their mythic status for many years to come.

When the announcement came that Pierre had won, I was standing on the convention floor and could see Joe Potts, an old friend and stalwart supporter in the riding, working his way toward me. When Joe finally arrived, he said, with a twinkle in his eye, "My guess would be that you're probably going to run again." If I hadn't already made up my mind, his comment propelled my decision. My man had won. I wanted to participate in whatever life experience came next. I smiled at Joe, and said, "Yes."

Sworn into office on April 20, Pierre Trudeau moved quickly to heal any possible wounds by inviting his main rivals to join his Cabinet. John Turner was named minister of consumer and corporate affairs and solicitor general; Paul Hellyer became minister of transport. There were several ministers without portfolio, including John Munro, Gérard Pelletier, Paul Martin Sr, and me. As I headed to Pierre's office to learn my involvement, I ran into Bob Winters and Martin. The individual manner of each man reflected their view of life and themselves.

Although Winters knew me, he gave no sign of recognition. It wasn't a snub, really, it was just as if he were saying, "You're part of the future and I'm not, so there's no point in talking." He looked grim and stooped as he walked away. I later learned that he had told Pierre he would not serve in his Cabinet. Winters died the following year of a heart attack while playing tennis.

Where Winters was sullen, Martin was as ebullient as ever in spite of his reduced status after five years as secretary of state for external affairs. The following year Martin would be named leader of the government in the Senate, but for now he was just another minister without portfolio in the new government, the same as me, despite my lack of experience compared with his arrival in 1935 on Parliament Hill.

Paul was always in love with life. In October 1984, he phoned and said, "I know how much you like baseball." He invited me to the fifth game of the World Series between the Detroit Tigers and San Diego Padres. We met in Windsor and went across the border by car. En route we stopped so Paul could buy a Sunday paper. The process took twenty minutes while he glad-handed well-wishers in the street and in the corner store despite this being almost ten years after his parliamentary career was over. He was just a people person and loved to swim in their adoration. His driver dropped us at Tiger Stadium and then waited throughout the game in that same spot. The Tigers, led by Kirk Gibson's two home runs, won the World Series that day, four games to one.

For me, the biggest casualty of the changing times in 1968 was that my mentor, Walter Gordon, left politics. His thoughtful voice, however, continued to be heard through speeches and books. In 1970, with University of Toronto economist Abe Rotstein, *Maclean's* editor Peter C. Newman, and others, Walter formed the Committee for an Independent Canada to promote nationalist views.

Three days after being sworn in, Pierre called an election for June 25. Pierre campaigned in a way never before seen by Canadians – bouncing on a trampoline and doing fancy dives into a swimming pool. In my speech at the Rosedale nomination meeting held at the King Edward Hotel on May 9, I stressed the importance of preserving Canadian unity. "Canadians must decide which leader and what policies offer the best promise of maintaining our Canadian nation. Many Canadians, engrossed as they are by more immediate problems, may not have recognized how serious is the threat of survival of Canada as a single political entity but it has already drawn attention abroad. The foreign vultures are already lining up," I said, citing George Ball, under secretary of state in the administrations of John F. Kennedy and Lyndon Johnson, who had recently predicted the eventual disappearance of Canada as a nation.

My second message was about creating a just society, the iconic phrase that would become forever associated with Pierre. "We cannot claim to be a truly just society when, as is now the case, the opportunity of a child to acquire a meaningful role through education is dependent more on circumstances than his own abilities. In the same way, we cannot afford to be complacent when an adult, through no misconduct of his own, finds that the skills learned in his youth have become obsolete. To meet both problems, we must be prepared through public policies – not just to cushion misfortune with a cheque – but also to help people help themselves out of their disadvantages," I said.[9]

Everywhere Pierre campaigned, crowds repeated the pandemonium of the Royal York Hotel ballroom. A very different scene unfolded during the St Jean Baptiste Day parade in Montreal the night before the vote. A mob gathered, shouting *Trudeau au poteau* (Trudeau to the gallows), then threw rocks and bottles at him as he sat in the viewing stand. While many members of the official party scuttled to safety, Pierre waved off those who urged him to do the same, and then stared down the mob while television cameras recorded the chaos for airplay on newscasts across the country.

Pierre's defiance in the face of such personal danger convinced any stragglers that he had the stuff of leadership and the courage of his convictions. The following day, June 25, 1968, we won a majority government, the first after three elections. The Liberals had 154 seats; the PCS under Stanfield, 72; Tommy Douglas and the NDP, 22; and Réal Caouette's Créditistes, 14 seats.

I was relieved and gratified that I had remained in office rather than announce my resignation. We had a prime minister whom I had known from our first meeting would be a winner, someone who symbolized tomorrow and the kind of country Canadians wanted – a place where pride reigned, justice prevailed, and equal opportunity was possible for all.

9

Inside the Cabinet Room

When Pierre first became prime minister in April 1968, I was named minister without portfolio and acting minister of justice. Finally, after six years and four elections, I was a member of the Queen's Privy Council for Canada. As such, I was granted the life designation "Honourable." I would do everything I could to uphold that title and work hard for the people of Canada.

As a lawyer, Justice seemed like a logical place for me. But in July, after the election, when more permanent posts were handed out, Pierre had other ideas. First word about what that would be came in a telephone call from Marc Lalonde, who was speaking to those like myself who had been close to Pierre during the leadership race. He told me that Pierre wanted me to be House leader and president of the Queen's Privy Council.

Immediately after the swearing-in ceremony at Rideau Hall on a sunny July 6, 1968, the full Cabinet gathered in the East Block on Parliament Hill. Sir John A. Macdonald's Cabinet had met in that same room, known as the Privy Council Chamber, as had Louis St Laurent's ministers in the 1950s. Despite his refreshingly new style, Pierre created a Cabinet that honoured the past. Seventeen of the twenty-nine ministers had served in the cabinets of St Laurent or Pearson, or both. Of the other twelve, nine of us had previously been M P s. Only three of the newly minted ministers had just been elected to Parliament for the first time. Although there were additions and subtractions during my nearly nine years as a minister, this Cabinet formed the core group for all my time at the table.

I think it was unusual that six of the ministers, more than one-fifth of the new Cabinet, had contested the party leadership. Once their attempts fell short, each set aside personal disappointment and began pulling on the oars in unison. Such an ambitious group also said something about Pierre's ability to keep so many egos in line and working full tilt.

When restoration of the Privy Council Chamber – a project approved in 1967 by Lester Pearson – began later in the year, meetings of the full Cabinet moved to Room 340-S in the Centre Block and never returned.[1] Above some of the doorways in the Centre Block are carved biblical phrases such as "Fear God" or "Honour the king." In the Cabinet room, the words read, "Love justice, you that are the rulers of the earth."

Pierre sat halfway down one side of the green-baize table with the rest of the Cabinet ranged around him according to their seniority. At each place there was a water glass, a pad of writing paper, and an ashtray. It was the 1960s, after all! Although many of the ministers smoked, Pierre did not. On occasion he would lead a silent protest by moving away from a cigar smoker to sit in a more remote chair.

The clerk of the Privy Council and secretary to the Cabinet, accompanied by a member of his staff, sat at a separate table to record discussions and decisions. The clerk functioned as the prime minister's deputy minister and the de facto head of the public service. But the clerk was no mere functionary. He had a policy role, too. For example, at the beginning of the October Crisis in 1970, Gordon Robertson, clerk from 1963 to 1975, suggested a scenario for resolution that came very close to what eventually happened.

In the Ottawa in which I grew up, senior public servants, particularly in the economic portfolios and at External Affairs, were revered. The public service was an honourable calling consisting of devoted individuals such as Hugh Keenleyside, Arnold Heeney, Norman Robertson, and O.D. Skelton. They set the tone for the cadre of officials with whom I worked. As a result, those I dealt with – including Bill Hood, Tommy Shoyama, Jack Austin, Bill Hopper, Mickey Cohen, and Fred Gorbet – were all of high calibre. Unlike the obsequious and conniving civil servants on the BBC television program *Yes Minister*, officials through my four portfolios were honest and outspoken. They backed down from no one when discussions became animated.

Ministers who had been in the Pearson Cabinet must have felt a stark contrast with Pierre's new ground rules. Sidebars, beyond a few whispered words, were not allowed. In the Pearson era, I was told, several discussions often took place at once. Under Pierre, unless the situation was an emergency, there were no oral presentations by ministers. Documents were circulated in advance and thoroughly discussed by one or more Cabinet committees before coming to full Cabinet.

Pierre also chaired Priorities and Planning, or P and P as that committee was universally known, but rarely attended any other Cabinet committees. P and P operated as an executive committee where many decisions were made. This orderly and rational approach closely mirrored Pierre's style: highly disciplined and accustomed to examining carefully all the evidence before arriving at a conclusion.

Decisions taken at Cabinet meetings covered a wide range of topics. One week we'd approve a donation for relief after an earthquake in a far-off land; the next week we'd extend Canada's fisheries jurisdiction further out to sea. As the years went by, the number of topics and briefing documents grew. In 1968, everything for full Cabinet could fit in a normal one-inch-thick three-ring binder. By 1977, my last year in Cabinet, I lugged around a four-ringed binder that was eighteen inches tall and three inches thick. I still have that binder, with my name embossed in gold. If the auditor general claims this as government property and wants it back, they can have it. In the intervening years, busy though I've been with a Royal Commission, a foreign posting, and serving on the boards of numerous large corporations, I never again found a use for this Brobdingnagian binder.

Regularly scheduled events filled most of each week. Cabinet committees met Tuesday mornings and afternoons, Wednesday afternoons, and sometimes Thursday afternoons. Caucus met Wednesday mornings; full Cabinet on Thursday mornings. All ministers were expected to be in the House of Commons daily for Question Period. Ministers also took turns on House duty during evening sittings.

On top of all that, there was constituency business and participation in local events; telephone calls from friends, colleagues, and favour-seekers; mail to read, answer, and sign; consultation with provincial and international counterparts; departmental briefings and meetings with staff or special interest groups; media interviews; and delivering speeches in the House or across the country. In addition, somehow you squeezed in French lessons, staying fit, and a family life. Plus there was always somebody saying, "Minister, have you got a minute?" when they really meant fifteen minutes or maybe half an hour. If you were very lucky, you might find some time every once in a while to reflect on what you'd done or blue sky about what might happen next.

What I missed most was any time to read for pure pleasure. Over the years, I have accumulated hundreds of books, most of which include marginalia in my own hand as I held one-way arguments with the author or simply recorded my thoughts. While I had a great ability to read and digest voluminous material overnight, by far the most capable person I ever saw was Pierre. I revised the wording from a famous hymn to describe his talent: "A thousand pages in his sight are like an evening gone."

Pierre was incontestably in charge. One of the many erroneous stories put around by the press was Pierre's supposed high-handed decision-making process that took no account of other views. Pierre was always cognizant that, ultimately, full Cabinet had to decide major questions. With very few exceptions, he neither forced his views on us nor cut short arguments from those who disagreed.

In fact, he could be too patient, rather than too domineering, and allowed protagonists of different views to argue at length around the Cabinet table. Sometimes, to keep moving forward, he would declare agreement on certain aspects and then focus on the areas remaining. But, on many occasions, when most of us had made up our minds, Pierre was prepared to hear the pros and cons rehashed one last time.

One minister, curious to learn why Pierre allowed such circuitous debate, asked why he didn't step in earlier and announce his decision on a particular matter. Because, said Pierre, the subject was not one he knew well, and he wanted to learn as much as possible before having to choose among the alternatives.

Conversely, on topics where he had a lifelong interest – the constitution, intricacies of Quebec politics, or certain fields of law and foreign relations – Pierre felt little need for more information. In those cases, he had no lack of confidence in himself or his knowledge built up over a lifetime. He was prepared to hear opposing views, but you had better make a good case because he could demolish a bad one. When it came to his areas of special interest, you learned to tread with caution and carefully consider whether a debate could turn into a debacle.

Two of the two elder statesmen, Paul Martin and Allan MacEachen, would wait until a topic about which they were knowledgeable had almost played out before finally adding their views. Most ministers usually commented only on their own departments, but there were always a few buttinskies who would offer their opinions on topics about which they knew nothing.

An example from my own bailiwick comes to mind. As House leader, I had the responsibility of putting to Cabinet and then to Parliament substantial changes in House of Commons procedure. Some were highly technical, while others were highly political in the sense that they would cause strenuous opposition. In areas where ministers had no expertise, they often said nothing; however, they all had experience serving in the House, so everyone had an opinion.

The changes – my first proposal to Cabinet – were given a rough ride. I left the meeting feeling a bit bruised. A colleague commiserated and said I should consider myself lucky that other ministers had intervened. First, he said, some had more experience than I did, and it was better to hear their criticisms behind closed doors rather than suffer slings and arrows in the House or across the country. Second, a full discussion transformed any individual proposal to one supported by the entire Cabinet. Thirdly, my colleague added, he wasn't surprised that I got beaten up. After all, he said, I was a frequent buttinksy on proposals from other ministers, so it was only poetic justice that I should get some of my own back.

Despite such differences of opinion, over the years we ministers formed lasting bonds. Although many are now deceased, ministers with whom I worked in common cause during the 1960s and 1970s remained among my closest friends for the longest time. There was only one occasion when Pierre condemned my opinion and I didn't fight back. Léo Cadieux, my predecessor as minister of defence, recommended a major reorganization and reduction of forces. He sought to eliminate some regiments, including the Black Watch. To my mind, the Black Watch held a particular place in Canada as the senior Highland Regiment. I said that killing it off was wrong.

Pierre exploded. He would brook no more discussion on the topic. "This has been decided," he snapped. "I don't want to hear anything more." I was so taken aback by Pierre's rudeness that I fell silent. The two regular army battalions were indeed wound up in 1970, but the third battalion – the reserve unit based in Montreal – continues, complete with a pipe and drum band. The unit's more than 200 members have volunteered for a wide range of duties, including service in Afghanistan and security at the Vancouver Olympics. In 2012, the Black Watch of Canada celebrated its 150th anniversary. I guess you could say that Pierre and I both won.

There were many other circumstances when I had differences of opinion with Pierre and let them be known in no uncertain terms. When Pierre visited the Soviet Union in 1971, he signed a Protocol of Consultations, one of his rare major steps taken without first discussing his plans with Cabinet. As minister of national defence, I was particularly upset to have been left out of the loop. I demanded that the Cabinet minutes record my displeasure. Don Jamieson said that he noticed a certain *froideur* in Pierre's relations with me for a time.

While I was House leader, I also took a stand on Canada's commitment to the North Atlantic Treaty Organization (NATO). I had previously come to believe that we were far too deferential to European opinion. One hundred thousand Canadians gave their lives while fighting the tribal wars of Europe twice in the twentieth century. We had no need to listen to scoldings from Europeans about the nature of our ongoing military involvement in their neighbourhood. In my speech at the United Nations in 1966, I had focused on economic development through aid and trade as solutions to world problems, not more military might.[2]

While I wanted to take Canada out of NATO entirely, some ministers, such as Mitchell Sharp and Léo Cadieux, defended the status quo. In their book about Canadian foreign policy under Pierre, *Pirouette*, Jack Granatstein and Robert Bothwell wrote:

One minister who definitely did not accept the wisdom of the establishment was Donald Macdonald, the president of the Privy

Council. Macdonald might have been taken to be an establishment type himself: cousin of a general, graduate of Toronto, Harvard, and Cambridge universities, and member of parliament for Toronto-Rosedale, which included some of Canada's most privileged turf. But 'Thumper' – a reference to his arguing style – was also iconoclastic and outspoken. The youngest man (and with Hellyer, the tallest) at the Cabinet table, he had not the slightest intention of being overawed or overborne by his seniors. With Eric Kierans, who had already broadcast his conclusions on foreign policy, Macdonald would lead the charge against NATO, and support would not be lacking.[3]

In addition to Eric Kierans and me, Jean Marchand and Gérard Pelletier also wanted Canada out of NATO. Debate in Cabinet lasted for weeks, first in the Priorities and Planning Committee, then in full Cabinet. Throughout, Pierre never revealed his own position, letting the arguments play out around him. In the end, he made a decision worthy of Solomon. We would stay in NATO but cut our troop commitment in Europe from 10,000 to 5,000.

Pierre was a pragmatist about such matters. He wanted to focus on other parts of the world, through aid not arms, rather than refight European wars. As historian John English has written in *Just Watch Me*, the second volume of his excellent biography about Pierre, "The Cold War was middle-aged when Pierre Trudeau became prime minister. The fears and ferocious enthusiasms of its early years had largely passed, and Trudeau well suited the new spirit."[4]

Still, the Cold War continued to have an impact on our foreign policy. For years, the Canadian Embassy in Moscow was bugged. Every time we thought all listening devices had been found and removed, they were somehow reinstalled. Even so, Canada had better relations with the Soviets than did the Americans. The closest we ever got to confrontation was an ancient cannon on a front lawn near the Soviet Embassy in Ottawa. That piece of equipment, went the joke at the time, was Canada's first line of defence.

Whether it was NATO or other matters, I think it's safe to say that I was no milquetoast minister. "Don was a good fighter, always very frank and outspoken. In fact, he was sometimes embarrassingly frank in the Cabinet: he would almost tell the prime minister – me – to go to hell, not much more gently than that. But I liked him, because he had a strong character. He was very intelligent, very vigorous," Pierre wrote in *Memoirs*.[5]

At the same time, I caused more than my share of problems for the government, but Pierre always gave me his full support even in my darkest days. After briefing him on whatever trouble I happened to be in, his response was always, "Okay, what are *we* going to do about it?" His use of the first person plural was reassuring. He never left me twisting in the wind – even in a gale of my own making.

Through it all, Pierre's style was more patrician than personal, except in the company of close friends from the past such as Jean Marchand and Gérard Pelletier. Pierre was a very private person and assumed everyone else wanted to be the same way. When ministers were going through rough periods in their private lives, and could have used a reassuring word, Pierre offered no such kindness. During the entire time after Ruth was diagnosed with cancer in 1975 and suffered through various stages of that fatal disease, Pierre never said a consoling word to me about it, never so much as inquired after her health. When his marriage to Margaret was coming apart, and she was acting shamelessly in public, he didn't share his feelings with anyone. As far as he was concerned, everyone's personal life was private, yours and his. His public persona was much different.

A comparison of Pierre with John Diefenbaker and Lester Pearson is instructive. Diefenbaker loved the House of Commons and could put a case in a speech better than anyone. Even when he was in the wrong, he would stitch together a counterattack that would include his strong points, misstatements of his opponent's position, and some contested material. His timing was superb; his sense of the dramatic, effective. Like Winston Churchill, Diefenbaker had read history and political biography widely, and had a penchant for the potent phrase. But what might seem formidable in full oratorical flight did not always translate well in media reports. Moreover, his capacity to lead a political party and appeal to all Canadians became limited. Diefenbaker eventually became a lonely figure, out of tune with the times.

Unlike Diefenbaker, Pearson didn't like either the House or the hustings. His strength showed in his personal dealings with members of

Cabinet and caucus as well as with friends in the media and business. He had a sunny personality and a ready wit that could ease any tension. Pearson's worst remonstration was, "Oh, for heaven's sake." He always claimed he'd rather manage a baseball team than run a government.

In the case of Pierre, his intelligence and education prepared him to handle most public policy questions, but his lifelong conviction about the importance of a united country and good relations between French- and English-speaking peoples lifted him to a higher plane. Prior to politics, he felt free to espouse positions without the necessity, which is fundamental for politicians, of persuading people to support the goals he sought. During the years we were colleagues, I witnessed the inexorable development of Pierre's persuasive skills.

Among my Cabinet colleagues, Gene Whelan and Don Jamieson were the best entertainment value. Gene could also be a pain in the neck because he would insist on bringing up issues that had already been decided by Cabinet. Pierre was remarkably patient with him. A lot of people thought Gene was a buffoon. Not I. The bones of those who underestimated Gene Whelan are still whitening on the battlefields of politics past.

Pierre admired self-made people like Don Jamieson, who began his professional life as a broadcaster in Newfoundland. Pierre would often turn to Don for a final comment on issues that had caused lengthy debates. Don had a broad national view, excellent judgment, and a wonderful sense of humour. He always had a hilarious story for any occasion or would dapple his comments with phrases that evoked laughter, such as how he would leave "no turd unstoned" to get a job done.

In addition to Jean Marchand and Gérard Pelletier, the other Quebec minister who had Pierre's ear was Marc Lalonde. For sheer brainpower, elegance, and capacity to persuade, Marc was in a class by himself. First elected to Parliament in 1972 and named minister of national health and welfare, his 1973 Orange Paper was one of the best documents ever written on the challenges of running a humane social security program in Canada.

Mitchell Sharp, who was twenty-one years my senior, was the most knowledgeable member of Cabinet when it came to the public service.

Of course, Sharp had been a bureaucrat for ten years in the departments of finance and trade and commerce. He was little bit prissy for me, but he had an excellent command of the problems in managing the Canadian economy. He probably thought I was a bit of a lug, compared to his more refined manner, but mostly I think he was upset with me because I was closer to Pierre than he was.

Roméo LeBlanc was a special individual, perhaps because as a New Brunswick Acadian he was part of a minority. In difficult circumstances, he always had the interests of others at heart. He had more international experience than the rest of us because of his broadcasting background with Radio-Canada in the United States and Britain. He was later a very effective governor general. His son Dominic, House leader under Liberal leader Justin Trudeau, will be a key player in the Liberal Party and in Canadian public life.

One of the least heralded but most interesting ministers was Horace Andrew Olson, known to everybody as "Bud." A businessman, he was first elected to Parliament as a member of the Social Credit Party. In 1967, when that party's time had passed, he became a Liberal. Changing sides is not easy; he did it with style. When I was minister of energy, mines and resources and took heat from Alberta politicians, Bud would remind me that the Albertans giving me grief were all football players from Calgary. As far as he was concerned, born as he was in the southern Alberta hamlet of Iddesleigh, Calgarians were a breed apart.

John Turner and I were never close. I don't think I ever sought his counsel on any matter. We worked well together, had lunch on occasion, but he always seemed to hold me at arm's length. I think, at root, he remained annoyed that I backed Pierre not him in 1968. I have a similar relationship with Paul Martin Jr. He has always kept his distance.

Of all the ministers, the one I most admired was Gérard Pelletier, my desk mate for much of my time in Parliament. He was a polished and articulate participant in discussions – except for economic matters, where he refrained from comment. He once said to me that anglophone ministers always seemed to feel obliged to speak on economic questions whether they had anything to say or not. Francophone ministers, he freely admitted, felt a similar need to participate whenever the topic was the constitution or bilingualism. Gérard was more concerned with the debate among the intelligentsia of Quebec and the future of Quebec in Confederation. When it came to media and communications, he could draw on his extensive experience, but only when called upon.

Gérard rarely took notes in Cabinet. Instead he made elaborate doodles on his scratch pad that reminded me of the op-art work by Hungarian-French artist Victor Vasarely. Despite what appeared to be a lack of interest, he was always listening intently. After retiring from politics in 1975, he was ambassador to France and then the United Nations. I'm sure he found some of the ceremonial matters tedious, but he would have matched wits with anyone.

As for an impartial assessment of me and my rapport with Pierre, what better source than the closest possible observer, Gordon Robertson, clerk of the Privy Council, who attended all Cabinet meetings and wrote in his memoir: "Donald Macdonald was another for whom confidence grew with his sure handling of the most difficult and critical departments. His intelligence and wit gave a special relaxed quality to their relationship."[6]

Cabinet also oversaw appointments for everything from the numerous government agencies and crown corporations to awarding of advertising contracts. As chief political minister for Ontario, a role conferred upon me by Pierre, I chaired a committee of all the Cabinet ministers from the province. Known as the Ontario Advisory Committee, we'd usually meet monthly. My colleagues would propose individuals for vacancies that existed, a discussion would follow, and our recommendations would go before Cabinet for final approval. In addition to Cabinet input, in the case of judicial appointments, for example, I'd also consult lawyers such as J.J. Robinette for their views.

Canada does not have anything like the spoils system of the United States where every incoming administration gets to fill the 5,000 jobs created when the party in power is defeated and its appointees resign, but we did play favourites. I have to admit that where two people were equal in background and merit, we'd usually pick the one who was an active Liberal. The more senior the appointment, the more merit-driven it would be.

Names flooded in from everywhere. In 1971, for example, Pierre decided he wanted a Prime Minister's Committee on Official Languages, so backbenchers and ministers alike sent me lengthy lists of their constituents for consideration. Party officials also offered their comments, not always of the kindest nature. In 1973, we were thinking about naming Bora Laskin as chief justice of the Supreme Court of Canada. A party official called on me in my Centre Block office to say that Laskin should not be given the job because he was Jewish. I was stunned and berated the individual for holding such a bigoted view.

Laskin had already suffered enough for his faith. After being called to the bar of Ontario in 1937, he could not find work with a law firm because of the anti-Semitism prevalent in the legal profession. As a result, he taught law beginning in 1940 until he was appointed to the Court of Appeal of Ontario in 1965. In 1970, Pierre named him as the first Jew on the Supreme Court. As far as I was concerned, no party official or anyone else was going to stop Laskin's further elevation. His appointment as chief justice went ahead, and he served with great distinction until his death in 1984.

Other appointments were contentious for different reasons. A name came up at one point for a possible Senate seat, and for whatever reason, Edgar Benson didn't want this individual in the Senate. Benson, who served in the cabinets of both Pierre and Lester Pearson, pulled out his calculator and figured out the total compensation the nominee would receive over the time of service involved. While the monetary argument could have applied to anyone, it was enough to dissuade the group. Another person was picked instead.

Of course, such appointments were only a small part of my role in Cabinet. While some will say I am biased, I believe the Trudeau Cabinet was by far the best Cabinet in the modern era. Each minister represented the interests of his portfolio with vigour and vision. Camaraderie and co-operation were our watchwords. In the forty-odd years since, I think it's fair to say that the quality of individuals running for public office has diminished. As a result, there are fewer good people to choose from when it comes to Cabinet making.

This diminution hurts us all. I don't make the claim about the quality of the Trudeau Cabinet to blow my own horn, but to assert that, as a nation, we need the best and brightest to run for Parliament.

Good political judgment and the ability to win the confidence of citizens come partly as a gift at birth and partly as growth through hard-won experience. Call it a combination of inborn knack and the hard knocks of life.

Herding Cats

When I was first named president of the Queen's Privy Council, I have to admit I was a bit mystified by that elegant but rather obscure title. I asked my mentor, Walter Gordon, who had held that same position in the Pearson government, exactly what the role entailed. He said that you never preside over anything, let alone a council, and in his two years in office he had never met Her Majesty. But, he assured me that the job had nothing whatsoever to do with a privy!

Pierre was the first prime minister to combine the ceremonial duties of the Queen's Privy Council with House leader. In that latter role, I managed the government's ambitious legislative agenda. I would have preferred Defence or one of the financial portfolios. But I thought, "Better to take the job that was offered and try for a worthier one later rather than walk away with nothing."

While some legislative procedures were to be changed, even under the restless leadership of Pierre Trudeau in 1968 other aspects were sacrosanct. New sessions of Parliament always begin with the Speech from the Throne, read by Her Majesty the Queen or the governor general, followed by eight days of debate. After the minister of finance brings down a budget, there are six days of debate. Once those set pieces were complete, the House then established itself in various iterations – from the Committee of the Whole, to the Committee of Supply, to the Committee of Ways and Means.

Like long trains on one track, almost all the business of the house – non-financial, supply (money), and taxation – was dealt with at the same time by all the MPs. A more disorganized method was hard to imagine. In addition, since there were no deadlines, even after all views had been presented, M P s procrastinated. M P s who did not need to be heard were able to talk "for the record" to their heart's content. The cumulative effect was that every piece of House business took far too long and often had to be carried over from one session to the next.

I finally understood why my father took no summer holidays in order to stay close to Parliament. He prepared spending estimates for the Forestry Branch early in the calendar year and then would wait months before finally being called to sit at a table on the floor of the House in front of the minister so he could provide his political master with details in answer to opposition questions. The entire House was tied up studying one aspect of one department's estimates even though the money under discussion had often already been advanced. There was no time limit, so in the dog days of summer, estimates for an individual branch could drone on simply because the opposition was feeling particularly obstreperous. Even as a boy, when I sat in the gallery, the process seemed protracted.

I believed that parliamentarians in general would gain public respect if proceedings were more efficient. Because the pace was so slow, M P s became bored, disruptive, and partisan. I agreed with Winston Churchill, who said that the House of Commons must be freed from the mass of business that clogged the system. "The essence and foundation of House of Commons' debating is formal conversation," he said. "The set speech, the harangue addressed to constituents, or to the wider public out of doors has never succeeded much in our small wisely-built chamber."[1]

In the previous parliament, an all-party committee of M P s had submitted nine reports to the House of Commons, all of which recommended ways to improve procedure. You'd think modernization of a such an archaic system, little changed since Confederation, would be straightforward given that we had a solid majority, but nothing is simple in a democracy. Compared with what I had to do, herding cats would have been far easier given the fact that the opposition saw its role as halting progress at every turn.

During the summer of 1968, Progressive Conservative House Leader Gerald Baldwin set the tone for the coming months. He seemed like a decent fellow, but even before we met for the first time to talk about the future business of the House, he gave an interview denouncing the undemocratic tendencies of Pierre Trudeau and attacking me in personal, derogatory terms. As a Stanfield loyalist, Baldwin had trouble keeping in line those members of his party who remained committed to Diefenbaker. Abuse about me and the government's position was the best way for him to defuse internal feuding by trying to focus his divided caucus on a common enemy.

In addition, I had to deal with NDP House Leader Stanley Knowles. First elected to the House of Commons from Winnipeg North Centre in 1942, Knowles knew parliamentary procedure better than anyone. He could argue every point with masterful authority and often did so ad nauseam. Knowles had a vested interest in stalemates. He had made his reputation during the pipeline debate that hastened the demise of the St Laurent government in 1957. (Knowles often remarked, with a wry smile, that he had been too successful. He lost his own seat in the 1958 Diefenbaker sweep.) But unnecessarily prolonging debate to delay a decision struck me as contrary to the core concept of democracy where a vote should eventually be taken and the majority view allowed to prevail.

Knowles was also in the habit of rising late in the evening at the end of a long session to offer a comment that did not always seem to be related to what had been under discussion. I once asked Deputy Speaker Hugh Faulkner what that was all about. "Nothing," he said. "He's just getting it on the record that he's there, to demonstrate his diligence."

Peter C. Newman swallowed such foot-dragging opposition tactics holus-bolus and wrote in his column, "It's becoming obvious even now – a week before the new Parliament meets – that one of the main deterrents to reaching a smooth intra-party agreement on these and other reforms will be the abrasive personality of Donald Macdonald."[2] Well, I thought, if they want a fight, then that's what they'll get. I'm not called Thumper for nothing.

Unlike a lot of new MPs, I'd made it my business to learn as much as I could about the workings of Parliament after I was first elected in 1962. I was active in the House, asking oral questions, speaking on bills of relevance, putting written questions on the order paper, and using every appropriate opportunity to state my views on items of interest to my constituents and me. But beyond the basics that I mastered, there were countless procedural rulings built on British experience in the Mother of Parliaments at Westminster, as well as entire books on the subject, such as Arthur Beauchesne's *Parliamentary Rules and Forms of the House of Commons of Canada.*

As House leader, I was fortunate to have knowledgeable help from John Stewart, who had been educated at Acadia University, held a doctorate from Columbia University, was on the faculty of St Francis Xavier University, and had been a member of the committee that wrote the nine reports. He'd been a Liberal M P from Nova Scotia since 1962 but lost in the 1968 election, so was available to act as a key adviser. He went on to publish, in 1977, the definitive work on this topic, *The Canadian House of Commons: Procedure and Reform.*

In 1969, I also hired Jerry Yanover, a recent political science graduate from Queen's University. I wrote Pierre to tell him I hoped he'd approve of my idea that Yanover would work with whoever became House leader in the years to come.[3] Pierre agreed, and Jerry advised me as well as all subsequent Liberal House leaders until his death in 2009. Of Jerry, *Maclean's* Paul Wells once said: "Yanover is to Liberalism what Yoda is to the Jedi Council: the most feared practitioner of an ancient craft."[4] Jerry's interest in Parliament began while he was growing up in Kingston, Ontario. He heard the Liberals promise during the 1957 election that if elected they would drop the tax on Fleers Dubble Bubble gum. He liked the idea because he knew each piece cost two cents in Canada but only one cent in the US. When the Diefenbaker Tories won, he realized the importance of which party was in power.

The recommendation made by the all-party group was that the House should create twenty-four standing committees, one for each major matter from Agriculture to Veterans Affairs. Each of these committees, consisting of twenty M P s, would do the work previously carried out by the Committee of the Whole. Individual committees could begin scrutinizing the estimates before April 1 and then refer matters back to the House for a vote, thereby setting a basic framework for an annual session of Parliament starting in the fall and ending around July 1.

Or so I hoped. But despite the all-party agreement prior to the 1968 election, once the House returned, the opposition changed its tune about the time allocation rules that would limit debate. We wanted to have both tools available, closure and time allocation. Closure involved a set number of hours of debate before a vote. Time allocation offered more flexibility. For example, a certain number of hours for debate on second reading and then a deadline by which time the committee studying the bill had to send it back to the House.

The British Parliament had already handled this dilemma. There, the Speaker can decide how much time will be spent on a bill. They also had a daily negotiation process between the government and the opposition called "The Usual Channels." Public servants were involved to ensure as much business gets done as possible. We had none of that. For the opposition, obstruction was their only way of having any impact on proceedings. For the divided Progressive Conservatives, parliamentary rule changes gave them a rare chance for public unity.

For Knowles, he could continue to cultivate his image with the press gallery as "the conscience of Parliament" when his real goal was more about partisan achievement and personal glory than he would ever admit. As I often said, "My idea of hell is an eternity spent debating points of procedure that only Stanley Knowles understands."

Looking back, I realize that my biggest mistake was never properly explaining to the public the case for parliamentary reform. Jack Pickersgill used to say that the one thing that ministers most detest is getting out on the stump to explain their plans to the country at large. "Only by the time you personally have become thoroughly sick to death of the speech that you were repeating does the public begin to understand what it is you are trying to do," he said.

But I was too tied up in the House to get out into the country. As a result, debate became cantankerous; the opposition saw me as intransigent. Still, the parliamentary process is never going to be tidy or capable of gratifying everyone's wish. I also had to deal with warring bureaucrats. At one meeting, several civil servants from different departments seemed to be in a turf battle that was delaying the drafting of a piece of legislation. I finally told them that they had a week to get their act together. They protested that such a deadline couldn't be met. "It can, if you work nights," I said. They met the deadline.

After a six-day debate about new rules on the use of closure, we faced the possibility of a filibuster that would prevent approval of all of the new rules. The situation was nothing if not ironic: a filibuster to stop the end of filibusters. In response, government agreed to send the question of time allocation back to the special committee for review and report. With that contentious matter hoisted, all the other rule changes were approved by the House on December 20, 1968.[5]

Six months later, on June 20, 1969, the committee recommended three new standing orders. The first, 75A, made it possible – if and when all House leaders agreed – for the House to decide without debate how much time should be set aside for one or all stages of a bill. Standing Order 75B permitted the government House leader, without notice, to propose a time-allocation motion for a stage of a bill if a majority of the parties agreed. The House would vote on this motion after a two-hour debate. The last, 75C, was a final resort that allowed the government to end a persistent filibuster. Even then, there were safeguards. For example, not only was 75C was restricted to one bill at a time, but also to only one stage of a bill at a time.

In order to the keep the pressure on, and bring matters to a satisfactory conclusion, I made sure that the House of Commons sat well into July, a month when MPs were usually free to go home to their ridings, mend fences, and attend picnics. I offered some amendments, but the opposition rejected them, so we decided to limit debate to two more days then call for a vote that we knew we would win. Syndicated columnist Charles Lynch called me a hippopotamus because, he said, I threw my weight around, all 220 pounds of it.

All the party leaders spoke on the motion, as did many other MPs. To my mind, the best speech was by John Roberts, the Liberal MP for York–Simcoe, who had been elected for the first time in 1968. He was a distinguished academic and a skilled orator. "The history of parliament, at least over the past century, has been a history of steady increase of government control in the House of Commons. Why? Not because of imperialistic government but because Parliament does not exist in a vacuum," said Roberts. "The rules of parliament correspond to social needs. We cannot freeze procedures so that they become irrelevant. We cannot look simply to the legacy of the past. We must look at the function of parliament in the context of the society in which it operates."

Some opposition MPs had quoted Edmund Burke, the eighteenth-century parliamentarian, in support of their arguments. Roberts admitted that Burke was not among his favourite thinkers but pointed out that "what Burke emphasized above all else was that political institutions, and society itself, were growing organisms which were developing through time, that they were moulded by time and that they must meet the changing interests of the society in which they exist," he said. "That is true in this parliament as well. The old rules of the past simply are not sufficient for the new era. That is the mistake which I think that the honourable member for Winnipeg North Centre has made in this debate."[6]

Roberts went on to note that Knowles had issued the ultimate threat: he would oppose *all* legislation. Knowles rose on a point of order and complained that he was being made fun of without proper regard to his considerable self-esteem. I think even some of the younger NDP members, who had to listen to Knowles week in and week out, were entertained by Roberts's attack on their colleague.

Roberts next turned his fire on Robert Stanfield. Citing Stanfield's complaint about the arrogance of Pierre Trudeau, Roberts pointed out that as premier of Nova Scotia, Stanfield had threatened to remove retroactively the protection of an elected member to speak freely in the legislature about another individual without fear of being sued for slander. Stanfield also rose in protest.

Not bad for a newly elected MP! Roberts had felled two birds with one speech. In both cases, the impression was created that good sense had been overcome by vanity. Sometimes, the self-appointed Great Men of Parliament run the risk of being mocked just like us lesser mortals. When the Speaker was finally able to put the motion to adopt the committee's report, it carried easily by a vote of 142–84.

Even with new rules in place, progress at first was slow. By Christmas 1969, of the eighty pieces of legislation we'd presented, only nine had been approved and many of those were minor. As we became more comfortable with the new rules, Parliament ran more smoothly. By June 1970, forty-six of the original eighty had passed.

But the result of all the changes was significant beyond just efficiency. Parliamentarians no longer had to rely on ministers or anonymous civil servants to assure the quality of legislation, policy, and administration in Canada. Through their work on the standing committees, M P s were engaged more intimately in law making. The House had taken a giant step away from its colonial origins and brought itself in touch with the needs of the country.[7]

Throughout, my relationship with the opposition parties was testy. One exchange will suffice to capture the tone. I was under attack by Stanley Knowles and Tommy Douglas from the N D P as well as Progressive Conservatives Lincoln Alexander and Robert Stanfield. They were complaining about not being able to fully discuss some aspect of housing policy. I pointed out that the P C critic on the topic, Lincoln Alexander, had not even attended the relevant committee hearings. Stanfield interjected, "Don't dig a deeper hole for yourself." I retorted, "I must say I can understand the mental block of the Leader of the Opposition because he is so deep in a hole in his present situation it will take a slingshot to feed him."[8]

Beyond such brief fusillades, history has rendered a favourable judgment on what I achieved. As a result of the rule changes I brought in, the House of Commons followed a set pattern when dealing with the government's requests for supply. As soon as the main estimates for the financial year were presented, in late January or early February, they were referred to the appropriate standing committee, which had until the end of May to study the numbers and make their reports. The House dealt with the bills by the end of June.

When, for example, the House dealt with a bill introduced by the minister of finance, the bill was sent to the committee for examination after second reading. Then the bill as reported could be amended before third and final reading and a vote. As a result, bills received a far more intensive scrutiny than was possible when all bills were dealt with by all M P s in the Committee of the Whole House. Meanwhile, the minister of finance could initiate tax changes without waiting until his next budget speech. Any additional estimates presented in the fall, and there usually were some, had to be tidied up by Christmas.

Closure using 75C was tried for the first time in December 1971 on a tax bill, more than a year after I had moved on from my role as House leader, and it worked just as intended. By then, Allan MacEachen was House leader, and the government was trying to pass C-259, a complicated 725-page bill intended to update the Income Tax Act. After the House spent forty days on the bill, it became clear that the opposition wasn't interested in passing C-259 in any form. MacEachen invoked Standing Order 75C, which meant there could only be four more days of debate before a vote. Even so, there had been more than enough debate to ensure that all views were considered.

While those standing orders may have seemed to some observers like powerful tools, they were not overused. In fact, it wasn't until 1994 that Standing Order 75B – by then called 78(2) – was used for the first time to limit debate. Long before that, in September 1970, my days as a procedural reformer were over – and none too soon for my liking. That's when I was named minister of defence and suffered my baptism by fire during the October Crisis that proved the validity of one of Oscar Wilde's maxims: "When the gods wish to punish us, they answer our prayers."

The October Crisis

Elgin Armstrong, deputy minister of national defence, strode into my office shortly after 9 a.m. on the morning of October 5, 1970. "Minister," he said, "during the last hour, James Cross, the British trade commissioner, has been kidnapped from his home in Montreal by a cell of the Front de Libération du Québec." I'd been in my new role for less than two weeks, barely enough time to be briefed about my duties. Suddenly, all previous priorities were swept aside.

The October Crisis was unleashed. As minister of national defence, I was involved in every major decision, including troop deployment during that stressful time, when the very roots of our democracy were imperilled. Because James Cross was a British envoy, news of the kidnapping flashed around the world.

Prime Minister Pierre Trudeau called an emergency meeting that included several ministers: Mitchell Sharp, Edgar Benson, Jean Marchand, Bud Drury, Don Jamieson, Arthur Laing, George McIlraith, and myself. As a first step, we vowed not to give in to the demands of the kidnappers: free seventeen felons already in jail or on parole, rehire 450 postal workers who had lost their jobs, send $500,000 in gold, and provide safe passage for the kidnappers and their families to Cuba or Algeria.

Ironically, I had sought this new role to escape my embattled position as House leader. Léo Cadieux, minister of national defence since 1967, had announced his retirement from Parliament and was appointed ambassador to France. I had pushed through the legislative changes to the House of Commons procedures that Pierre wanted, but rancour with the opposition parties resulted. The new rules, I told Pierre, would work better if I were no longer House leader, so I asked him to appoint me to Defence. I felt he owed me the move; this was a major Cabinet vacancy, and I wanted the job. Said Pierre, "What do you know about defence? You were never in the armed forces." Pierre was right. The closest I came to military service was as a teenaged corporal in the cadet corps at my prep school, Ashbury College.

Pierre had other reservations. During the 1968–69 defence policy review, I was in favour of neutrality and had pushed for Canada to get out of NATO. The debate became so heated that when Pierre called me, he'd say, "You haven't resigned yet, have you?" Pierre said that if he named me minister of defence, I couldn't get angry and leave in a huff. He further said that I couldn't reopen issues previously decided, such as NATO, and that I must seek compromise with other ministers. Finally, I had to live with the departmental budget freeze already in place. I agreed to his terms, and the role was mine.

The armed forces were still in turmoil over unification carried out by Defence Minister Paul Hellyer during the Lester Pearson government when the three separate services were abolished. Traditional ranks and uniforms were replaced by a common rank structure and a single green uniform.

I had supported unification. Now, part of my mandate was to raise morale, although there was widespread doubt among the military that I could handle the job. After all, I was the first defence minister who had not served in the military since Grote Stirling in the 1930s government of R.B. Bennett. "His appointment has probably heightened the concern of many senior officers who have begun to suspect that there is little room for the Armed Forces in Pierre Trudeau's vision of the future," wrote John Burns in the *Globe and Mail*.[1]

On Saturday, October 10, the October Crisis escalated when Quebec labour minister Pierre Laporte was kidnapped in front of his house by a second FLQ cell. With two men now held hostage, and FLQ communiqués threatening more mayhem, we had to protect innocent parties. Using the National Defence Act, which allowed the Government of Canada to come to the aid of civil powers, on October 12, I ordered 3,000 troops to guard Cabinet ministers, diplomats, and federal buildings in Ottawa.

My family was among the first to feel the impact. Around midnight, we awoke to the sound of heavy trucks and jeeps rumbling down our street. The next noise was boots on the pavement as soldiers in full battledress, armed with submachine guns and automatic rifles, took up positions. The *Toronto Star* published a page-one photo of me, wearing my bathrobe and pyjamas, solemnly greeting seven soldiers at my front door before they dispersed in the neighbourhood.[2]

At the next Cabinet meeting, Pierre made a chilling announcement. If a spouse or child of a Cabinet minister were kidnapped, there would be no concessions. We were not giving in to blackmail in the case of Cross or Laporte, so our loved ones would be treated no differently. When journalist Burns asked me how my children were getting to school, I retorted, "None of your business." Why make special arrangements, and then tell the world? On October 14, at a crucial meeting of a special Cabinet committee chaired by Pierre, attendees included Minister of Justice John Turner, Solicitor General George McIlraith, and me. We decided to recommend to full Cabinet the War Measures Act, a draconian piece of legislation that had been around since the First World War, but had never been used during peacetime. The act gave Ottawa control over arrest, detention, deportation, censorship, and all forms of trade, transport, and production.

Meanwhile, the situation in Montreal and Quebec City was rapidly deteriorating. Marc Lalonde, Pierre's principal secretary, and Jean Marchand, minister of regional economic expansion, fed information to Cabinet that they gleaned from officials and police sources about the FLQ's growing strength. Jean called the FLQ a state within a state and reported they had two tons of dynamite in their control in Montreal. Their plan was to load trucks with dynamite, park them near large buildings, and detonate them remotely. If radio equipment had worked the day before, he said, there would have been an explosion in Montreal.[3]

As Cabinet continued to meet in emergency session, it became apparent that law enforcement in Quebec was becoming overwhelmed. We agreed that there was no time to draft and present to the House any new legislation to deal with the situation. Our Criminal Code was – and remains – inadequate to deal with extreme political violence.

I sat in on phone calls between an emotionally distraught Premier Robert Bourassa and an implacable Pierre. At thirty-seven, elected just six months earlier as Quebec's youngest-ever premier, Bourassa was only a year younger than I, but he seemed immature and incapable. During one call with Pierre, Premier Bourassa actually cried as he pleaded for more help. By contrast, Pierre was patient and restrained.

Cabinet unanimously agreed to proclaim the War Measures Act and send in the army. As thousands of FLQ sympathizers gathered in Montreal's Paul Sauvé Arena on the evening of October 15, Pierre informed opposition leaders of his plans. Official letters, one from the provincial government and the other from Montreal civic authorities, arrived in the early hours of Friday, October 16. Both requested special powers and, with those letters in hand, the War Measures Act was duly proclaimed at 4 a.m.

Troops and tanks were deployed, hundreds of citizens were arrested in Montreal, and everyone was on high alert. Even after that bold intervention, Pierre Laporte was found strangled in the trunk of an abandoned green Chevrolet at Saint-Hubert Airport just before midnight on October 17. Murder for political ends was alien to our experience in Canada.

Cabinet had been closely following the escalating tensions in Quebec. On July 23, the RCMP Security Service had presented a comprehensive report on subversive threats in Canada. At the top of the list was Quebec separatism and related terrorism. Conjecture was that there were up to a dozen FLQ cells with three to five members in each cell. "Their strategy appears to be to promote direct confrontation with authority in any form over issues generally formulated in the shape of unreasonable demands in order to trick authority into using force against them," said the report.

Some members of the media seemed to have taken sides. "The FLQ were getting full radio and TV coverage; they had the PR initiative, with the connivance of the news media, who were, in some cases, obstructing police work by the way they handled the FLQ communiqués and destroyed potential fingerprints," said a memorandum to the prime minister by E.A. Côté, deputy solicitor general. The document, dated November 3, 1970, said that some members of the FLQ had trained with Al Fatah, founded by Yasser Arafat, and predicted more bombing of public buildings as well as assassination attempts of prominent French-Canadians and federalists.[4]

The October Crisis underscored not only the inability of Premier Bourassa to cope but also the inherent failings of two other leaders. If Robert Stanfield had been elected leader of the Progressive Conservative Party twenty years earlier, he might well have become prime minister. But, in my opinion, by the late 1960s and early 1970s, it was too late for a unilingual anglophone to be prime minister of Canada – and I apply that harsh judgment to myself as well. If it came to a confrontation with separatists over a united Canada, a unilingual – or barely bilingual – anglophone would be at a great disadvantage. But Stanfield was at least thoughtful and responsible in his comments.

On the other hand, Tommy Douglas's speech in the House after the imposition of the War Measures Act was totally inappropriate in both content and tone. The leader of the New Democratic Party clearly had no sympathy for either public opinion in Quebec or the sudden collapse of law and order. Douglas compared the FLQ situation to the 1919 Winnipeg General Strike. "But there was no kidnapping then," Mitchell Sharp reminded him from across the floor in a comment that was not recorded by *Hansard*. For Douglas, the government was "using a sledgehammer to crack a peanut. This is over-kill on a gargantuan scale," he said.[5] At that point, the House erupted with shouts and catcalls by numerous Quebec MPs from both the Liberal and Créditiste parties about his out-of-touch views.

NDP House Leader Stanley Knowles was equally out of tune with the times. When Pierre Laporte was found dead, the House of Commons was sitting in an unusual late-night weekend session. Someone passed a note to Robert Borrie (L–Prince George–Peace River), who was speaking at the time. After announcing the news to shocked MPs, Borrie stopped speaking and sat down.

The next scheduled speaker was Knowles, who acknowledged the event but then launched into his prepared remarks just as if no tragedy had occurred. *Hansard* records that some honourable members shouted "Enough," but Knowles carried on until Marcel Prud'homme

(L–Saint-Denis) rose to say, "Mr Speaker, under the circumstances, the best thing the honourable member could do would be to offer his silence for a better, united Canada." Knowles finally relented, and the House rose for the night. To my mind, Knowles demonstrated unbelievable insensitivity by trying to get his speech on the record rather than honouring a life taken in such a horrific manner.

In making our momentous decision to impose the War Measures Act, Cabinet was responding not only to immediate events but also to a seven-year pattern of FLQ violence. During that time, terrorists had blown up Montreal mailboxes and planted bombs in liquor stores, homes of union leaders, and the Montreal Stock Exchange. One such device detonated outside the Ottawa headquarters of the Department of National Defence (DND), killing a female employee.

I have no regrets, nor did Pierre, about the potency of our response. The Criminal Code and police authorities were inadequate to deal with violence by this criminal minority in our midst. As Pierre said to CBC's Tim Ralfe in that famous "Just watch me" interview outside the west door of the Centre Block: "There are a lot of bleeding hearts around who just don't like to see people with helmets and guns. All I can say is, go on and bleed, but it is more important to keep law and order in the society than to be worried about weak-kneed people."[6] Still, I listened with trepidation to the radio news every morning to hear if a soldier had lost his cool and shot someone. One day, a soldier did shoot himself accidently, but hundreds of other armed combatants did their jobs without incident.

My mother-in-law, who also lived in Ottawa, was certainly up for a fight. With tensions high, Lillian Hutchison arrived at our door carrying a duffle bag containing five pistols and a Beretta submachine gun, ostensibly for our self-protection. None of the guns, liberated by her husband George during the Second World War, had been registered. I turned everything over to the RCMP, who disabled the Beretta, a prohibited weapon. After the handguns were registered, I tried one of them, a .25 caliber Browning, on a DND range. I discovered that whatever challenge I might face, I could not bring myself to fire at another human being. I returned the guns so the family could continue to keep them as souvenirs.

In fact, my family and I had security aplenty. An armed infantry-man always accompanied me; others constantly guarded the house.[7] Even when we took a brief holiday to Lady Lake, north of Ottawa, soldiers came along. There was so little for them to do that my wife Ruth had them build a tree house for the three girls. The two burglars who broke into the house next door to the residence of Jean-Luc Pépin, minister of industry, trade and commerce, must have been surprised to suddenly be surrounded by soldiers armed with rifles. As Jean-Luc later remarked, "That will teach them to not read the political news."

On another occasion, guards just got in the way. Adrian, my second wife, then married to Otto Lang, minister of manpower and immigration, was expecting twins at any moment. As she and her mother hurried from the house to the car on October 31 for the urgent drive to Ottawa Civic Hospital, they were stopped by one of the young guards. Adrian told the soldier that she had previously given birth to five children, knew the signals, and warned him there was no time to waste. "My orders are to go with you," he said. Replied Adrian, "You are not accompanying me, and if you continue to argue with me, you may have to deliver the babies here." The guard blanched and beat a retreat. Amanda and Adrian were born safely at the hospital soon after, without soldiers on hand.

For the next few weeks, while police hunted for Laporte's killers and Cross's captors, I carried on with my other ministerial duties. Among those tasks was hosting a visit by NATO's Nuclear Planning Group. The committee's cross-country schedule included meetings in Calgary, where Mayor Rod Sykes hijacked the occasion to lambaste both Ottawa and me. Airing domestic differences seemed a most unsuitable act in front of our international guests. I could not let his attack pass.

In my remarks, I noted that members of the armed forces stationed in Winnipeg, Edmonton, and Victoria had been sent to Eastern Canada to help during the October Crisis. Those cities, I said, could spare their troops because they were well managed and were unlikely to have security problems. The regiment posted at Calgary, however, remained in place because, given the quality of local government, it was impossible to say what might happen if those troops were sent elsewhere!

My comments caused a surprisingly positive response among my NATO guests. As a new boy in NATO, I was relatively unknown. Most of them had been subjected to similar, unwarranted personal attacks in their home countries so they enjoyed my response and complimented me for my quick comeback.

The final act in the October Crisis played out early in December when I was attending the annual meeting of defence ministers at NATO headquarters in Brussels.[8] Police and the army surrounded an apartment in Montreal where James Cross was being held prisoner. Negotiations ensued and Cross was freed. Some of the kidnappers were sent to Cuba while others stood trial. Later that month, the murderers of Pierre Laporte were captured at a farmhouse outside Montreal and were subsequently jailed.

At least two Cabinet ministers have since questioned the necessity of the War Measures Act, but they offered no such view at the time. Popular support in Canada was overwhelming. Only in the rear-view mirror are events made to look different. I have even heard claims that Laporte's killing was accidental and that the FLQ cell didn't mean to strangle him. Such revisionism is misplaced and misguided. I'll take the rule of law over villainy any day.

Many historians agree. Military historian Jack Granatstein, for example, later changed his mind and admitted he was wrong to oppose the War Measures Act. Other historians also support our action. Robert Bothwell, Ian Drummond, and John English, in their book, *Canada since 1945: Power, Politics, and Provincialism*, wrote: "In retrospect it is difficult to understand what else, legally and politically, could have been done. The government was bound to uphold the law and its application. It would have been ultimately foolish to concede much of the terrorist program, and it may have been unwise to concede any." They further added: "In this [the government] acted wisely and properly."[9]

Throughout the October Crisis, the tact and professionalism shown by the armed forces was superb. Their security work gave them something useful and important to do; the positive reaction by the public boosted military morale. Once James Cross was liberated, none of the authorities in Quebec – including my federal colleagues from Quebec – showed any interest in post-mortems. My query back then remains unaddressed today: What role did prominent separatists play in supporting, or turning a blind eye to, those behind the kidnappings? While the inquiry by Mr Justice David McDonald looked at the activities of the RCMP, no one wanted to investigate the murder of Pierre Laporte.

I give the final word to Pierre, who, in *Memoirs* quoted a comment in *La Presse* by René Lévesque, leader of the Parti Québécois just formed in 1968 – "One day, the police and army will be gone and Trudeau's stupidity will not have prevented more kidnappings."[10] In fact, the action we took snuffed out the FLQ. Several decades of debate have followed about the place of Quebec in Canada, but such talk has always taken the form of legitimate political discussion culminating in decisions by the electorate. The use of terror was never again a factor.

When I assumed the defence portfolio in 1970, some aspects of the department's role had already been determined. The budget had been frozen in 1968 at $1.8 billion a year for the next three years. In a speech to Parliament on April 3, 1969, Pierre had redrawn Canada's military priorities. Peacekeeping and NATO, previously first and second in importance, were replaced by Canadian sovereignty and the defence of North America in co-operation with the United States. A start on Arctic sovereignty had already been made with the establishment in May 1970 of the Canadian Forces Northern Region headquartered in Yellowknife. Fulfillment of our NATO obligations fell to third place and international peacekeeping was fourth.

In that context, I was told to devise a more fully formed policy. In August 1971, I released a fifty-page white paper called *Defence in the 70s*.[11] Among other recommendations, the document declared that the military would assist civil authorities in any future civil emergency, from natural disasters to violence by urban guerillas. Our continued participation in NATO was confirmed, but the white paper proposed a role change in Europe because our Centurion heavy tanks were at the end of their useful life. As for peacekeeping, Canada was prepared to send troops abroad only when such action was effective. We also announced plans to scrap our two Bomarc missile bases (in North Bay, Ontario, and La Macaza, Quebec) as well as stabilize the strength of the armed forces, which had been dropping steadily, at 83,000.

"The most striking thing about the defence White Paper is its realism, and in this it reflects the outlook of its principal author, Defence Minister Donald Macdonald," wrote newspaper columnist Charles Lynch. "He deals more in brass tacks than brass hats, and his preference for the direct over the evasive approach, which made him so abrasive in his former role as government House leader, obviously makes him an ideal defence minister."[12]

Approval by Cabinet was tortuous. Every time the white paper was on the agenda, somehow Pierre managed to avoid it. At one meeting, I showed my anger and frustration by walking out when the topic was once again postponed. When discussion finally took place in July 1972, approval was relatively easy. I never understood what Pierre's stalling was all about.

Some aspects of my job were more hair-raising than others. On one occasion, while I was aboard a navy supply ship off the East Coast, a single cable was strung to a nearby destroyer. With the two vessels pitching wildly in the high seas, I was strapped into a bosun's chair. Just as they were about to send me swinging alone out over the briny deep via what is known as a jackstay transfer, I gamely said, "I hope you're not planning on going anywhere." After what seemed like a terrifying amount of time, I arrived on the destroyer in one piece, shaken but safe. Never had a ship's deck felt so welcome. On that same trip, I was awakened during the night, taken on deck, and shown the lights of a line of Russian trawlers on the horizon. They were fishing right on the international line. One of the navy's roles was to make sure they didn't stray into Canadian waters.

For me, defence was a fascinating portfolio, one to which I continued to pay close attention during the rest of my time in Ottawa. Even in November 1975, three years after I'd left that post and was minister of finance, I was still fighting a rearguard action against the reintroduction of a heavy-tank role for Canadian forces in Europe. Cabinet had decided to replace our decrepit Centurions with lighter, tracked vehicles that could be more easily moved by air. I approved that approach. However, West German Chancellor Helmut Schmidt put the heat on Pierre, and Canada ended up buying the German-made Leopard battle tanks.

Of all the comments made about my eighteen months as minister of national defence, the one I treasure most came in a letter from Major General Donald C. Laubman, who was twice awarded the Distinguished Flying Cross during the Second World War and had a consummate career in the military. "You held the Defence portfolio during a particularly difficult period in the history of the Canadian Armed Forces and it is to your credit that we emerged from that period with much more confidence than we entered. The Department in general, and the Laubmans in particular, are sorry to see you leave." Not bad for a mere civilian.

Blue-Eyed Sheiks

In my role as minister of national defence, whenever I landed at Canadian Forces Base Downsview, a colonel would greet me on the tarmac with a brisk salute and a cheery "Good morning, Minister," then usher me to a waiting taxi for my meetings in downtown Toronto. When I became minister of energy, mines and resources (EMR), all that heady protocol disappeared. There was no colonel, just a corporal kicking the chocks under the wheels. "Hello," I said. "Hiya," he replied, and walked away. Among the members of the armed forces, I was suddenly a non-person.

I did, however, quickly establish myself with my new cadre of bureaucrats at EMR. I called an all-day meeting so assistant deputy ministers and directors-general could tell me what they did. The first to speak began with a feeble joke at my expense, saying, "Minister, it's too bad you weren't here two weeks ago because I gave a full-day presentation. Now, they've given me fifteen minutes." There was some chortling in the room until I said, "Take ten minutes and I'll ask questions for five."

During my first few months as energy minister in early 1972, I met with Alberta premier Peter Lougheed, consulted petroleum industry leaders, and visited a Panarctic Oils Ltd drilling site on the Arctic islands. Barely was my initiation over, when my new portfolio was caught up in the energy crisis that came to dominate the headlines and Parliament. Finding appropriate pricing and supply solutions would not only redefine relations between Ottawa and Alberta but also transform energy policy in Canada for decades to come.

The stakes were high: Would Alberta control the price of energy because of the location of resources or would that wealth be shared with all Canadians? If Alberta won, what would happen to our fragile federation if every province sought similar rights for other special interests? Such a precedent could contribute to the rise of Quebec separatism and the dissolution of Canada.

Canada's energy situation was complicated by the fact that in 1961 the Diefenbaker government had created an imaginary north-south line running through the Ottawa Valley. The reason was that foreign oil could be imported into Montreal at a lower price than it cost to deliver oil from Western Canada by pipeline. The Ottawa Valley line created a two-price system; the East enjoyed cheaper imports while higher prices in most of Ontario and the West aided growth in Alberta.[1]

When Premier Lougheed announced he would raise prices, thereby boosting his provincial revenue, Premier Bill Davis of Ontario was not pleased. After all, for more than a decade, Alberta enjoyed a premium over international prices and a guaranteed market in Ontario. One estimate of the increased cost to Ontario was $750 million.

While these issues were occupying me, Canadians were turning their backs on the Liberal Party. During the October 1972 election, unhappy voters complained about everything from bilingualism to unemployment insurance. Our slogan, "The Land is Strong," may have been true, but the people were feeling truculent. Public esteem for Pierre had fallen so far that in my riding we did not use his name on our campaign literature. Robert Stanfield's improved image over 1968, coupled with a strong showing by the NDP that took votes from us, allowed Stanfield to sneak up the middle.[2]

The result was a minority Liberal government with 109 seats, 107 PCs, and the NDP holding the balance of power with 31. My 1968 majority of 9,328 dropped to 1,217. Rather than be gracious to my opponents in my victory speech, I called the election the "dirtiest, nastiest, meanest" ever and expressed gratitude that Rosedale wouldn't be represented by a "Tory redneck point of view."[3] I delivered other speeches that might have been more boring, but that was the only speech I ever gave that I wish I could take back.

Dealing with a minority Parliament was difficult, but we tried to balance what we thought best for the country with opposition views. No one wanted another election. I focused on my portfolio and in June 1973 released a green paper, *An Energy Policy for Canada*, that predicted oil might reach $5 a barrel by 2000. How wrong I was! We also proposed the concept of "economic rent," a way of sharing the available petroleum money among industry and governments after covering the costs of exploration, production, transportation, and overhead.

As a first step, in September we asked the oil companies to freeze Canadian oil prices voluntarily. We levied an export tax of forty cents per barrel on oil that was exported to the US and used that money to subsidize prices in eastern Canada. Previously, the US price had determined the value of our oil. Now, the Government of Canada would set prices and ensure future research and development of resources in the national interest.[4]

All of this put us on a collision course with Big Oil Companies and Alberta. In response, Alberta's minister of federal and intergovernmental affairs, Don Getty, vowed to cut off oil to Eastern Canada. Our war of words led to a most memorable bumper sticker: "Let the Eastern bastards freeze in the dark!"

On October 6, 1973, the energy crisis suddenly went global after a coalition of Arab states led by Egypt and Syria invaded Israel. In what became known as the Yom Kippur War, Israel fought back, coming within forty kilometres of Damascus and a hundred kilometres of Cairo, before a ceasefire was declared. Arab oil-producing states embargoed oil exports to nations friendly to Israel, which in turn sent world oil prices to $5 a barrel by mid-month. I was beginning to think I was a jinx, like Joe Btfsplk, the character in the Li'l Abner comic strip who always had a rain cloud above his head. It seemed that every Cabinet post I assumed was suddenly confronted with more problems than the rest of my colleagues combined.

I was bombarded daily with questions in the House of Commons. Alvin Hamilton (PC–Qu'Appelle–Moose Mountain) posed a particularly long-winded inquiry, wondering if I'd be prepared to make a statement about *force majeure* and other highfalutin topics.

"I suppose I would be," I replied, "if I thought it were more than empty rhetoric."

On another occasion, I discovered an unlikely ally. In his preamble to a question, John Diefenbaker said, "Mr Speaker, I do not often do this, but I want to commend the Minister of Energy, Mines and Resources for the manner he has answered questions during the last several days." Amid much desk thumping from the Liberal benches, and surprised faces among his colleagues, he added, "It is worthy of the best traditions of Parliament."

Although the OPEC embargo did not specifically include Canada, it had the effect of reducing our supply in Eastern Canada because some imported oil arrived in Montreal via a pipeline from Portland, Maine. In response, we increased the shipment of Western oil through the St Lawrence Seaway to Montreal to 100,000 barrels a day. We organized another 50,000 barrels a day by tanker from Vancouver via the Panama Canal. We approved a pipeline from Sarnia to Montreal[5] and announced a $40-million research fund for developing the Athabasca tar sands.

Moreover, we twice raised the export tax on a barrel of oil from forty cents to $1.90 and then $2.20. Without the tax, US refineries could buy oil from Canada at frozen prices, a windfall for American companies. I believed that the interests of all Canadians, not the bottom line of Big Oil or the Alberta treasury, should come first, particularly when more than half of our output went to the US. We also announced conservation measures for the federal government aimed at saving $125 million annually. I urged Canadians to lower their thermostats and reduce highway speeds from sixty miles per hour to fifty miles per hour. My neighbour Gordon Robertson and I did our small part by carpooling. Canadians responded in kind. When I spoke to the Ottawa Kiwanis Club, they gave me a bottle labelled "No. 2 Fuel Oil" as a memento. The McGill Young Alumni presented me with a coal-oil lamp.

Still, we knew prices had to rise eventually. "The days of abundant, cheap energy for Canadians must come to an end," Pierre told the House on December 6, 1973. "We must in the long run allow the price of domestically produced oil to rise toward a level high enough to ensure the development of the Alberta oil sands, and other Canadian resources, but not one bit higher."

As part of our new national oil policy, Pierre pledged to create a national petroleum company that I had been recommending in order to achieve security of supply, help develop the oil sands, and promote Canadian development of our resources. Our critics saw what would become Petro-Canada as some sort of wild-eyed social experiment. But we were not nationalizing anyone's assets. Cabinet had considered but rejected buying a controlling interest in Shell Canada or Gulf Oil Canada because of the cost ($600 million for fifty per cent of Gulf or $480 million for fifty per cent of Shell)[6] and decided instead to create something new. In fact, the private sector seemed to welcome Petro-Canada. I was inundated with letters from bankers, auditors, search firms, and other suppliants all looking to work with the new entity.[7]

Pierre wanted Jack Austin, my former deputy in Energy who became Pierre's chief of staff, to head Petro-Canada. I thought Petro-Canada should be led by someone with experience in the petroleum sector. Pierre referred repeatedly to troubles at other Crown corporations where the bosses felt no obligation to take into account the government's wishes. I pointed out that Cabinet had unique powers over Petro-Canada. In the end, Pierre appointed Austin to the Senate. Maurice Strong, who'd been in business and at the United Nations, became chairman and chief executive officer (CEO). Bill Hopper, with experience in both the energy sector and government, was named president, and later became chairman and CEO.

As a result of defending the interests of all Canadians by dampening the rise in prices, I was portrayed in Alberta as the bad guy. A Calgary TV station invited me to participate in what I was told would be a one-on-one debate with Don Getty. As we took our places in the studio, a curtain rose to reveal a bleacher full of Alberta journalists who fired loaded questions at me. "I don't have to put up with this," I said, and walked out. Whenever I told that story elsewhere in Canada, the audience always applauded.

On another occasion in Alberta, I was given a Stetson, not the usual white hat, but a black one. I didn't mind. When I returned to Ottawa,

I proudly wore my black Stetson to the next Cabinet meeting. To me, it was a badge of honour. I represented a nation that consisted of more energy consumers than producers. At one point, Marc Lalonde passed me a note in Cabinet that read, "It is nice to see you in fighting form again. You have become the good old arrogant Liberal that you were when you were House Leader!"

Relations with the US were equally difficult, but I didn't buckle. On the eve of my January 1974 meeting in Washington, DC, with President Richard Nixon's energy czar, William Simon, the State Department officially protested our export tax and the Senate passed a resolution proposing punitive action. I went on NBC's *Today* show and spoke at the National Press Club in Washington, pointing out that without the export tax, we were paying more on the East Coast to import the 1 million barrels a day of foreign oil we needed from the Middle East and Venezuela than we were getting for the 1 million barrels a day of Western Canadian oil we sold to the US.[8]

After I explained our strategy at a meeting with Bill Simon and his officials, all heads turned to hear his reaction. To my surprise and delight, he replied, "If I were in Mr Macdonald's position, his policy is exactly what I would do." Because he had the president's ear, the US did not retaliate.

For my tough-guy stance, I was named *Report on Business* Man of the Year[9] and became the focus of a satirical song at the annual Parliamentary Press Gallery dinner in March 1974. As usual, the evening included off-the-record speeches by the party leaders and the governor general as well as a show written and staged by the media and political assistants. One of my aides, Ian Macdonald (no relation), performed a song to the tune of Helen Reddy's "Delta Dawn" that had these opening lines:

Thumper Don,
What's that crisis you got on?
Has that oil and gas you're sniffing got you high?
And did I hear you say
You're gonna be PM some day,
According to your pipeline in the sky.[10]

In an attempt to find more oil from other sources, I twice visited Venezuela and went to Iran and Saudi Arabia in February 1974. My warmest welcome was in Saudi Arabia, where my friend from Harvard, Ahmed Zaki Yamani, was minister of petroleum. Zaki held a dinner in my honour at his home in Jeddah, one of his five residences in the Middle East and Europe. The family occasion included friends and relatives ranging from his seventy-seven-year-old widowed mother to an adopted daughter of Chinese ancestry. We arrived at 10 p.m. and the musicians were still playing when we left at 3 a.m. At one point, someone coaxed me into a martial arts dance, complete with staves. Thankfully, after a few minutes, our ambassador, Jacques Gignac, rescued me.[11]

OPEC ended its embargo in March 1974, thereby reducing some of the pressure on Canada. At the end of the month, at a three-hour working lunch with first ministers held at 24 Sussex, we agreed that the price per barrel in Canada would increase to $6.50 while the world price headed for $12, quadruple what it had been before the Yom Kippur War. Looking back, it's hard to imagine we were arguing about such modest amounts. In June 1974, gas cost sixty-nine cents a gallon or about fifteen cents a liter in Ontario compared to $1.30 a litre today. We have somehow managed to deal with constant increases in the forty years since.

Despite our best efforts, the pricing issue was far from settled. Within days of the agreement, Alberta and Saskatchewan raised their royalty rates to increase their share of oil revenues at the expense of the rest of Canada. We responded in the May 6 budget by announcing that royalties paid to the provinces by oil companies would no longer be deductible from their corporate income tax.

The NDP stopped supporting us in Parliament. The government was defeated, and an election called for July 8, 1974. We won a 141-seat majority as the Tories slid from 107 seats to 95. The NDP suffered most from their minority performance, going from 31 to 16 seats.

By the fall of 1974, rising energy prices and a slowing global economy had combined to create a new phenomenon: stagflation – no or slow growth coupled with rising inflation. That latter problem would hound me in my next portfolio, Finance. Still, in July 1975, it was clear that our energy policy had worked, notwithstanding so much international turmoil. The price of oil in Canada was almost $2.50 a barrel lower than in the US and $4 lower than in most other countries. We had accomplished our goal, shielding Canadians from sharp increases. Meanwhile, a new issue arose that would test my patience with the Government of Alberta one last time.

On December 4, 1974, Atlantic Richfield Canada Ltd. pulled out of Syncrude Canada Ltd, a synthetic crude oil extraction plant planned for Alberta's oil sands. Cost estimates had ballooned from $900 million to $2 billion. In this case, the problem was bigger than just one commercial development. If Canada were to stand a chance of achieving energy self-sufficiency and of continuing as a major exporter, the oil sands were our last, best hope.[12]

Atlantic Richfield, Imperial Oil, and Cities Service each owned thirty per cent of Syncrude, with Gulf Oil holding ten per cent. A replacement had to be found for Atlantic Richfield or the other partners threatened to shelve the project. It was Bill Mooney who brought everyone together. Mooney joined Cities Service as a geologist in 1957, rose to executive vice president, and was one of the few people in the industry who had good relations with Ottawa.[13]

One day in January 1975, Mooney showed up at my office without an appointment. My assistant, Annette Léger, told him I was busy, but he said he'd wait. When I returned, we talked briefly. Cabinet had approved participation in Syncrude, so I told Mooney we were prepared to invest up to $400 million, but warned him, "If you say a word, I'll call you a liar, but get out there and get it done. It's important for Canada."

Because it was early in the calendar year, I had extra daily planners, and Annette had given him one. When he asked me to autograph it, I wrote, "To Bill Mooney, that great supporter of the National Oil Policy," and signed my name. "I'll get killed out west, but thanks," said Mooney. Mooney next met with Don Getty to see if Alberta would also invest. There was no firm commitment, but Mooney showed Getty my comment in his planner and asked for Getty's autograph, too. Getty wrote, "To Bill Mooney, anybody who can understand the

National Oil Policy is a genius," and signed his name. At least Getty and I were now talking, if only in Bill Mooney's calendar.

On Monday February 3, the companies and interested governments – Ottawa, Alberta, and Ontario – met at the International Inn near the Winnipeg airport. The hotel originally set up a long, narrow table with seats on both sides, but Mooney had it reconfigured into a square, so everyone could look directly at each other, with Ottawa opposite Alberta, the three oil companies to our right, Ontario and Shell to our left. The Alberta delegation was the largest: Premier Lougheed, Don Getty, Attorney General Merv Leitch, Minister of Energy Bill Dickie, and Deputy Provincial Treasurer Chip Collins. For Ontario, Premier Bill Davis attended with Treasurer Darcy McKeough, Energy Minister Dennis Timbrell, and Deputy Minister of Energy Dick Dillon. The senior industry representatives included Jerry McAfee of Gulf Oil Canada Ltd, Jack Armstrong of Imperial Oil Ltd, Bob Sellers of Canada-Cities Service Ltd, and Bill Daniel from Shell Canada.

Ottawa was represented by myself; my deputy minister, Tommy Shoyama, who had been a central figure in policy-making in Saskatchewan before moving to the federal civil service; and Terry Trushak, also with the ministry. As president of the Treasury Board, Jean Chrétien had asked Pierre if he could attend since public money was involved. But Jean hadn't been previously involved with the issue and didn't understand the details, so at one point, he and Imperial's Armstrong were on their hands and knees on the floor while Armstrong used a black marker and a large sheet of paper to explain the project's financing to Jean.

This was, above all, a risky venture. We didn't know if this extraction process would work, and if it did, whether it would be economic. The only other company that had tried was Great Canadian Oil Sands (GCOS), and they were just breaking even after starting production in 1967. Moreover, plans for Syncrude called for 125,000 barrels a day, three times the output of GCOS.

The meeting began at 9:30 a.m. and got off to a rocky start. As a possible new participant, Daniel said Shell would only consider investing the necessary $600 million if there were a government guarantee on a floor price of $19 a barrel for Syncrude production. His demand was rejected and he left.

Premier Lougheed and Imperial's Armstrong were supposed to be co-chairmen, but Lougheed dominated. He pretended that he didn't understand that I represented the Government of Canada and could cut a deal on the spot. Lougheed kept needling me by saying, "Why don't you go and call the prime minister?" I didn't take the bait, and I didn't make the call. I said we'd put in $300 million, Alberta agreed to $200 million, and Premier Davis said Ontario would invest $50 million.

Premier Lougheed was rude to Davis and dismissive of Ontario's offer. "The chips at this table are one hundred million, not fifty. Perhaps you should withdraw and see if you can do better." Premier Davis reacted calmly, saying, "Mr Premier, I'll take your advice on that. If you have further things that we should know about, I hope you'll keep in touch with us. Let's see if we can do a deal," and proceeded to leave the room. Premier Davis was, as always, a gentleman in the face of discourtesy.

Of the many senior political people I saw during my career, Davis was among those I most admired. By contrast, Premier Lougheed treated Premier Davis poorly, kept him isolated for two hours, and continued the discussions in his absence. Finally, I brought Premier Davis back into the meeting, and he announced that Ontario would contribute $100 million, an amount acceptable to Lougheed. Premier Davis said he hoped that some of the new petrochemical plants would be located in Ontario. "I want to feel wanted in this deal," said Premier Davis. Premier Lougheed gave him no undertakings.

The total amount of government money, $600 million, replaced Atlantic Richfield's portion. For our $300 million, the Government of Canada would own fifteen per cent of Syncrude; Alberta would own ten per cent, and Ontario, five per cent. For their seventy per cent interest, the three companies agreed to increase their total investment from $1 billion to $1.4 billion in order to reach the $2 billion needed.[14] The Government of Canada's lead investment in the oil sands was timely. Syncrude shipped its first barrel of oil in 1978 and by 1998 had produced 1 billion barrels. Today, the oil sands supply about half of Canada's oil production.

Although we had just negotiated the largest public–private joint venture in Canadian history, instead of bringing the meeting to an agreeable conclusion, Premier Lougheed launched into a long harangue of his grievances with the federal government. I was annoyed. When his tirade was over, silence descended. I stared at him for a long time and finally said, "On those questions, you might want to pick up the phone and call the prime minister." At the close of that meeting, I would have been happy never to see Premier Lougheed again.[15]

While the din of disagreements during my time as minister of energy received much public attention, the fact is that we always found the middle ground. It's the substance of the results, not the rhetoric of the debate, that's important. If the federal government had not forcefully intervened by taking over oil pricing from the international market, Canada might have emerged from the 1970s as a balkanized collection of mini-states, each selfishly guarding its own local interests with no thought for the country as a whole.

Eventually, I reconciled with both Don Getty and Peter Lougheed. In 1978, I sent Getty a book about Clint Eastwood. In his letter of thanks, Getty said, "My family, especially my two youngest sons, have found any comparison between myself and Clint Eastwood to be a real laugh." He closed by saying, "Please say hello to your charming wife for me since she may now be right in that you are not nearly as nasty a person as you used to appear to be."

When I left politics in 1978, among the corporate boards I joined was Alberta Energy Co., fifty per cent owned by the Alberta government. When CEO David Mitchell asked Premier Lougheed to approve my appointment as a director, the premier said, "You're testing me, aren't you?" Mitchell smiled and nodded. After a brief pause, Premier Lougheed said, "That will be all right."

That act of consent was both a truce and a triumph. When Peter died in 2012, 2,500 mourners attended his funeral in Calgary's Jubilee Auditorium. He and I had certainly battled, he for his province and I for my country, but at that service I was honoured to sit in the row immediately behind his family.

Pierre is about to quaff whatever's in the jug
during the 1974 election campaign. Standing
to the left is his wife, Margaret, wearing a hat.
I'm behind Pierre and my wife, Ruth, is behind
Margaret. (*The Toronto Star*)

Part of the job as minister of energy was negotiating with other elected officials. Here I'm flanked by Ontario treasurer Darcy McKeough, left, and Alberta premier Peter Lougheed. (*The Toronto Star*)

At the official opening of the Libby Dam in 1975, I told President Gerald Ford that Canada would look after its own energy needs first before exporting any oil to the US.

A rare Santa Claus performance as minister of finance in 1976 with Barbara Frum and Alan Maitland, co-hosts of CBC Radio's *As It Happens*.

A farewell visit with Pierre in 1978 after I'd left public life.

Ruth and me at our farm with daughters Althea (top) and, from left, Nikki, Leigh, and Sonja.

While chairing the 1982–85 Royal Commission that led to free trade. I was aided by a dozen commissioners, including Jean Casselman Wadds. (*The Toronto Star*)

Duncan Macpherson's portrayal of Supermac taking free trade to the canyons of Wall Street. (*The Toronto Star*)

After Ruth died, I married Adrian Merchant (Lang) in 1988, and we immediately moved to London where I was posted as Canadian High Commissioner. Here we are with our newly acquired Labrador, Teal, in Grosvenor Square Gardens.

We entertained royalty at the High Commission residence – none more enjoyably than the Queen Mother. In the doorway, behind Adrian, is Ernest "Smokey" Smith, a Canadian winner of the Victoria Cross.

To Donald Macdonald
with every good wish
Margaret Thatcher

After a fierce windstorm felled millions of trees in Britain, Prime Minister Margaret Thatcher gratefully received 35,000 trees and 26 million evergreen seeds donated by the Canadian forestry industry.

Queen Elizabeth II and I were shown around *The True North*, a 1991 celebration of Canadian landscape and contemporary artists held at the Barbican Art Gallery, by an unidentified official.

Prime Minister Brian Mulroney and his wife, Mila were among the many
Canadian visitors Adrian and I hosted in London.

University of Toronto president Rob Prichard (left) and chancellor Hal Jackman (centre) with me, a newly minted honorary Doctor of Laws in 2000.

Our extended family at our 1988 wedding. Front row, from left: Amanda, Althea, Timothy, Leigh, Maria (killed in an auto accident in 1991), Adrian, Elisabeth, and Adrian. In the back row from left, with me: Sonja, Nikki, and Andrew. (Gregory was in Europe playing for the Canadian Ultimate Team.)

13

Zap, You're Frozen

On September 10, 1975, John Turner abruptly resigned as minister of finance, a post he'd held for three years. John's timing couldn't have been worse, eight days before a provincial election in Ontario. Pierre asked him to postpone his action until after the vote, but John refused, thus adding to Liberal leader Robert Nixon's woes. The Liberals finished third; Stephen Lewis and the NDP replaced them as the official opposition. Bill Davis remained in government but with a minority.

I first heard the news when Jean Chrétien called me and said, "John Turner has resigned, saying that as ministers we failed to support him." "That's bullshit," I replied. "We gave him all the support that he sought from us in whatever he wanted to do." John's problem was not with us. Cabinet had discussed the possibility of mandatory wage and price controls as a way to fight inflation, but John never brought us a specific proposal. Instead, he spent months unsuccessfully trying to convince labour, business, and provincial governments to embrace voluntary restraints.[1]

I phoned Pierre, who said John had indeed tendered his resignation but gave no reasons for doing so. Pierre told me that he'd offered John various roles, but he refused any appointment. I offered to denounce John to the world if he went public with criticisms. But after Pierre and I further discussed any such action, I cooled down. My final words to Pierre were, "C'est une bonne situation pour moi à se taire." (This is a good time for me to shut up.) Soon after, John and I met and talked while we each demolished three Scotches. John insisted Pierre had forced his hand. None of the facts as I knew them bore this out. He seemed weary and filled with concern that he was doing the right thing.

I had other matters of greater personal import on my mind. A few months earlier, in March 1975, Ruth had been diagnosed with breast cancer and underwent a mastectomy at Toronto General Hospital. I brought a bottle of Dry Sack and two glasses to her room for a quiet celebration. While she ate dinner, I fell asleep in the chair, a combination of relief and the sherry.

Her doctors were confident they'd got everything so did not recommend Ruth undergo radiation or chemotherapy. But recurrence of cancer is always possible, so I began thinking about leaving politics and returning to my law practice and a less hectic and more private life.

Pierre and I talked about my becoming minister of finance, but I was worried about Ruth, and said I was not interested. Several friends and colleagues, including Walter Gordon and Tommy Shoyama, my former deputy minister at Energy and now deputy at Finance, urged me to take the job. Well, I thought, for all the negatives, there was at least the exhilaration of not backing off from a fight.

When Pierre and I met again, this time he said not only that he wanted me in Finance but also that he needed me. Pierre wasn't always so direct with other ministers in similar situations. If they showed hesitancy, he did not push his case. With me, Pierre always showed his true feelings. On that basis, I accepted and was sworn in on September 26.

For the first fifteen years of the post-war era, Canada's inflation was benign, then prices began rising in the 1960s. When I took on Finance, Canadians had experienced double-digit inflation for twenty-one months in a row. Wage settlements with annual increases of twenty per cent were commonplace.

Inflation was the major issue in the 1974 election when we regained our majority. Robert Stanfield had campaigned on controls, beginning with a ninety-day wage and price freeze, to break inflation's momentum. We ran television ads that mocked Stanfield by saying: "Zap, you're frozen!" Fifteen months later, the Progressive Conservative Party was replacing Stanfield as leader, and we were actively contemplating the very policy that we had fought against.

In fact, Cabinet had been preparing a contingency plan for price and income controls for almost two years. In February 1974, the Cabinet Committee on Economic Policy had considered a memorandum dated November 30, 1973 from Consumer and Corporate Affairs Minister Herb Gray on the topic.[2] The committee decided to proceed with further preparations and asked several departments (Finance, Justice, Labour, Consumer and Corporate Affairs, and National Revenue) to complete draft legislation as well as make recommendations for staff requirements and an information campaign.

At the Cabinet meeting held on July 24, 1975, John Turner urged a heightened state of readiness and said he would bring to Cabinet in September a review of the inflation outlook and overall economic situation. Some ministers favoured continuing the contingency preparations while others had specific views. Postmaster General Bryce Mackasey, for example, said we should seek other means of controlling inflation rather than through wage controls.

I was not at all happy about the direction matters were heading. I opposed John's recommendations on the grounds that we had declared our opposition to controls and shouldn't be proceeding to draw up such measures. For me, it was a matter of principle. I was the only minister to be so categorical. Pierre said that, despite his own and the government's distaste for controls, the economic situation required us to consider all possible options. Pierre also said that he was inclined to agree with all of John's recommendations.[3] Such support made the timing of John's resignation all the more remarkable.

But resign he did, without delivering his promised September update. "My choice of Donald Macdonald as Turner's successor was a last-ditch attempt to rescue the voluntary consensus effort and avoid controls," Pierre wrote in *Memoirs*. "Macdonald had been one of the most vehement opponents of controls, and I knew that if there was any way to avoid them, Don would find it."[4]

Even prior to my appointment as minister of finance, a September 11, 1975, Cabinet memorandum left little wriggle room. "The news from the inflation front has been consistently bad over the past three months," said the memo. "We are thus faced with a very real threat of continuing double-digit inflation which in turn would choke off the incipient recovery of real output and lead to continuing increases in unemployment. In such a scenario, our cash requirements would rise to extraordinary levels and the task of fiscal management would become virtually unmanageable."

An ad hoc committee of officials presented three choices to Priorities and Planning on September 30: one, selective controls on strategic industries and key wage settlements; two, a more comprehensive approach that included a ninety-day freeze, during which talks with the provinces would lead to some flexibility; three, a sixty- to ninety-day freeze to allow talks that would choose between the selective or comprehensive approach.

To me, none of the options was palatable. The words of one of my Harvard professors, Lon Fuller, rang in my ears. He'd warned about the difficulties caused by direct public action in a market economy. Elsewhere, controls had mixed results. President Nixon invoked a ninety-day freeze on prices in 1971 but saw unemployment grow. When the US re-imposed controls in 1973, inflation and unemployment both rose at an alarming rate.

Edmund Dell, paymaster general in the Harold Wilson government and right-hand man to Denis Healey, chancellor of the exchequer, happened to be in Ottawa during our considerations. Dell told us that Britain's recent experience with price controls demonstrated that we should aim to regulate only big business and large labour unions. That kind of program would set a pattern; trying to control the entire economy was impossible.

By the time of the next meetings of the Priorities and Planning Committee on October 7 and 8, I had become convinced of the necessity of controls, and we had come up with the broad outlines for a focused approach. Pierre and I got into a philosophical discussion. As a lawyer trained in Ontario, I followed English common law. "We need rules so people know what they're doing. We have to lay it all out," I said. Pierre was more familiar with the Civil Code of Quebec that's based on the Napoleonic Code. "Just make a statement of principle. Tell people, 'Don't raise your price unless it's appropriate.' Let them figure it out," he said. We went back and forth for about fifteen minutes until Pierre finally gave in and agreed with me.

On October 9, I told P and P Committee that there was no other choice but to bring in a program of mandatory controls. Speaking to the media after, I expressed my fears. "The kind of restraints we have in mind are unprecedented in peacetime. We are moving into an era of government intervention in the economy. If you don't find that as frightening as I do, then let me know."

On October 13, Thanksgiving Day, Pierre went on television to announce mandatory wage and price controls that would take effect at midnight. There would be no ninety-day freeze, thus giving political cover for our recent election stance. Wage and salary increases would be limited to eight per cent in the first year, six per cent in the second, and four per cent in the third. Prices would rise only at the same rate as cost increases. Controls would apply to the federal government, the 1,500 largest companies in Canada, construction companies with more than twenty employees, and all professionals.[5]

In my speech the next day in the House, I joked about how I faced a sudden crisis in the early days of three consecutive Cabinet posts. "A funny thing happened to me on the way to retirement. Somehow – and I still haven't quite figured out how – I found myself diverted a little over two weeks ago when I was called on to assume an even stiffer workload as Minister of Finance. I must confess that I would have liked to have had a little more time in which to learn the ropes."[6]

We created the Anti-Inflation Board (AIB) as well as an Administrator with powers to roll back prices and wages and impose penalties. Named AIB chairman was Jean-Luc Pépin, who had retired from politics after being defeated in 1972. Vice-chairman was Beryl Plumptre, a straight-talker formerly on the Food Prices Review Board. We froze salaries of MPs, Supreme Court judges, senior officers in the Armed Forces and RCMP, and senior executives of all government boards, commissions, agencies, and Crown corporations.

Initially, we expected to monitor a few thousand large firms, but the number grew to 6,500 when associated companies were included. Once we added construction firms, the total was 9,500. We later included companies that bargained together, bringing the total number of businesses under AIB to more than 20,000. The impact was immediate. The first year of the anti-inflation program brought the year-over-year increase of consumer prices down to 6.2 per cent from 10.6 per cent. Wage settlements, after increasing 20 per cent in 1975, fell to 8.8 per cent in the first quarter of 1977.[7]

Public response was generally positive. "Donald Stovel Macdonald is emerging as his own kind of finance minister with a style different not only from that of John Turner but also from what might have been expected from Macdonald's own past record," wrote columnist Don McGillivray in the *Gazette*. "The man who has been coolly and carefully playing for provincial agreement to the anti-inflation program is not the 'Thumper' Macdonald who stirred up such a storm in the Commons when he was government house leader and in the West when he was battling Alberta's Premier Lougheed over oil."[8]

On October 14, 1976, the first anniversary of controls, the Canadian Labour Congress held a national day of protest. One million workers failed to show up for work. Business had become irritable, too. By the end of July, we'd fielded 500 complaints from companies, many worried about what they saw as increasing state control. One forest products executive called us communists for invoking controls. I was ready to remind him that President Nixon had brought in a similar program and no one could be more anti-communist, given his actions in the late 1940s as the most virulent Red-baiter on the House Un-American Activities Committee. Tommy Shoyama wisely advised me to keep quiet. Some price increases were granted, such as a five-cent rise in the cost of a chocolate bar to twenty-five cents, based on a fifty-one per cent jump in the cost of cocoa. "The kids of this country are going to hate you," Steve Paproski (PC–Edmonton Centre) called across the House floor. "Just like everybody else," I replied.[9]

The pressure of House sittings, Cabinet, caucus, and sessions with angry delegations made me feel like a prisoner, crowded and oppressed, the very fate that I had feared. As far as my colleagues were concerned, if controls succeeded, they would bask in a policy of their own making. If controls failed, they would regard the event much like a body newly washed up on shore. Mine.

In my first budget, on May 25, 1976, we simplified the program, loosened rules on profits, and gave tax credits on business investment.[10] Among the slashed expenses was the traditional post-budget party in the minister's office. "This," I said, "is the year of the cheapskate." Amid such seriousness, there was time for frivolity. The night before that budget, I neither rehearsed my speech nor studied macroeconomics. I watched *The Big Store*, a Marx Brothers movie, on TV. Moreover, I snuck out of my mother-in-law's birthday party to do so, even though I had seen my favourite comedians save the Phelps Department Store many times.

Whenever I needed a laugh in life, I turned to the Marx Brothers for their zany antics and intricate word plays. I was forever organizing Marx Brothers film fests for family and friends. Once when we were on some outing, our daughters fell behind. When I looked around, I saw all four of them mimicking Groucho's signature walk, complete with pretend cigars at their lips, and those bouncing eyebrows.

When you're in politics, it's also important to be able to laugh at yourself. I'd been parodied at the Parliamentary Press Gallery dinner when I was minister of energy. In 1977, another of my assistants, Terry Wills, wrote and performed a song about me, called "Big Mac Attacks," to the tune of the McDonald's commercial. Here's an excerpt:

> While I'm stuck in Finance,
> Beggars won't stand a chance.
> You won't get no break today,
> Bugger off and pay your way.
> Thump the masses, lads and lasses,
> Lower class, no free passes.
> From Macdonald ... we'll screw it up for you.

I attended the 1976 Remembrance Day ceremony at the War Memorial with Nikki and Sonja. John Diefenbaker greeted the girls, and a Canadian Legion official moved Sonja up front with Justin and Sacha Trudeau.[11] After the ceremony, I met with Pierre, Treasury Board President Bob Andras, Bank of Canada Governor Gerald Bouey, Clerk of the Privy Council Michael Pitfield, Pierre's Chief of Staff Jim Coutts, and several Finance officials.

Associate Deputy Minister Bill Hood confirmed that we had outperformed our expectations on inflation but reducing unemployment would take more time. I urged winter works programs in specific regions, but mostly we talked about the Quebec election just four days away. We were right to worry. The Parti Québécois, led by René Lévesque, won. I felt devastated that night by the separatist threat. The Canadian dollar, worth US$1.03 that summer, fell below par by month's end, the beginning of a long ten-year slide to US$0.70 that drove up the cost of imports.

As a result, my principal concern continued to be controls. MPS paid so little attention to one budget speech that no one noticed when

I inadvertently turned two pages at once and did not deliver an entire section of text. According to the editors of *Hansard*, I had to speak the missing words in the House the next day so they could officially be "on the record." After a discussion with my staff, we found a better solution. Since no one else seemed aware of my blunder, the speech was published just as if I had delivered every scintillating sentence. Ending controls wasn't quite so easy. Former US secretary of the treasury George Shultz, then an executive at Bechtel Group, gave me the best advice I received on the topic: "Declare victory and withdraw."[12]

Other matters dominated international gatherings. At the May 1977 G7 summit in London, British prime minister James Callaghan came to the end of the agenda and asked if anyone wanted to raise an issue. Yes, I said, and brought up the restrictive measures used by the European Union to keep Canadian products, such as grain, out of their markets.

German chancellor Helmut Schmidt was livid. "I'm not here to talk about your grain," he said. For a moment, there was pregnant silence, and then President Jimmy Carter said, in his Georgia drawl, "Mistah Chairman, I'm not sure I totally agree with that. I think we *should* be talking about EU policies, but if Chancellor Schmidt doesn't want to, then we'll get together with the Canadians and agree on the kind of trade policy we want the Europeans to follow." Schmidt was suddenly very conciliatory. After two days of meetings, we hammered out the Downing Street Declaration that undertook to create more jobs, reduce inflation, and seek additional resources for the International Monetary Fund. Nothing was done about grain, but at least we were able to tell Canadian farmers that we'd begun the process toward more open borders.

All the while, I was wrestling with my own future. After delivering the March 31, 1977 budget, I told the media, "I don't know if I'll be here for another budget. Sometime in the course of 1977, I will have to decide whether I will remain for another election."[13] For me, there was nothing more to do in politics. I had no interest in becoming party leader and said so in December 1976. "I don't have the driving ambition to be the prime minister as other people do," I said on CTV's *Question Period*. "I think it's important to have that little extra quality of royal jelly in the person who is going to be in the position. I haven't got it." A few days later, Senator Keith Davey sent me a package of sweets called "Royal Jelly" and a note saying, "Now, you have it."

The subject of my departure came to a head during an August 1977 family vacation on the aptly named Ugo-Igo Island in Georgian Bay. I'd wake up in the morning, gaze at the rugged granite and windswept pines, and tell myself I was determined to retire from politics. By late afternoon, I'd talked myself back into loyally soldiering on.

Toward the end of our holiday, I had a visit from Jim Coutts, Tommy Shoyama, and a colleague of Tommy's in Finance, Ian Stewart. Pierre was considering calling an election for October 24 and wanted my views. Polls showed the electorate had confidence in Pierre but was feeling unsettled about the economy. Should we go to the people then, or work through what could be a difficult winter with a new economic policy? And, they asked, as the economic minister with the widest public support, would I be participating in the next election?

I said the October date was fine with me but I told them I had doubts about being a candidate, a comment that was greeted by stares and silence. Coutts finally mumbled that was a matter for resolution between Pierre and me. They left after an hour and a half. Ten minutes later, I was playing tennis.

Their visit had gelled my thinking. Not only was I not going to run in the next election but I would also resign immediately as minister of finance. My diplomatic passport showed I'd visited eleven countries in four years, including Britain, the United States, Japan, Hong Kong, Lebanon, Cyprus, Iran, Saudi Arabia, Argentina, Venezuela, and Brazil. It was time to get off the treadmill of politics and see more of life and my family.

I met Pierre for lunch at 24 Sussex on August 30 and told him my decision. There was a chilly atmosphere of unease that was typical of Pierre whenever he faced personal dealings with his colleagues.

"Is this your final decision?"

"Yes."

"Do you want to be pressed to stay on?"

"No."

This moment seemed the logical end of my political career. Reluctantly, Pierre agreed, adding that at some point he would be taking a similar step. We discussed possible successors for my portfolio. Pierre favoured Jean Chrétien, although he held out hope that Jean would leave Ottawa to lead the Quebec Liberal Party against René Lévesque.

I waited over Labour Day weekend to make my announcement so Pierre had time to consider my replacement. On Tuesday, I met the media in my parliamentary office and told them that I was resigning from Cabinet but would remain an MP until February. "I've had differences with my colleagues, but I have none on policy questions now," I said. "The reasons were personal in terms of my family, my own career."

Commentary was generally positive. "He has been Mr Trudeau's strongest English-speaking minister – one of the few strong figures in a weak Cabinet. Mr Macdonald is a good man and his leaving is a loss," wrote columnist Geoffrey Stevens in the *Globe and Mail*. *Le Devoir* said, "On voyait en lui le successeur éventuel de M. Trudeau," echoing the headline on a John Gray column in the *Ottawa Citizen*, "Trudeau loses his logical successor."

Even the *Calgary Herald* found fine things to say. "There was a time not long ago when Donald Macdonald's departure from public life would have been greeted with rejoicing in this part of the country," said an editorial. "Now that the passage of time has made it possible to view Macdonald's career as energy minister in perspective, it is possible still to disagree with Ottawa's energy policy and the manner of its implementation, while at the same time regretting the loss of a devoted and able public servant."[14]

At the next caucus meeting, there was a standing ovation when I entered the room. I received best wishes from world leaders, including Chancellor Schmidt, Prime Minister Callaghan, US Federal Reserve Chairman Arthur Burns, and Vice President Walter Mondale.[15] By another measure, my career came full circle. When I was first nominated in 1961, the *Telegram* had carefully told readers that I was not the much better known CCF leader Donald C. MacDonald. In September 1977, the *Wall Street Journal* headline said, *Financial Minister Resigns in Canada*. The accompanying photo showed an NDP member of the Manitoba Legislature. So much for a higher profile after all those years in public life.

In November, Jean Chrétien, Canada's first French-Canadian finance minister, announced that controls would be phased out beginning April 14, 1978, six months ahead of schedule. The timing of imposition was right; controls had succeeded. According to a paper by Professor W. Craig Riddell of the University of British Columbia, "Econometric studies generally conclude that wage and price controls reduced new wage settlements by 3–4 percent in each of the three years of the program, and price inflation by 1–3 percent a year, with the reduction in price inflation concentrated in the second half of the program and continuing well beyond the end."[16]

As for my future, I had made no arrangements. Conflict-of-interest rules prohibited a minister from job-hunting while still in Cabinet.[17] On the one hand, such career uncertainty was intimidating; on the other hand, it was liberating. I no longer had to consider the political implications of my every move. I could choose the life I wanted. After fifteen years of answering to constituents, and nine years of Cabinet solidarity, a new and wider world opened to me.

14

Meetings of the Minds

During my time as minister in various portfolios, I met many of the world's leaders, including Soviet premier Alexei Kosygin, US presidents Richard Nixon and Gerald Ford, British prime minister Edward Heath, Chinese premier Chou En-lai, and the Shah of Iran. I learned something about leadership from each of them and always came away with a better understanding of them as individuals, their nations, and how to deal with the major issues of the day.

Leaders can achieve great goals through cables, negotiations, carefully crafted statements, and grand public occasions, but when it comes to really knowing people on the other side, nothing beats face-to-face meetings for a frank exchange of views and the likelihood of progress toward greater understanding.

Premier Kosygin was portrayed in the West as a liberal reformer, although First Secretary Leonid Brezhnev denied most of his efforts for change. Even so, during Kosygin's weeklong visit to Canada in October 1971, his comments were not repressed and he was comfortable discussing any subject. We spent several enjoyable hours talking about politics, world affairs, and Soviet life.[1]

I was fascinated with Joseph Stalin, Soviet leader from the 1920s to the 1950s, so Kosygin's relationship with Stalin was the first topic I raised. During the Second World War, as Kosygin rose through the Soviet hierarchy, his contact with Stalin increased until they met daily. Kosygin said that Stalin's greatest attribute was his self-confidence. Even in 1941 and 1942, at the height of the German onslaught, Stalin never doubted his own judgment or leadership. Although Stalin often lost his temper, you could disagree with him, said Premier Kosygin, "But you had to be tactful."

Surprisingly, Stalin had a sense of humour and could laugh at his own comrades. Nikolai Bulganin, who played a leading role in the Red Army, often took salutes in Red Square. An effective soldier, Bulganin was a poor rider with no military bearing on horseback, a sight that Stalin found amusing.

In later years, Stalin became grim and difficult to deal with. I remarked that being close to Stalin for so long, Premier Kosygin must have had to perform a difficult balancing act. When Paul Martin Sr and I met the premier that night, his first words were directed at me. He said he might not have fully comprehended the meaning of my remark, but added that he had never followed "a policy of balancing." Behind the polite diplomatic facade, there was a flash of the regime's brutal nature. But for the most part, I found him an intelligent and civilized man. He was not the demon that his detractors claimed.

When I next saw Premier Kosygin a few days later in Toronto, he was staying at the Inn on the Park. The hotel in northeast Toronto was surrounded by open space and served by few roads so the area could be fully secure. Anti-Soviet demonstrators were isolated at the entrance to the hotel's long driveway. I expressed embarrassment and apologized for their noisy show, but he brushed it off. Premier Kosygin's attitude was far different than the Czechoslovakian ambassador who once reproached me for allowing protests outside the Soviet embassy in Ottawa.

The final morning, October 26, as we drove to the airport, Premier Kosygin talked about the decision by the United Nations General Assembly the previous day – despite US opposition – to replace the Nationalist Government with the People's Republic of China (PRC) as the recognized government of China. It was an historic step, one that Pierre and I had urged five years earlier as UN observers.

Premier Kosygin approved of the change but wondered, given US support for Taiwan, whether the United States was playing a "double game." I said that it was unusual for the Americans to be opposed by their traditional friends: the UK, France, and Canada. I offered the opinion that the decision simplified matters for the US. They did their best for Taiwan, and now, with the UN vote, they had been relieved of promoting the interests of the Nationalist Government.

Premier Kosygin agreed but noted that the US continued to maintain bilateral dealings with Taiwan and the PRC, a link that might make for difficulties in US relations with the Soviet Union. Paul Martin added that the charged atmosphere at the Security Council reminded him of the post-war period when some of the leading powers had difficulty making up their minds on important matters.

If Premier Kosygin understood, he refused to be drawn in. He did agree, however, that the admission of China to the UN was significant. Just before we said our goodbyes, Paul noted that because US Secretary of State Henry Kissinger was in China, our talks were easier since none of us was involved in persuading Kissinger. Instead, we were just having conversations. To my mind, that was the best part of the visit, the fact that we were able to just have conversations across the great divide that separated democracy from communism.

Visiting the White House in the halcyon days long before 9/11 was relatively simple. For the event on February 11, 1974, our names were vetted in advance. There were document checks at the wrought-iron gates on Pennsylvania Avenue, but that was the extent of it. Today's Super Bowl has tighter security. Inside, we were taken through a series of rooms and hallways filled with paintings of former presidents and bucolic landscapes hanging above magnificent pieces of nineteenth-century furniture and displays of bone china used by first families.

In the receiving line, when I shook hands with President Richard Nixon, I told him that I was the minister of energy he'd referred to as "that tough minister from Canada." He laughed and said, "I meant that as a compliment." I said, "I took it that way." I'm not sure that either of us really meant what we said.

Our delegation included Secretary of State Mitchell Sharp, Minister of Finance John Turner, Deputy Minister of Energy Jack Austin, Chairman of the National Energy Board Marshall Crowe, and Marcel Cadieux, Canadian ambassador to the US. Other guests included a wide range of individuals, from Japanese business leaders to, sitting beside me, US secretary of commerce Frederick Dent, a former textile company president.

The evening was billed as a working dinner, but it was little more than an exercise in public relations. After the sirloin and soufflé, the president spoke without notes for fifteen minutes. He was gracious and at ease as he outlined US aims that could be boiled down to this: the Americans were willing to assist in the wider interests of the world economy and political stability, but were more than happy to go it alone if need be.

Nixon was deeply mired in Watergate, but that night we speculated more on his skin tone than his political future. In the depths of winter, he had such a good tan that I assumed he must have been wearing television makeup. Mitchell Sharp, who sat to Nixon's immediate left, said the source was more likely a sun lamp.

Just three months earlier, Nixon told a press conference he was innocent of any wrongdoing in Watergate, saying, "I'm not a crook." But his world was disintegrating. In July, six months after our dinner, Congress began impeachment proceedings. Nixon resigned on August 8, 1974. When I watched on TV as his helicopter lifted off from the White House lawn, and he raised his arms with two fingers on each hand forming a V, I couldn't help but wonder how he'd brought himself to such a low estate. One thing was certain: President Nixon was a performer right to the end.

The day before my scheduled meeting at 10 Downing Street with British prime minister Edward Heath, he called a general election for February 28, 1974. Our group included Ward Cornell, agent general for Ontario in London; Jake Warren, Canadian High Commissioner to the UK; Harold Smith, chief engineer at Ontario Hydro; and Darcy McKeough, Ontario minister of energy. Darcy's father-in-law was David Walker, the sitting MP I defeated in the 1962 election, but Darcy never let that get in the way of our ability to work together, and I have admired his prowess over the years.

Our mission was selling to Britain the Canadian-built CANDU nuclear reactor. The pressurized heavy-water reactor, developed in the 1950s and 1960s, operates in Ontario, Quebec, and New Brunswick, and has been sold to India, South Korea, Argentina, Romania, China, and Pakistan.

Lord Bridges, the prime minister's private secretary, guided us to a book-lined ground-floor waiting room. I was immediately transported back to my grandfather's library in Winnipeg. In the summers, when Janet and I visited, we'd play in Peanut Park across the street and visit Polo Park to see the bears. My grandfather would often come home from the office for an afternoon nap. To ensure peace and quiet, he'd tell his chauffeur to take Janet and me to Ringer's Drug Store for ice cream sodas.

He needn't have bothered. As a bookish boy, I'd happily spend hours on my own in his library. Janet remembers my saying, when I first saw the shelves filled with books, "Can I read them all?" Over the years I devoured many of them and so admired an illustrated series compiled by the *Times of London* about the First World War, that when my grandfather died, I asked if I could have it. I enjoyed the volumes for decades and donated them in 2011 to the Royal Canadian Military Institute in Toronto.

The collection at 10 Downing Street was similar and included English classics by Thomas Babington Macaulay and George Eliot; the Colonel Edward Mandell House Letter, which is not a letter but an official report on the First World War; several biographies of nineteenth-century politicians; and contemporary works by such Labour Party frontbenchers as Douglas Jay and Roy Jenkins.

The prime minister then led us up one flight of stairs to a sitting room. Along the way, we paused at a cluster of television cameras and still photographers for the requisite photo opportunity. Once seated, we were offered Chinese or Indian tea and then briefly discussed the election. As might be expected, the prime minister felt he was on strong ground.

We pitched CANDU for about fifteen minutes. At the end of our presentation, the prime minister smiled and said that Britain would be pleased to sell us one of *their* nuclear reactors. We laughed and left. Given the imminent election, the prime minister was likely just going through the motions with us, rather than cancel our appointment on such short notice.

Even if Edward Heath had agreed to buy a C A N D U, the deal would likely never have gone through. Like President Nixon, he was on his way out. During his four years in office, the Conservative Party had been severely damaged by miners' strikes, among other events. Even so, I thought the prime minister was in good spirits, but Jake Warren said that our host nervously drummed his fingers on the side of his chair the whole time.

The February election ended in a hung parliament. Prime Minister Heath tried but failed to form a coalition then gave way to a minority government led by Harold Wilson of the Labour Party. Heath carried on as Conservative leader until 1975 when he and other contenders were defeated by Margaret Thatcher, his former education and science secretary, who would become prime minister in 1979.

During my time as High Commissioner to the United Kingdom, Adrian and I were invited to Heath's home, Arundells, in Salisbury's Cathedral Close. The occasion was lunch followed by a stroll in his beautiful garden. He served as a backbench M P until 2001 and died in 2006. I still think fondly of him for listening to our sales pitch on that first full day of an election when he had far better things to do with his precious time.

Meetings with foreign leaders always involve formality and scripted procedure, but none more so than in China. In late April and early May 1973, I led a thirty-five–member Canadian oil mission to China. We visited Shanghai and Peking, as Beijing was then called, Harbin in Manchuria, and the oil fields at Taching. Invitations for talks with Premier Chou En-lai were rare and always announced at the last minute. After several days of meetings with Minister of Foreign Trade Pai Hsiang-kuo and Vice-Minister of Minerals and Chemicals Tang Ke, there was some free time so I went sightseeing and shopping.

The Canadian Embassy tracked me down in the market to say that our request to see Premier Chou En-lai had been granted and I must return to the hotel immediately to dress appropriately. Although there was a translator, initially I spoke to Chou En-lai in French. He replied in French, but admitted he spoke it rarely, so switched to Chinese. The interpreter, Nancy Tang, was the best I'd ever heard. As the daughter of a former ambassador to the United Nations in the government of Chiang Kai-shek, she had been educated in the US, so spoke English with an American accent. Her translation included gestures and expressions that mimicked Chou En-lai. Only later did I learn that while growing up he had been schooled in English. His English was probably good enough to hold a conversation, but in those days the leadership in China wanted to keep themselves at a discreet distance.

The premier asked about Canadian views on the continental shelf and our preparations for the 1974 Law of the Sea Conference. I said that Canada's experience on our Atlantic coast was similar to China's in the Yellow and South China seas. He disagreed, saying that Canada had no neighbouring states with conflicting claims. I corrected him, pointing out that the United States, France (through Saint-Pierre and Miquelon), and Denmark (through Greenland) all had divergent views from Canada.

For the most part, he controlled the conversation and at times would make an amusing remark so deftly that it was difficult to respond before he had steered the discussions elsewhere. Inadvertently, I found a ploy to keep the talks on track, at least during the Law of the Sea topic. As he spoke, I sketched on the pad between us a rough illustration of our continental shelf including the slope and rise. Curiosity got the better of him. He stopped talking and looked at my drawing, giving me an opportunity both to respond to his earlier remarks and describe Canada's maritime strategy in more detail.

My chief impression of the premier was that he had a quick mind, a good sense of humour, and the vigour of someone much younger than his seventy-four years. As our time came to a close, I asked about China's priorities for the next twenty-five years. He forecast continuity with their current concerns: agriculture, light industry, and heavy industry. He expressed the hope that the nation's annual population growth of 20 million could be reduced by half but, even then, admitted that great efforts would be necessary to produce the amount of food required. I suggested that perhaps China should focus more on making farm machinery than passenger vehicles, but he said they would produce both.

The following day, May 1, is one of China's important holidays. We were in the market and could see Chou En-lai walking nearby. When people spotted the charismatic leader in their midst, they rushed closer to him with such a frenzy that guards and army personnel could barely restrain them from trampling flower beds and each other.

Without any prior notice, we were introduced to Jiang Qing, wife of Mao, who was also in the market. Compared to Chou En-lai, the diplomat of the regime, she was more aggressive and wore a bright red jumpsuit for the occasion, a colour we were told would likely be adopted by others now that she had appeared in it. The normal garb, for women as well as men, was grey or blue jumpsuits. Looking back, I don't think anyone, not even an optimistic Chou En-lai, could have predicted the successful modernization of China. In 2012, China topped the United States as the world's largest trading nation.

The Shah of Iran was short, physically fit, and trim of figure. At fifty-five, he was quiet, intelligent, and greying at the temples, so looked older than in the propaganda photos that watched over us everywhere in the capital, Tehran. He spoke fluent English and French, likely learned during his education at Le Rosey, the Swiss boarding school known as the "School of Kings" because so many monarchs attended. When I called on Shah Mohammad Reza Pahlavi of Persia in 1974, the Niavaran Palace was heavily guarded. Inside the gates were manicured gardens, nineteenth-century French furniture, and museum-quality paintings. Oddly, I saw nothing from the Persian Empire or its Arabic successor. I found the Shah to be solemn, pretentious, and totally lacking in the humility that one might expect from the wise ruler of a country who had made some progress but still had much to do.

My time with the Shah reminded me of British prime minister Benjamin Disraeli's comment to the poet Matthew Arnold: "Everyone likes flattery, and when you come to royalty you should lay it on with a trowel." The Shah did some trowel work, too, boasting that within a generation his country would rank with France and Great Britain among the top half dozen nations in economic, military, and political terms.

The oil shock of 1973–74 had elevated Iran's place in the world. Tehran had become a boom town. Increased trade and joint ventures were on every caller's agenda. Canada's previous relations with Iran had mostly been ceremonial. Now, as fellow oil exporters, we had matters of mutual interest to discuss. We also wanted to help them spend their oil money by selling them a CANDU nuclear reactor. The Shah told us that he found our objection to rising oil prices difficult to understand. His argument, and it was a good one, was that oil prices should not be restrained any more than any other commodity.

During the next two days, we met with a number of senior ministers. The most likeable and the one with the greatest depth was Amir-Abbas Hoveyda, prime minister since 1965. In talking of his dealings with the Arabs, for example, he pointed at his forehead, his mouth, and then his heart, and said that Arabs have trouble getting all three together. According to him, you hold a meeting with them in which they seem to agree with you, but then they leave and say something entirely different.

I commiserated that prime ministers must find it lonely at the top. "On the contrary," he said, smiling. "The concept of loneliness is a myth fostered by prime ministers. What a successful prime minister does is to shift the ultimate decision and responsibility to one of his ministers who can then take the responsibility if things don't work out." While I admired his frank assessment, I wasn't sure how well that political strategy would work in Canada.

There was a power struggle underway between Iran and Saudi Arabia as to which country would lead the Organization of the Petroleum Exporting Countries, a clash that the Saudis would eventually win because they were the biggest operators. For Canada, I saw a possible role bringing together consuming and producing states. As Sheik Yamani had told me, "You have one foot in each camp."

The revolution in 1979 forced Iran's last monarch to flee. The Shah died in 1980 in exile in Egypt. His government, haughty though I found its style, was vastly preferable to the sectarian regimes that have followed.

My encounter in August 1975 with US president Gerald Ford was one of those grand occasions when we actually made progress with our southern neighbour. As minister of energy, I attended the dedication of the Libby Dam on the Kootenay River, a tributary of the Columbia River, near Libby, Montana. The $450-million US-built dam was forty-two storeys high and more than 3,000 feet wide.

About half of the ninety-mile long Lake Koocanusa created behind the dam was in British Columbia. The electricity it produced was distributed to eight states.

My involvement with the project began in 1963 as a member of a special parliamentary committee studying the Columbia River agreement between Canada and the US. Pierre could not attend, so I represented Canada on this occasion. Others in the platform party included President Ford; Senator Mike Mansfield and Governor Thomas Lee Judge, both of Montana; Senator Wayne Morse of Oregon; Minister of Mines and Petroleum Resources Gary Lauk of British Columbia; and Jake Warren, who was by then Canadian ambassador to the US.

To my mind, this was the perfect occasion to make a forthright statement about Canada's position on energy exports. Ambassador Warren disagreed, saying that the speech should not be substantive. I wasn't about to serve up platitudes, so I pressed ahead with my plan to say that Canada would be pursuing an energy policy of enlightened self-interest. We would look after ourselves first and then share our resources with the US only after careful study on a case-by-case basis.

To ensure bureaucrats didn't massage my message into meaninglessness, I sent advance copies of my speech to the US media. "Canadian objectives rule out a comprehensive resource trade package," I said. "They rule out the so-called continental energy deal."[2] Such a significant assertion and early communication paid off. When President Ford learned of my views, he tossed away his prepared text and accepted my position, declaring that the US would also focus on self-reliance first and discuss any shared arrangements later.

"Energy Minister Donald Macdonald not only outshone his peers in representing Canada but he also won wide applause from Americans for his personal performance. Ford immediately understood him and they got on like a pair of locker room chums," wrote Frank Rutter in the *Vancouver Sun*. "Mr Macdonald got a message across to Mr Ford in a style that dam-ducker Pierre Trudeau could never emulate. When Mr Ford responded in terms as blunt as Mr Macdonald it was the frankest bilateral exchange since the days of [treasury secretary in the Nixon administration] John Connally – only this one was in public."

During our private conversation after the ceremony, President Ford seemed genuine and uncomplicated. As a result of being raised in

Grand Rapids, Michigan, the president knew Canada far better than most Americans. He asked about Canada's plans for a northern pipeline in the Mackenzie River valley, and I told him we were still in the early stages of discussion and consultation. I knew that the US was hoping the approval process would move along quickly. I pointed out that any haste was politically impossible and any appearance of pressure by the US would cause the Canadian government grave difficulties.[3]

In 1976, President Ford invited Canada to join the second annual gathering of the world's wealthiest industrialized countries, what had been the G6 – France, West Germany, Italy, Japan, the United Kingdom, and the United States. Initially, the French did not want to include Canada, but President Ford and West Germany's Chancellor Helmut Schmidt – who both liked Pierre – insisted.

Pierre, Secretary of State for External Affairs Allan MacEachen, and I attended that first G7 meeting in Puerto Rico. Membership elevated Pierre and Canada on the world stage. When the British pound needed support, Canada contributed the same amount of money as France, proof that we could play a significant international role. I'd like to think my rapport with President Ford at the Libby Dam that day two years earlier helped pave the way for Canada's inclusion in the G7 as well as our ongoing role in its powerful successor groups, the G8, and the G20.

15

Heir Rampant

My family was relieved when I left politics and was ready to see more of me at home. Our four girls then ranged in age from fifteen to five. Today, my grown daughters have children of their own. The eldest, Leigh, now living in Peterborough, Ontario, is an artist and has a teenaged son, Angus, named for my father and grandfather. Nikki is executive director of government relations at the University of Victoria, is working on a Ph.D. in public administration, and with her husband, Ned Jackson, has two children, Sarah and Meghan. Althea sang as a mezzosoprano with the British Youth Opera at Sadler's Wells, lives in Montreal, and has three children, Lucas, Cecil, and Sydney. Their father, Christopher Carty, has a business in Kingston, Ontario. Sonja lives in Hamilton, Ontario, with husband Paul Shaker and son Salim (Sam) Macdonald, is a Ph.D. candidate in communications, and runs an urban research firm with her husband.

After I left politics and returned to practice law at McCarthys in Toronto, we bought a house at 29 Dunvegan Road in Forest Hill as well as a forty-seven-acre farm in Uxbridge Township on the moraine northeast of the city, which we used on weekends. Previously owned by Dr Taylor Statten II, long-time director of Camp Ahmek and Camp Wapomeo in Algonquin Park, the house was designed by architect Napier Simpson and sat on the highest point of land between Lake Ontario and Lake Simcoe so there was a magnificent 360-degree vista. It was a restorative place to withdraw.

Borrowing a phrase from the children's song, "Old MacDonald Had a Farm," Sonja – who was then six – named the farm E I E I O and made a sign for the gate. Over the years, I planted thousands of trees on the property, including white pine, tamarack, black locust, and other species. My forester father might well have had something to do with that pastime. Although I read, and played tennis and squash, the only recreation I put in my *Who's Who* listing was silviculture.

Several ministers stepped down around the same time I did for a variety of reasons. Bud Drury was shuffled from Cabinet after he'd spoken to the judge hearing a contempt of court case involving fellow minister André Ouellet; Bryce Mackasey and Jean Marchand both left to run for the Quebec Legislature[1]; and James Richardson resigned in protest of official bilingualism, later leaving the caucus to sit as an independent. By the time I resigned as an MP at the end of February 1978, the government was stale and out of ideas.

On October 16, 1978, fifteen by-elections were held in six provinces. Liberals were defeated in thirteen of them, including my old seat of Rosedale. We had recruited an excellent candidate, Dr John Evans, a Rhodes Scholar and president of the University of Toronto, but former Toronto mayor David Crombie, who ran for the Progressive Conservative Party, won.

When Pierre called an election for May 22, 1979, Joe Clark and the PCs won a minority government. I'd never paid that much attention to Clark, who first came to Parliament in 1972. On the government side, we called him "Deep Throat" because he regularly shouted partisan comments during Question Period or while one of us was delivering a speech. Clark's good luck was his bad luck. He was called to responsibility as prime minister without sufficient experience, but my admiration for him has since grown. His service as secretary of state for external affairs in the Mulroney government was exemplary; he shows intelligence and integrity in his thinking; and his contribution to Canadian society has continued apace since he left public office.

In early November 1978, while visiting in Ottawa, I played squash with Jean Chrétien. He was still smarting from Pierre's televised address that summer announcing major economic reforms and spending cuts without consulting Jean, his minister of finance. I had the opposite problem. Pierre once wrote me an eleven-page letter detailing his views on economic strategy. Pierre apologized to Jean but that did not alleviate Jean's humiliation.

I told Jean that Pierre was so disliked in the country that it was time he resigned. But who would succeed him? I said that John Turner would not run if there was the slightest possibility that he might become leader of the opposition rather than prime minister. Jean felt he personally would have to run so there was at least one French-Canadian candidate. He did not think he could win, adding, "Losing is no fun." Then he asked, "How about you?" "No way," I said. "I'm not going to run."

In July 1979, after Joe Clark had become prime minister, I saw Pierre at a party in Toronto where he was accompanied by classical guitarist Liona Boyd. At one point during the evening, he and I talked privately about his future. He said he knew he could not remain leader much longer, but expressed concern about the manner of his leaving, saying that the tone and timing had to be just right.

Pierre was also worried about constitutional issues. He did not want his successor to give Quebec special status, and he feared that John Turner might make just such a concession. "If you were a candidate, I'd be prepared to announce my retirement in three weeks or three months," Pierre said. He then referred to my description about lacking "royal jelly" and admitted that he had similar self-doubts when he succeeded Lester Pearson. "I don't agree you lack royal jelly," he said, "but you must decide yourself if you want to be leader."

"I don't want to go back into politics," I said, "but I am worried about the Liberal Party. I don't see a leadership candidate with whom I could be happy."

As a final note, Pierre referred to a recent press conference when he'd said, "I am the best." He complained that he couldn't even make a jocular remark about himself without the press misconstruing it. In retrospect, he wondered if he would have enjoyed more support from the media if he'd catered to journalists rather than confront them. "The basis for their hostility," I said, "is that they envy you."[2]

We'd had many such frank exchanges ever since we first got to know each other at the United Nations in 1966. But what was I supposed to do with this new information about his support? Pierre's backing was a gift of great value. Would I run for leader or remain happily where I was? I thought of little else in the days ahead.

Jim Coutts phoned me early Saturday morning, November 17, to see if Pierre could come to my house that afternoon. After he'd settled into a chair in the living room, Pierre confided that he would be stepping down soon. I should decide about running for leader, he said, and make all necessary preparations. "If you need more time, I can wait until December, but I need a decision soon. I might announce early next week if you're ready to go."

As he gazed around, he added, "Seeing your surroundings is enough to make me feel that my visit is fruitless." I was thinking along similar lines. "My distaste for the pettiness of politics, the House, and the endless speech-making are additional reasons to stay put." Pierre countered by saying the unpleasant parts can be made tolerable. "The value is the opportunity to carry out your objectives." I told him I would consider everything he said and call him.

Before I could do so, Jim Coutts phoned again four days later to say that Pierre was announcing his resignation that very morning. After I hung up, I headed for a scheduled meeting with Ontario Liberal leader Stuart Smith in my fundraising capacity as chairman of the Ontario Leader's Foundation. When I told Smith about my dilemma, his training in psychiatry prompted advice in the form of a comment from Sigmund Freud, the father of psychiatry. "On little decisions it's appropriate to set down in a balance sheet the arguments for and against. But in really big decisions, trust to your feelings as to what you consider to be the right thing to do – unless there is an absolutely irrefutable reason for not doing it."

The Legislative Press Gallery, hearing that I was at Smith's office, gathered to ask me how I felt about Pierre's resignation. My voice quavered and broke. I could barely talk about my friend. It was, truly, the end of an era. By sheer coincidence, I was scheduled to have lunch the next day with John Turner at the York Club. We did not discuss the leadership. And yet there we were, two potential candidates with similar backgrounds as lawyers and ministers of finance, a Cabinet post often described as the graveyard of politicians. Now we were both practicing law in downtown Toronto. He was with McMillan, Binch in the golden glow of the Royal Bank Plaza. I was across the street at McCarthys in the black spires of the Toronto-Dominion Centre. In medieval times, we could have been two knights-errant in our respective towers girding for battle.

With the leadership convention set for March 1980 in Winnipeg, I tried to clear my head and listen to my heart. Literally hundreds of people contacted me by phone, telex, and mail. Their plea was always the same: you should run for leader; the country needs you. They told me there wasn't a better candidate. They reminded me that the party had a tradition of alternating between French and English leaders. It was English Canada's turn. They pointed out that there had never been a prime minister from Toronto. I could be the first.[3]

Among my many fans was David Mitchell, CEO of Alberta Energy. While in Toronto on business, he took a cab from his hotel to my house and put a handwritten note of encouragement through the mailbox. Senior party figures such as Keith Davey and Jim Coutts offered their support. Cabinet ministers urging me to run included Marc Lalonde, Ron Basford, Barney Danson, Monique Bégin, Roméo LeBlanc, Jean-Jacques Blais, Otto Lang, and Alastair Gillespie.

Joe Potts, later an Ontario Supreme Court judge, read me a passage from Lester Pearson's memoirs. "Despite my doubts about my qualifications, however, it seemed to me that a member of a party who had benefitted from the years in power – unless he had an unassailable reason – had no right to reject the invitation of his friends to allow his name to go before the convention. Whatever his personal feelings, his public obligation was overriding. Having enjoyed ministerial responsibility in those great years, it seemed churlish now to run away from the difficulties of the new challenge facing us."[4]

Even the media was positive. "To many Liberals the ideal candidate would be Donald Macdonald. Those close to the political process – including MPs of all parties – regard Macdonald as one of the finest politicians of the decade. His stint as Energy minister (1973–75) included a lot of innovative policymaking under extremely tense circumstances. He still draws praise and admiration from top officials in Ottawa," said the *Financial Post*.[5]

I decided to test the waters, so on December 9, I gathered a group of people at the house to talk about my possible candidacy. Among the ten MPs who supported me were four who were able to attend: Aideen Nicholson, Charles Caccia, Roy MacLaren, and Peter Stollery.⁶ Also there were Joe Potts, who would help with the organization; David Wishart, as fundraiser; Michael Kirby, president of the Institute for Research on Public Policy, on polling and the public mood; U of T law professor Rob Prichard, overseeing policy; and Kathryn Robinson, a lawyer at the Toronto firm of Goodman & Goodman, who had agreed to be campaign chair. I told the group that I wanted an issues-oriented campaign. The party needed intellectual renewal; we would release a policy paper on a different topic every week.

Everyone said they were prepared to help. Peter Stollery offered to step aside in Spadina so I could run in his riding. I was flattered by the positive reaction, but I must admit that I had very little enthusiasm for the task. I thought the best outcome would be for me to run but lose at the convention. That way I would have done my duty but wouldn't have to take on the job.

We lined up a headquarters location, and I even got so far along in my thinking that I drafted an announcement.

In 1977 when I resigned from Cabinet, I indicated that it would not be my intention to seek public office again. During the course of the past several months, and in particular since the Rt Hon. P.E. Trudeau announced his decision to stand down as leader of the Liberal Party, I have been urged by friends to reverse that decision and, recently, to let my name stand as a candidate for the Liberal Party leadership.

After careful consideration of that advice and discussion within my family, I have decided to seek the leadership. I feel that with my experience in public office, particularly in the portfolios of energy and finance, I can make a positive contribution to the government of our country in this critical campaign and, during the general election, offer the opportunity to discuss with Canadians the tasks before us in the '80s and our need for strong, decisive government.

My candidacy received an unexpected boost on December 10 when, to everyone's surprise, John Turner announced he would not be running.[7] I'm not privy to his thinking, but one likely reason was animosity among party members. After a political lifetime of wanting to be leader, he left office and proceeded, along with law partner Bill Macdonald, to write and circulate newsletters about the economy that were little more than virulent anti-government diatribes. Not surprisingly, many Liberals were angered by his constant sniping from the sidelines. When John took soundings about his chances, the response likely ranged from hostility to indifference. With John gone, suddenly, I was the heir rampant.

The next day, John Crosbie, minister of finance in the Clark government, delivered a budget that included an eighteen-cent tax on every gallon of gas. Prime Minister Clark was operating as if he had a majority and did not seem worried about losing a non-confidence vote.

Opposition to the tax was immediate and widespread. The Liberals saw their chance to bring down the government. On December 13, I was in Montreal on business. I spent several hours calling Liberal MPs, urging them not to vote against the budget later that same day. We didn't even have a leader, I reminded them. Why precipitate an election? But they could taste blood. A Gallup Poll put the Liberals at forty-seven per cent, the Conservatives at twenty-eight, and the NDP at twenty-three. That night, the government was defeated 139–133, and Joe Clark called an election for February 18, 1980.

The group backing me immediately tapped lawyer Ian Scott, who wrote a legal opinion saying that the national executive of the Liberal Party could designate me as leader. The momentum, however, was shifting elsewhere. Keith Davey and Jim Coutts, who had been pressing me to run, now urged Pierre to reconsider his resignation. Allan MacEachen gave a rousing speech to caucus urging MPs to bring back Pierre. During a meeting of supporters at my house on Sunday, December 16, I excused myself to call Pierre, who was still equivocating but reiterated his view that I was his choice to replace him. I told him that if he decided to return as leader that was fine with me. But, I added, if he decided to stay out, then I would be a candidate for leader. He had a question: "If I decide to come back, would you run for

Parliament?" I said I would not. He said he'd call when he'd made up his mind.

On Tuesday morning, expecting to hear from Pierre, I waited at home while journalists camped on my doorstep. Pierre finally phoned, apologized for causing me so much uncertainty, and said that he had decided to lead the party in the next election. He offered two reasons. First, he wanted to halt what he called "the Turner revival." Second, he did not want a potentially divisive leadership campaign in the midst of an election. "I'm sorry," he said. "I know what you've been through, but this is what I've decided to do." All I said was, "Don't worry about it," and wished him good luck.

An enormous sense of relief washed over me. I felt like Sisyphus pushing the stone up the hill when, suddenly, someone took away the stone. I called Ruth and then Kathy Robinson with the news. Ruth, who hadn't been eager about my candidacy but was willing to support me if that's what I wanted, was glad the race was over before it really began. I listened on the car radio to Pierre's news conference announcement as I drove downtown to meet Ruth, Kathy, Steven Goudge, and Rob Prichard for lunch at Trader Vic's to celebrate the world's shortest non-leadership race. I spent the rest of the afternoon happily doing my Christmas shopping, free from any encumbrances – including, and especially, trying to fulfill the expectations of friends and supporters.

I worked as hard in the 1980 election as if I were running myself. I campaigned in nine different Metro Toronto ridings and visited Rosedale four times. I appeared in support of Liberal candidates in another twenty Ontario constituencies as well as a dozen more in Quebec, New Brunswick, Nova Scotia, Saskatchewan, and British Columbia.[8] In February, we won a majority government with 147 seats to 103 for the PCs. On election night, Pierre appeared before a cheering throng in the very ballroom at Ottawa's Château Laurier hotel where he'd conceded defeat to Joe Clark only nine months earlier. This time, he said, "Well, welcome to the 1980s!"

Being a national leader is a singular calling, particularly when you know, as I do, what people have to go through to attain the role and how hard they work to keep it. I always felt hampered by my inadequate French. Mr Pearson's French was less than faultless, but in those years the standards required of an anglophone leader were not as demanding.

But the biggest drawback was my own perception of myself, what I called my lack of royal jelly. I define royal jelly not as any particular talent, but the relentless drive of personal aspiration. Pierre and others possessed that need to lead. They would think less of themselves if they had not become prime minister. I never felt that deep yearning. I am content within myself, proud of my accomplishments, and harbour no regrets. Not everyone who has been in politics can say the same.

16

Private Life, Public Duty

From the moment I resigned from Cabinet in September 1977, the phone didn't ring as often, there were no more briefing books, and much of the stress in my life vanished. I felt a bit like a deep-sea diver suffering from the bends after coming up from the ocean floor. I soon realized, however, that a wider world awaited. Even before I resigned as minister of finance, my name was being bandied about for secretary general of NATO. US secretary of state Cyrus Vance supported the idea.

I sought advice from John Aird, a Liberal Senator and later lieutenant governor of Ontario. His pertinent question was, "After three years in Brussels, then what?" I said I could return to the law and join some corporate boards. He said my personal and professional standing was at its peak and I should capitalize on that status now.

His views were quickly confirmed. Because financial services came under my purview, I couldn't join the board of any bank or life insurance company for two years after resigning as minister of finance. Still, I heard from several firms interested in my services once the quiet period had expired. In the first month after my resignation, Ken MacGregor, chairman of the Mutual Life Assurance Company of Canada, approached me about going on their board. So did President Syd Jackson at Manufacturers Life Insurance Company. Ced Ritchie, chairman and CEO of the Bank of Nova Scotia, also told me he wanted to talk about opportunities.

In March 1978, I saw Paul Desmarais, chairman and CEO of Power Corp., when I was in New York to hear Pierre speak at the Economic

Club. Desmarais wanted my involvement with any one of his many holdings. He suggested Consolidated-Bathurst Inc., but by then I was already on the board of a competitor, Boise Cascade Corp., so that was a non-starter. Investors Group? Power? The guidelines made both impossible for now. Finally, Desmarais said, "If you can find me a way of getting control of Argus, I'll make you chairman."

Power's 1975 attempt to acquire Argus Corp. Ltd had led to establishment of the Royal Commission on Corporate Concentration, which reported in 1978. I spent some time looking into the matter, but in the end took no action. It was clear I could be as busy as I wanted. I was delighted not only at the range of possibilities but also at the prospect of making some real money. Public service has many rewards, but top remuneration is not among them.

When I returned to McCarthys as a senior partner, the firm had grown to almost one hundred lawyers plus support staff. In addition to my legal work on corporate and commercial matters, I also became a director of Shell Canada Ltd, Siemens Electric Ltd., and McDonnell Douglas Corp. Once the required two-year waiting period had passed, I joined the boards of Manulife and Scotiabank. In those days, board work paid an annual fee in the $5,000 range plus $300–$500 for each meeting. Today's directors can earn twenty times as much.

They probably get to ask more questions, too. At my first Scotiabank board meeting, I interrupted Chairman and CEO Ced Ritchie at some point by saying, "May I ask a question?" All heads around the boardroom table swivelled to look at me in astonishment that I could be so bold. They put up with me until I went to London as High Commissioner and resigned all my directorships. After my tour of duty was over and I returned to Toronto, I was not invited to rejoin the board.

Like politics, corporate boards are all about relationships. For example, when I joined the board of McDonnell Douglas, where I served as a director for ten years, their twin-engine CF-18 was on the short list to replace Canada's aging fighter jets. Barney Danson, minister of national defence, called me to say that he wanted McDonnell Douglas to remain in the running. He'd heard rumours that the firm expected not to be chosen so was losing interest in continuing the costly process of competitive bidding.

Barney said he wanted to meet James McDonnell in person so he could make sure the company's founder fully understood Canada's enthusiasm for his company's bid. McDonnell, who was at the firm's headquarters in St Louis, Missouri, was almost eighty. The closest most people got in terms of familiarity was to call him Mr Mac, but when he'd invited me on the board, he insisted that I call him Jim. He always called me Big Mac. I relayed Barney's request and impressed on him the merits of going to Ottawa. He was in Barney's office the following day at 10 a.m.

As a result, McDonnell Douglas stayed in the competition and, in 1980, was awarded a $3-billion contract for 123 jets that created hundreds of manufacturing jobs in Canada. The CF-18 successfully participated in NORAD patrols, the 1991 Gulf War, the 1999 Kosovo War, and the Libya no-fly zone in 2011.[1]

My activities also included attending meetings of the Bilderberg Group, named after the hotel in the Netherlands where the first gathering was held in 1954. Bilderberg is a unique institution that once a year offers a forum for intelligent talk among 150 business leaders, academics, and members of government, labour, and the media from Canada, the United States, the United Kingdom, and a score of European nations.[2] During the 1980s and 1990s, the meetings were held in Austria, England, Norway, Scotland, Greece, the United States, and twice in Canada – at Le Château Montebello in Quebec in 1983 (where I was host) and in King City, north of Toronto, in 1996.

Participants during those years included Henry Kissinger, George Soros, Nigel Lawson, William F. Buckley Jr, Marie-Josée Drouin, the Queen of Spain, Lord Carrington, Olof Palme, David Rockefeller, the Prince of Wales, Peter Jennings, Paddy Ashdown, Helmut Schmidt, and Bill Bundy, editor of *Foreign Affairs*.

From Canada came business leaders Alf Powis, Anthony Griffin, Bill Mulholland, and Paul Desmarais; politicians Pierre Trudeau, John Roberts, Allan MacEachen, and Gilles Lamontagne; as well as author Margaret MacMillan, and Lise Bissonnette, editor of *Le Devoir*. Among the many off-the-record topics were politics (fall of the Berlin Wall, the European Union, the growth of China,) business (productivity, trade, technology), and public policy (arms control, employment, deficits).

Attendees were in a half-circle of tables facing a raised dais where the chairman and secretary sat. Beside them was what looked like a horizontal traffic light with the usual three colours: green, orange, and red. When green was lit, the speaker had three minutes left; orange indicated one minute remaining; and red meant time was up. I remember one speaker rambling through his preliminary remarks until the red light was on. "And now, Mr Chairman," he said, "I would like to get down to the genesis of the problem." Interjected the chairman, Alec Douglas-Home, British prime minister in the 1960s, "My dear sir, you've already passed through Genesis. You're now in Exodus," and then called upon the next speaker.

I would usually extend my trips for other meetings in the region on behalf of McCarthys. In 1979, for example, while attending Bilderberg in Baden, Austria, I also met in Zurich with Dr Werner B. Schick, Basel-based manager of the Swiss Bank Corporation, a company looking at opening branches in Montreal and Toronto. Salomon Brothers arranged a lunch in my honour that was attended by senior officials from the Union Bank of Switzerland. In Frankfurt, I met with Bank für Gemeinwirtschaft, a commercial bank with trade union roots, and Commerzbank, which was about to open a representative office in Toronto.[3]

At home, I taught a course in public policy formation from 1979–82 at the University of Toronto Law School in conjunction with political science professor Marsha Chandler; Hugh Segal, who'd been principal secretary to Bill Davis; and Rob Prichard, dean of the law school. Among the many bright students we taught was Michael Bryant who went on to be attorney general of Ontario.

Using case studies on topics such as wage and price controls, the evolution of Canadian oil and gas policy, and the Tokyo round of GATT negotiations, one of the messages I tried to get across during the three-hour seminar held every week was that, in addition to enacting legislation, governments had other means to accomplish their goals. As an example, I cited a plan by Steve Roman, CEO of Denison Mines Ltd, to sell uranium in France. As minister of energy, I didn't think this specific deal was appropriate, but there was no legal way we could intervene. Finally, I came up with the idea of simply issuing a press release that said, in effect, this sale was not in Canada's best interest. The statement had no teeth but the mere declaration was sufficient to stop the planned arrangement.[4]

Private life turned out to be just as unpredictable as elected office. In the fall of 1982, Michael Kirby, by then deputy clerk of the Privy Council, came to see me at my Toronto home. "The prime minister wants you to chair a Royal Commission that would go coast-to-coast, talk to people, and recommend a new set of economic policies," said Kirby. Pierre wanted a broader study of economic issues than could be effectively dealt with inside the formal structure of the public service. If the recommendations were not acceptable to the government, a smiling Kirby told me, "The chairman should be shot!"

I was excited by the idea and met Pierre to talk further about the role. "I'd like you to do this, and I'm glad you are prepared to do it, but I don't want you to regard this as a reason why you wouldn't be a candidate for the Liberal leadership when the time comes," he said. I told him I was not interested in the leadership, saying, "I was there once, as you know, but for personal reasons I don't ever want to run again, so there's no problem." Pierre wouldn't let the matter drop. "All the same," he said, "I don't want to hear from you, 'I'd like to run, but I'm chairman of the Royal Commission and I can't.'" I repeated my assurance about my lack of political ambition and accepted the role as chairman of what would officially be called The Royal Commission on the Economic Union and Development Prospects for Canada.

Looking back, I think Pierre would have been wise to resign at the same time as the Commission was established. Patriating Canada's constitution earlier that year was his greatest achievement. By the time he took his famous "walk in the snow" on February 29, 1984, and decided to step down for good, the Liberal Party had been in power too long.

At that point in 1984, I had no interest in running, just as I had predicted. The Royal Commission was by then halfway completed. We were about to issue our interim report. As chairman, I had set aside partisan politics. It wasn't that I thought of myself as some sort of elder statesman; I just didn't believe the twain should meet. I was confident I could make a difference by staying where I was. Why jump somewhere else?

Pierre wrote a few weeks after he resigned to say that he valued our years together and my dedication to the Royal Commission. "Your period of time in the government was indeed a very exciting and I hope rewarding one for you," he said in a letter dated 9 April 1984. "I will always appreciate having had in Cabinet an individual who was so deeply committed to the ideals for which we were fighting and who never backed away from a challenge no matter how imposing."

When John Turner succeeded Pierre, I initially thought he would make a strong prime minister, but it quickly became clear that he had passed his "best before date." John did poorly in the debates, and the 1984 election was a debacle. The Progressive Conservative Party won a majority with 211 seats compared to the Liberals with a paltry 40 seats.

Initially, the purpose of the Royal Commission was sidetracked by the media's misguided focus on my daily stipend of $800, even though the amount was only half what I could make on any given day doing legal work. The next question was: What is a Royal Commission on the Economic Union, anyway? Over time, I came up with an answer by using a story I heard from University of Toronto economics professor Ed Safarian. It seems there was a scientific breakthrough at the Cavendish Laboratories in Cambridge on a Monday. On Tuesday, the Americans discovered a practical application. On Wednesday, the Soviets declared they had made the same discovery thirty years earlier. On Thursday, the Japanese exported to the US the first product based on the discovery. On Friday, the Koreans exported to Japan *their* first product based on the discovery. And on the following Monday, the Government of Canada appointed a Royal Commission to determine whether the discovery was a federal or provincial responsibility.

Once in every generation, a Royal Commission like this comes along and provides an opportunity to discover Canada's place in a changing world. My mentor, Walter Gordon, conducted the previous study, with exactly the same name, in the 1950s. The initial emphasis of this new Royal Commission was about interprovincial trade barriers such as Ontario's restrictions on alcohol or Quebec's obstacles to out-of-province workers. As we drew up the terms of reference, however, it soon became clear that any attempt to redesign internal trade could only begin once we knew the global direction of the Canadian economy.

When the Commission was officially announced on November 5, 1982, the terms of reference ran to three single-spaced pages. The over-arching mandate was "to inquire into and report upon the long-term economic potential, prospects and challenges facing the Canadian federation and its respective regions, as well as the implications that such prospects and challenges have for Canada's economic and governmental institutions and for the management of Canada's economic affairs." Despite such an all-encompassing directive, we were given just three years to accomplish our task.[5]

As a first step, we appointed senior staff. Gerry Godsoe became executive director; Alan Nymark, director of policy; and the directors of research were Ivan Bernier, Alan Cairns, and David Smith, who later left to become president of Queen's University.

Michael Pitfield was personally involved in selecting the twelve commissioners. Such a large number was necessary to ensure a wide range of people who could make policy recommendations as well as represent the regions of Canada, both genders, the two major language groups, business, labour, academe, and the three principal political parties. The twelve commissioners were: Clarence Barber, professor of economics at the University of Manitoba; Albert Breton, professor of economics at the University of Toronto; Gérard Docquier, national director of the United Steelworkers of America; William Hamilton, postmaster general in the Diefenbaker government and president of the Employers' Council of British Columbia; Jack Messer, former minister of energy and resources in the Allan Blakeney NDP government in Saskatchewan; Angela Cantwell Peters, chairman and CEO of Bowring Brothers, St John's; Laurent Picard, dean of the Faculty of Management at McGill University and former president and CEO of the CBC; Michel Robert, a Montreal constitutional lawyer and former president of the Law Societies of Canada; Daryl Seaman, chairman of Bow Valley Industries Ltd, Calgary; Thomas Shoyama, my former deputy minister at Finance; Jean Casselman Wadds, a former Progressive Conservative MP and High Commissioner to the United Kingdom; and Dr Catherine Wallace, chairman of the Maritime Provinces Higher Education Commission.

For me, the Royal Commission was an exhilarating opportunity to assess Canada's strengths, weaknesses, and potential. In the first year, we held more than ninety meetings with provincial and federal government departments, business organizations, labour, churches, women's organizations, and other groups. On September 6, 1983, we embarked on the busiest and most far-flung round of public hearings ever undertaken in Canada. Commissioners visited twenty-eight cities and nine Arctic communities, a gruelling odyssey of 65,000 kilometres that took four months.

On one leg of the journey, I headed north by bus from Calgary to Edmonton. I was just beginning to relax and doze off when I heard someone call out in an alarmed voice: "Does anyone here know *anything*?" Several passengers, including a nurse, rushed to his side. He thought his companion was having a heart attack. As it turned out, he had only tossed violently in his sleep. The human drama was brief, and I'm sure was quickly forgotten by my fellow passengers. For me, however, his fear and uncertainty about how to respond was a metaphor for the mood of Canadians who had just been through the worst economic recession since the Dirty Thirties.

While the media did not cover the hearings to any great extent, Canadians were eager to appear and help us find solutions. We often had to expand the number of sitting days in a city to accommodate all the requests. In some locations, the commissioners worked shifts, sitting mornings, afternoons, evenings, and weekends. In all, we received more than 1,100 briefs containing some 40,000 pages. In addition, there were 16,000 pages of transcribed oral evidence delivered by 700 witnesses ranging from single parents to CEOs.

Four specific presentations stick in my mind. First, in Prince George, British Columbia, L. Dino, the head of the local library system, urged governments to endow all libraries with the means of using the newest version of communications, the Internet. I had no idea what Ms Dino was talking about; she was at least a decade ahead of her time. The second was in Saint-Georges de Beauce, Quebec, a region known for its entrepreneurial culture. I began by advising the audience that they could address the commissioners in either official language. The next presenter said, "That's all right, Mr Macdonald, when we sell our sawmill equipment in Australia, we sell it in the English language." They reminded us that Canadians in every corner of the country could be globally competitive.

The third memorable message came from the Mining Association of Canada. They warned that new mines under development in Canada contained lower grades of ore than competitors in South America and the developing world. Commissioners quite properly concluded that Canada's resources would not provide prosperity at the same high levels as in the past. We would have to rely less on our natural resources and more on our human resources and innovative skills.

Fourth, we learned in downtown Toronto that some of the government social policies meant to help the working poor often provided disincentives. If an individual found a job and earned a little extra money, rent payments increased and income taxes not previously collected were suddenly levied. In such circumstances, people concluded that they were better off doing nothing.

Other briefs aided in setting the agenda for Commissioners. "Economic activity is not an end in itself," Environment Canada told us, "but a means to achieving a better quality of life for present and future generations." Said the Atlantic Provinces Economic Council: "We see a need to move closer to a system which allows the market to make major economic decisions. At the same time, and of equal importance, we must be careful not to lose the gains we have made with respect to redistributing the benefits of economic growth." Finally, as the brief from Dow Chemical Canada Inc. put it, "The key to the future economic welfare of everyone in Canada is not tradition or structure. It is adaptability."

If there was a single *cri de coeur*, it was a plea for Commissioners to make clear what this country stood for. Everyone knew all the challenges that had to be confronted but worried that we were too preoccupied with past internal conflicts to be able to act boldly and in unison.

We saw five themes in what we'd heard and read. First, unemployed Canadians wanted to work rather than rely on government. Second, Canadians believed social and economic policy should bring the country together rather than tear it apart as had happened in the past. Third, they sought to be part of the decision-making process. Fourth, they desired an end to unnecessary confrontations among the regions or between the people and their politicians. Fifth, Canadians needed uncertainty replaced by leadership with a clear sense of national direction.

In addition to the hearings, we created three research divisions: politics and political institutions, legal and constitutional, and economics. More than 500 researchers from universities, think tanks, and the private sector conducted 300 surveys, studies, and symposia that resulted in seventy-two published volumes. "When we prepare for a journey, we try to predict the climate and terrain of our destination, so that we may prepare everything we will require to make our voyage as valuable and enriching as possible. This is what the Commission hopes to achieve in preparing for a Canada twenty-five years hence," I said in a speech to the University of Toronto faculty of law on March 21, 1984. "We have one advantage in that we can attempt to modify the conditions and possibly unsteady climate by recommending that new policies be implemented and attitudes be modified in order to make life tomorrow better for us, both individually and collectively as a nation."[6]

A few weeks later, I visited Sweden with fellow commissioner Albert Breton. We were amazed to see what they had done with a population half the size of Canada's. Often cited as a model for social policy, Sweden also offered an outstanding example of a successful trade policy. Unlike Canada, Sweden had never used the barrier of protective tariffs. As a result, the Swedes had been able to create a large number of global giants: Electrolux, Alfa Laval, Atlas Copco, Saab-Scania, and Volvo. None of those firms would have become so eminent if they had confined themselves to a small, protected market. Swedish industrial and export success came about because business was prepared to confront competition from other far more populous industrial states.

Breton was a key member of the Royal Commission. As an economist born in Saskatchewan, he was interested in reassuring all Canadians that national institutions could provide economic results equally and fairly right across the country as well as lead to optimum results for the welfare of all. He and I had many vigorous debates, and I was delighted when he, along with all the other commissioners, agreed with our major recommendations and signed the final report.

In his supplementary statement, Breton talked about creating a "competitive federalism" that stimulated rivalries among governments. I did not anticipate such a lively group would be automatons. In that regard, and in so many others, they fulfilled all my expectations.

Somewhere along the way, the name was abbreviated. The Royal Commission on the Economic Union and Development Prospects for Canada became known simply as the Macdonald Commission. For some individuals, such nomenclature might mean intimations of immortality. For me, it only heightened expectations. The entire country was watching and waiting. I did not want to fail.

17

Leap of Faith

When Brian Mulroney was elected prime minister in September 1984, we worried he would kill the Royal Commission that had been launched by a Liberal government. There was a collective sigh of relief when his letter to us dated November 2, 1984, left the mandate untouched. He declared a special interest in five topics: deficits, entrepreneurship, trade, employment, and youth. We were well covered on the first four, less so on the fifth, so we focused additional attention on youth during our final few months.

By then, some of our recommendations were becoming obvious: the need for a globally competitive economy, a better balance between wealth distribution and economic growth, an appreciation that resources no longer offered the clout they once did, and freer trade, particularly with the US. Trade had been a lifelong interest of mine. I first learned about the importance of trade from John Read at Sunday school. The General Agreement on Tariffs and Trade (GATT) was the subject of my Cambridge thesis. The international economy had an impact on my portfolios of Defence, Energy, and Finance.

Canada was built on trade with Britain and France. They supplied finished goods in return for our fish and furs. Our growing relationship with the US over the years led to the exploration of various policy alternatives. Sir John A. Macdonald's National Policy, a protected market, almost gave way to free trade in 1911, but the concept was rejected by the electorate. Protectionism was reinforced in the 1930s with higher tariffs against the US. In the 1940s, Prime Minister Mackenzie King again considered free trade with the US but turned back. The rise of nationalism in the 1960s put us at loggerheads with the US for a while, but the Auto Pact and various Defence Production Sharing Agreements launched us on the road toward a more integrated North American economy.

About 3 million jobs – one-quarter of Canada's workforce – depended on exports. Only West Germany exported more per capita than Canada. Almost eighty per cent of our trade was with the US, but while tariffs were falling, we continued to face non-tariff barriers, a protectionist Congress, and US tribunals that punished Canada for perceived wrongdoings. It seemed to me the only way we could improve growth and enjoy something approaching equality with our biggest trading partner was by signing a bilateral agreement that ended the unfairness in our relationship. Prosperity would flow from a level playing field.

If anyone had asked me when I began my role as chairman of the Royal Commission if I favoured free trade with the US, I would have instinctively said no. Nor was there any groundswell for free trade at the public hearings. In his book, *Continentalizing Canada*, Gregory J. Inwood claims that a major influence toward my embrace of free trade was my role as a director on several multinationals. According to Inwood, I was "simultaneously comprador and national bourgeoisie, fully implicated in the continental corporate structure."[1] Such a hypothesis is nonsense on stilts.

My change of heart took place over several years. As a protege of Walter Gordon, I had been an economic nationalist in the 1960s. But in a speech I delivered in 1977 while minister of finance, I said that Canada must face the challenge of doing business in a world where trade barriers were being replaced by a more open international trading system. "Whether we like it or not, international pressure is going to be against long-term protectionism for our industries. We are going to be compelled to adjust to a new environment," I told The Canadian Club of Montreal.[2]

Upon my return to law at McCarthys, I saw first-hand the deleterious impact of the Foreign Investment Review Agency (FIRA). I was a fan when our government created FIRA in 1973, but in practice, it meant that Canadian companies could buy their Canadian competitors, thereby concentrating their power, because too often foreigners were unable to make a bid and expand the number of domestic players. I was prepared to abandon FIRA entirely because it had become a form of bureaucratic protectionism that was doing Canadians no good.[3]

During my seminars at the U of T law school from 1978 to 1982, one of the assignments I gave students each year was to write a proposal for the prime minister in favour of free trade with the US. At the same time, I re-read several Canadian economists who were long-time free traders: John Young in the 1950s, Harry Johnson in the 1960s, and a more recent group that included Ron and Paul Wonnacott. I found myself agreeing with many of the ideas that I'd previously rejected.

In the summer of 1984, some of the Commission staff and researchers began discussing the possibility of Canada–US free trade, but there was no consensus either for or against. The more I listened, the more I concluded that Canadians had to renounce our protected past and move toward a more open future. We could no longer rely so heavily on our natural resources; we had to become a manufacturing economy. Only by doing so could we improve household incomes and be able to afford our treasured social programs.

But if Canadian manufacturers were to be the engine of this new economy, they would need better access to bigger markets. Without a secure entree, they would neither achieve the scale needed to create a variety of products nor innovate to the extent required for success. In my view, we could no longer act like second-class citizens of the world. We were a well-educated society that was capable of rising to the challenge of change.

Politically, the time was ripe. President Ronald Reagan had declared himself in favour of a free trade pact with Canada. As chairman, I had to assume a leadership role. I concluded that we must be daring and make certain that the Commission's report was a substantive document with a bold new idea.

I was scheduled to give a speech on Canada–US relations in November 1984 at Arden House, a conference centre in Harriman, New York, that had been the former home of Averell Harriman, commerce secretary under President Harry Truman. It was there that I chose to reveal my idea of free trade between the two countries by calling for a "leap of faith," a phrase that became even more widely quoted than my earlier reference to royal jelly. In religion, a leap of faith means accepting an idea or concept that's unprovable or for which you have no evidence. You either believe in your heart or you don't. For me, free trade was the new religion. I believed in free trade. In my gut.

The weekend sessions at Arden House were off the record. Among the attendees was *Globe and Mail* journalist William Johnson. After my speech, he asked for an on-the-record interview so he could write a story about my proposal for publication. I'd spent enough years in politics to know that sometimes the best way to gauge public support for a new idea was to float a trial balloon. That way, if the balloon got shot down, little was lost, least of all the reputation of the one who sent the idea aloft.

I agreed to Johnson's request. Such coverage would spur debate and put pressure on the other commissioners to consider what I thought could be a key recommendation in our final report due out the following year. Without secure and unhindered access to American markets, Canada would continue to run into foolish protectionist barriers such as the New York law that said all steel used in highway construction must be made in that state.

Johnson's page-one story ran on Monday, November 19, under the headline, "'Leap of Faith' Canada must act on free trade, Macdonald says." "Many Canadians are nervous about the prospect of putting in jeopardy that perhaps rather fragile structure of national sovereignty that was built in a country called Canada – a country that started off, after all, with a plain defiance of the north-south economic pressures," I was quoted as saying. "If we do get down to a point where it's going to be a leap of faith, then I think at some point some Canadians are going to have to be bold and say, yes, we will do that. It's another step in our evolution, and we've got enough confidence in ourselves to do it."[4]

The article caused, shall we say, some surprise and not a little consternation among commissioners. Some, like Clarence Barber, Gérard Docquier, and Jack Messer, were opposed to free trade. The rest were lukewarm or outright in favour. My case was helped by the fact that a growing number of Canadians were coming around to my point of view on their own. I just crystallized their thinking. "In many ways, Macdonald personified the changes in society. As a newly elected M P in the 1960s, he had prided himself on being labeled an economic nationalist. As a senior government minister in the 1970s, he had seen himself as a pragmatist in the mold of Lester Pearson, Mitchell Sharp and Bud Drury," wrote authors Michael Hart, Bill Dymond, and Colin Robertson in *Decision at Midnight: Inside the Canada-US Free-Trade Negotiations.* "As chair of the Commission in the 1980s, he accepted the new realities and saw a need to return to the discipline of market-driven economics. It would be the theme of the Commission's report."[5]

All thirteen commissioners signed the final text – including the recommendation for free trade. I was astonished that we achieved consensus among so many diverse and opinionated individuals. Six commissioners wrote supplementary statements setting forth specific views on various topics. The toughest talk against free trade came from Docquier, the labour representative, who called free trade "a dangerous idea, a blind and imprudent act."[6] He also complained that we failed to solve unemployment.

Still, no one wanted free trade at any price, not even the pro-trade Business Council on National Issues (B C N I). "We support the idea of a Comprehensive Trade Agreement only if in fact it produces concrete, beneficial results for the vast majority of working Canadians and our industries. Only the outcome of detailed and tough negotiations will tell us that," said B C N I Chairman Rowland Frazee, former chairman and C E O of the Royal Bank of Canada.[7]

But the four Western premiers announced they supported free trade. So did the Canadian Manufacturers Association, despite the fact that lower tariffs might hurt their members' sales by increasing competition from the US. Opponents included Mel Hurtig, chairman of The Council of Canadians, who said free trade would mean negative economic consequences for Canada and the end of our political independence.

While free trade dominated debate about the report, there were fifty-nine pages of other recommendations. Aware that an unemployment rate below 6.5 per cent was likely to cause inflation, we proposed a system of voluntary wage and price controls. We urged replacing the crutch of unemployment insurance with something called the Transitional Adjustment Assistance Program. This new arrangement would eliminate disincentives to work through retraining and compensation so families could move where jobs were more plentiful.

In addition, we suggested replacing a hodge-podge of social security programs for low-income Canadians with a universal income security program – a guaranteed annual income. We affirmed our traditional parliamentary government by calling for an elected Senate that would respond to Western alienation. We urged a commercial-free CBC fully funded by public money.

My overall conclusion was that Canadians did not suffer from a lack of will; they were suffocating from a failure in policy. Canadians had to learn to rely less on governments and discover within themselves the strength and solutions for a changing environment. The man on the bus seeking help for his friend found that he had overestimated the problem. Many Canadians make the same mistake. Too often, we think we cannot succeed when, if we try, we can.

The total cost and duration of the Macdonald Commission was far less than the Royal Commission on Bilingualism and Biculturalism in the 1960s, the last commission on a similar scale. That report took six years and cost more than $50 million in 1985 dollars. We had been given three years and delivered a three-volume, 2,000-page report on September 5, 1985, two months ahead of schedule. We spent $20 million, just under our original budget of $21.7 million, or about eighty cents per Canadian.[8]

The report was generally well received by the media. "The massive report, delivered to the government and issued to the public, marks the end of the commission's work. The analysis will now probably sit there, like a beached whale, and, as in the case of such rarely to be seen monsters, people will walk around it trying to comprehend its mysteries and plan for its disposal," said Dalton Robertson in the *Financial Post*. "But, and this is what should give pause to the complacent and purpose to the concerned, don't wait too long before doing something. Because the generations to come, yours and everybody else's, will hold you accountable."[9]

Bill Robson, now president and CEO of the C.D. Howe Institute, aptly captured the tone of the final report when he said that we moved

"decisively away from further dirigisme and towards economic liberalism."[10] That was a significant change for me, given that in the 1970s,
I was the minister responsible for some of government's most highly
dirigiste policies. In Energy I had brought in the National Oil Policy,
created Petro-Canada, and invested public money in Syncrude. In
Finance, I oversaw wage and price controls, the ultimate in economic
intervention. Times had changed and so had my views.

As it turned out, so had Prime Minister Mulroney changed his
views, and he was prepared to act immediately. Only two years earlier,
while he was leader of the opposition, he had declared himself against
free trade. By the time of the March 1985 Shamrock Summit in Quebec
City, he was in favour. He and President Reagan signed a declaration
to create "a more secure and predictable environment for trade."

That summer, our report was available to the government while it
was being translated so Mulroney was well aware of our views in
advance of their official release.[11] Many Royal Commissions are simply shelved. Not ours. Three weeks after our report was made public
on September 5, Prime Minister Mulroney invited President Reagan
to negotiate a free trade deal.

That was a courageous act. No Canadian prime minister had been
prepared to stake the life of his government on the negotiation of a
comprehensive trade agreement with the US since Sir Wilfrid Laurier.
In that instance, Laurier lost the 1911 election to the Conservatives led
by Sir Robert Borden, who used the slogan, "No truck or trade with
the Yankees."

In November 1985, Prime Minister Mulroney appointed Simon
Reisman, who had negotiated the Auto Pact, as chief negotiator.
Business leaders swung in behind. A group led by David Culver, chairman and CEO of Alcan Aluminum Ltd, formed the Canadian Alliance
for Trade and Job Opportunities that drew support from about three
dozen organizations. Other key players included Tom d'Aquino, CEO
of the Business Council on National Issues, and former Ontario treasurer Darcy McKeough.

My one-time nemesis Peter Lougheed and I co-chaired the campaign that was aimed at convincing not only Canadians to accept
free trade but also thought leaders in the US. In April 1987, I spoke
at the Johns Hopkins School of Advanced International Studies in
Washington, DC, as well as the annual meeting of the American

Society of International Law in Boston. During the months that followed, I gave more speeches on a single topic at more locations than during any other period of my life.[12]

Ranged against free trade were the New Democratic Party and the Canadian Auto Workers (CAW) union, not to mention Pierre himself, as I later learned. I well remember attending one public meeting with John Crispo, an outspoken professor at the University of Toronto who backed free trade. After we'd listened to a presentation from the CAW, Crispo responded by saying, "Ladies and gentlemen, you have just heard from the biggest hypocrites in Canada! These people have their own free trade agreement – it's called the Auto Pact. They enjoy the benefits of free trade with the United States and they don't want the rest of us to enjoy the same." After a few more meetings with similar exchanges, the CAW stopped attending. The most sustained attack came from my own Liberal Party. As leader of the opposition, John Turner said he would "rip up" the free trade agreement. My response was, "I hope he's strong – it'll be four inches thick."

I was disappointed by his stance. When the report came out, John called to congratulate me and said it was a great piece of work. I took him at his word. I had every reason to believe that he accepted the general conclusions, but it turned out I was naive to think he was being forthright. I was also surprised by Ontario premier David Peterson's negative view. After all, manufacturers in southwest Ontario would have better access to the massive American market next door. Even to this day, Peterson is glib about the gains we've made. "We are still hewers of wood and drawers of water," he said in 2012 on the twenty-fifth anniversary of the two countries agreeing to a deal.[13] Such thinking demeans Canadian companies and individuals who have worked hard to be competitive and prospered as a result of free trade.

In the end, however, such political backbiting did not matter. Canadians made the ultimate decision on November 21, 1988 – in the election that became a referendum on free trade – when the Mulroney government won a second majority. Despite Liberal Party TV advertisements predicting the end of the Canada–US border, we have retained our independence and sovereignty.

Parliament approved free trade the following month and the Canada–US Free Trade Agreement (FTA) came into effect on January

1, 1989. Since then, two-way annual trade has soared to $700 billion, or about $2 billion a day. That's a long way from the $150 billion a year in 1985 when the Commission reported. The proportion of total commerce involved in trade disputes between the two countries has dropped to less than one per cent. Success with the US gave us the confidence to strike other deals, including the North American Free Trade Agreement (NAFTA) and pacts with numerous individual countries such as Israel, Chile, and South Korea.

Other nations became equally active. Argentina and Brazil formed a free trade zone with their neighbours known as Mercosur. The countries of the Pacific Rim formed Asia-Pacific Economic Cooperation. GATT, with the participation of other states, created the World Trade Organization that eventually included the USSR and China.

Canadians cannot boast that their "leap of faith" was responsible for that global revolution, but they can be thankful that we were among the first to see the potential of freer trade and fewer rules. With the perspective of twenty years, an editorial in the *Globe and Mail* on September 19, 2005, called the Commission's report "a road map into the 21st century." "Most of its proposals, which once provoked near-riots, now seem like solid common sense. Its chairman, former federal finance minister Donald Macdonald, once the object of nationalist derision, is now viewed as a visionary."

The editorial noted that, in addition to free trade, the report led to other advances such as Employment Insurance reforms that made it more difficult for workers to alternate short spells of work with long and lucrative stretches of federal support. "In the end, the Macdonald Commission was a tonic at a time when governments had simply run out of inspiration."[14]

As a result of free trade, no country is better placed to make a positive contribution to a changing world than Canada. No people are better able to play a constructive role in the face of new challenges than Canadians. I first served in Ottawa under a great Canadian, Lester B. Pearson, who looked upon difficult circumstances as creative opportunities. I have always followed that optimistic view. But I also heeded economist John Maynard Keynes who once said, "When the facts change, I change my mind. What do you do, sir?" I took that to heart when it came to transforming my point of view from a nationalist to a free trader.

Canada crossed a watershed with the arrival of free trade. "The FTA, and then NAFTA, were critical ingredients in helping modernize the Canadian economy, and have ultimately played a big role in transforming Canada from a relative underachiever among industrial world economies to a relative overachiever," wrote Douglas Porter, deputy chief economist of BMO Capital Markets, in *Inside Policy*, published by The Macdonald-Laurier Institute in 2012.[15]

The economic upheaval was valuable, but even more relevant was the psychological boost. We became more confident. Rather than rely heavily on our natural resources, we became a resourceful people prepared to compete on the world's terms through more innovative sectors such as biotechnology as well as a growing number of global players like Bombardier in planes and trains, Magna in auto parts, and Toronto-Dominion Bank, which now has more branches in the US than in Canada. It wasn't easy, and there continue to be setbacks that must be overcome, but we have forever lost our fear that somehow we are not good enough. I was proud to play a role in that maturation to true nationhood.

18

Coup de foudre

While I was chairing the Royal Commission, Ruth was able to pursue her own interests, something she could not freely do as a political wife when we were in Ottawa. She joined the Toronto-based Canadian Institute for Advanced Research (CIFAR), an organization founded by Fraser Mustard, a physician who did cancer research, studied childhood development, and generally was a force to be reckoned with. CIFAR brought together researchers in such diverse fields as education, economics, health, and high tech.

Because of Ruth's fundraising efforts, the Mulroney government provided $7 million, an amount matched by the private sector. "We would not have survived if she had not joined us," Mustard told Craig Brown, author of a book about CIFAR, *A Generation of Excellence*. "She brought in money. She brought in the federal government. She was a very shrewd woman."[1]

Ruth's cancer had come back while we were still living in Ottawa, but then went into remission; however, when it returned again in 1986, Ruth decided to undergo chemo and radiation treatments. Nikki, who had just completed her undergraduate degree at McMaster, came home to live and help her mother. During the last few months of Ruth's life, Nikki drove her to and from CIFAR, where she worked until two days before her death on March 6, 1987, at St Michael's Hospital. At fifty-two, she was taken far too soon.

For the next few months, I was sad and lonely. Family and friends helped, but that period remains a blur. The mind works in mysterious ways to deal with grief and let you get on with life. Adrian Lang, who was living in Winnipeg, had been a loyal friend and a regular visitor during Ruth's illness. Of course, I knew Adrian and Otto in Ottawa, where Adrian was a vibrant presence socially and on Parliament Hill where she worked for Otto as a $1-a-year assistant.

At the time of Ruth's death, Adrian and Otto were living under the same roof, but they had been separated for some months. Otto worked at Pioneer Grain Company Ltd; Adrian operated a government relations and public affairs business. After Ruth died, when Adrian came to Toronto on business, she continued to stay with us, as she always had.

I can vividly remember the exact moment when I fell in love with this lively and lovely woman who was ten years younger than I. I had invited a few people to Dunvegan for drinks. Late arriving from the farm, I walked into the garden, and saw Adrian sitting with guests. I was wearing my country clothes with the dog bounding along at my side; Adrian was in a royal-blue sundress. Our eyes locked and we smiled at each other. It was far from our first meeting, but for both of us, that instant was what the French call *coup de foudre* (love at first sight). We decided to marry. A few people were scandalized, believing that my period of grieving was too brief. All I can say is this: if you had just gone through a time of mourning and melancholy and then found love and laughter, I would wish you and your new partner every happiness.

On July 25, 1988, I appeared before a parliamentary committee studying Canada–US free trade. After the hearing, I walked to the Langevin Block on Wellington Street for a meeting requested by Derek Burney, Prime Minister Mulroney's chief of staff. I assumed he wanted a debrief, but Burney had another topic in mind. "The prime minister would like you to accept the role of High Commissioner for Canada to the United Kingdom of Great Britain and Northern Ireland."

I managed to stammer, "I'm just about to be married."

"The prime minister knows that and suggests this would be a great way to start a new marriage," said Burney.

I agreed to consider the offer, assuming that after a polite period, I'd turn it down. My main concern was financial. At fifty-six, the remaining nine years to sixty-five were my prime earning period. Why take a job for three of those years for less than half of what I was making?

But everyone urged me to accept. The reaction of my Montreal friend, Ron Chorlton, was typical: "Go for it. If you don't, you'll spend the rest of your life regretting it." So, after a few days of thought and consultation with our children, Adrian and I agreed we would take on this once-in-a-lifetime challenge.

On September 10, we were married at Holy Rosary Church in Toronto. The 200 guests who celebrated with us in our new home at 27 Marlborough Avenue included Keith and Dorothy Davey; Manitoba Liberal leader Sharon Carstairs and her husband, John, with whom I'd gone to Ashbury; Gordon and Kilby Gibson; Heather Reisman and Gerry Schwartz; former Cabinet ministers Alastair Gillespie and Don Johnston; philanthropists Bluma and Bram Appel; and future Liberal leader Paul Martin Jr, who was a close friend of Adrian and her family.

Second marriages are difficult for offspring, but everyone now gets along and I give Adrian all the credit. Adrian had seven children to go with my four, and we share fifteen grandchildren. Adrian's eldest, Maria, a promising young lawyer with the Winnipeg firm of Monk Goodwin, was killed in a car accident in Manitoba just as we returned from London in 1991.

Timothy is vice-president advancement at St Francis Xavier University. He and his wife, Jennifer, have two children, Matthew and Jacqueline. Gregory lives in Toronto and is director, major accounts, Canada, at Silver Bullet Corp. Andrew is a media relations specialist in Toronto. Both he and Timothy have been federal candidates for the Liberal Party, and Gregory ran for Toronto city council.

Elisabeth is director general, program policy and regulatory affairs, Office of the Superintendent of Bankruptcy. Married to lawyer Paul Amirault, they have three children: Kate, Jane, and Claire. Amanda is CBC News senior business correspondent, won a Gemini for *The Lang & O'Leary Exchange*, and wrote *The Power of Why*. She was married to Vince Borg and has a son, Julian. Adrian, the youngest by two minutes and an identical twin to Amanda, is associate general counsel at Bank of Montreal. Married to Ashley Taylor, a partner at the law firm Stikeman Elliott, they have two children, Gavin and Victoria.

And so I left Canada three weeks after our wedding, with a new partner and a new and expanded family, ready to be received by Her Majesty the Queen. As part of my diplomatic life, I resigned from all my boards. I set self aside, took a cut in pay, said to hell with worrying about my golden years, and went to work for Canada. Again.

As someone of Scottish ancestry, I looked forward to living and working in the United Kingdom. Adrian had her own unique connection. She was named after Adrian IV, the only Englishman ever elected pope. Our home for the next three years was in Macdonald House (named after Sir John A., not me) on Grosvenor Square in Mayfair. The Chancery, or office, was at Number 1, the residence at Number 3. The building had been the American Embassy until they moved across the Square in 1961. With additional offices in Canada House on Trafalgar Square, the High Commission employed about one hundred people and had an annual budget of $14 million.

My predecessor, Roy McMurtry, and his wife Ria, lived for part of their posting on Upper Brook Street. The landlord, the Duke of Westminster, reduced the term of the lease and raised the rent, so Ottawa gave up the house. When we later met the Duke, Adrian said we were disappointed Canada no longer had that lovely residence. He was unaware and said he would have ensured continuity if the bureaucrats had but asked.

As a result of losing Upper Brook Street, some of the offices at 3 Grosvenor Square were turned into residential space. On the main floor were created two drawing-rooms, a dining room with a mahogany table that could seat twenty-four, a glass-roofed conservatory, a library, and a sizable chef's kitchen. On the second floor, there was a small sitting room, a master bedroom, a galley kitchen, and four guest bedrooms, one of which was occupied by Sonja, who attended The American School while we were in London.

Our bedroom was also the "safe room," with a steel door and bulletproof glass on the one sealed window. Under siege, everyone was supposed to squeeze in, lock up, and ride it out. The American ambassador, Henry Catto Jr, claimed there was a tunnel linking his embassy with ours. If attacked, he said they'd flee through the tunnel to our safe room. Fortunately, no such event occurred nor did we ever see any sign of a tunnel. We just heard the rattle and roar of the Piccadilly Line under the salon.

We sought to replace some of the art that we irreverently referred to as "CPR gothic," but the reply from the civil service in Ottawa was, "There is no art, and if there were, you wouldn't get it." Adrian spoke to Shirley Thomson, director of the National Gallery of Canada, who said, "We've got vaults of art. I'll give you some slides, pick what you want, and we'll send it over." When Adrian informed External Affairs of our plan, they suddenly had plenty from which to choose.[2]

The staff included a chef, Frank Flanagan; a household manager, Barry Stacey; a chauffeur, Brian Griffith; and three housemaids. As a newly wedded couple, we treasured our private time together. I recalled a story about 1920s movie stars Douglas Fairbanks and Mary Pickford making love in each of the formal rooms of their mansion, Pickfair. We did the same. We also demonstrated our love on more public occasions. My secretary came into my office once and found Adrian sitting in my lap. When she told the chauffeur, he said, "You should drive the car!"

The Canadian High Commission in London is a complex post compared to the Embassy in Washington, DC. While Washington is home to the world's only superpower, the city is neither a business nor cultural hub. London has politics and the Queen, and is one of the world's top financial and cultural centres.

In addition to diplomatic duties, I was responsible for British firms doing business with Canada, and the more than 150 Canadian companies operating in the UK. I was involved, for example, in helping Canadian Utilities Limited, of Edmonton, a partner in the Thames power project, and persuaded British and European governments to increase their duty-free quotas on Canadian newsprint. London is also a magnet for Canadian politicians, business leaders, writers, artists, and friends, so we did a lot of entertaining. Grand occasions, such as the opening of Parliament, Trooping the Colour, and relations with other diplomats and organizations automatically took up twenty-five per cent of my time.

In the first few weeks, I made courtesy calls on two dozen diplomats, a similar number of business leaders, and the editors of all major newspapers. I also called on the prime minister, other parliamentarians, and, of course, Her Majesty. Ambassadors must stand in Her Majesty's presence, but because Canada is a Commonwealth country, we are considered family, so Adrian and I sat for tea with the Queen.

Adrian and I were a team in London. I couldn't have functioned without her. Adrian was not only an extra pair of eyes and ears at gatherings; she represented Canada with élan. At one dinner, the Dowager Duchess of Hamilton called Adrian "a fairy princess." "Here, in what he calls 'this important world crossroads,' Macdonald, 56, has plunged into his duties as head of the largest Commonwealth diplomatic post with the pragmatism of a political pro. And the zest of a lottery winner," wrote Ellie Tesher in the *Toronto Star*. "Heads turn when the couple enter a room – he, robust and towering at 6'5"; she, a perky, attractive woman whose 5'4" brings her smack up to his shoulder where she frequently nestles her head. This is no ordinary diplomatic couple."[3]

Tradition and pageantry play a major role in British life. During one November week, there was a British Legion event at Royal Albert Hall, a Remembrance Day ceremony, the Lord Mayor's banquet at Guildhall, a Royal occasion at the British Museum, and the annual reception for diplomats at Buckingham Palace.

Only High Commissioners are invited to take part in Remembrance Day. It's understandable why the Germans, Italians, and Japanese are not welcome, but beyond my ken why an ally like the US was excluded. An officer of the Grenadier Guards led us through a rehearsal of our choreographed wreath laying. In my row, I was the first, followed by Australia and New Zealand. When the officer said "Sir" to me, I snapped to attention. "Sir, you have an advantage. You have long legs. In the interest of your colleagues you might like to take shorter steps." I looked to the end of my line and saw that my Malaysian counterpart was five feet tall.

The recent Winter Olympics in Calgary and the G7 Summit in Toronto had raised Canada's international profile. While those successes garnered worldwide praise, Canada's relationship with Britain continued to struggle under the residue of colonial status. Our sophisticated lifestyle, particularly in urban centres, seemed unknown to

British tastemakers, despite numerous Canadians with high profiles. Writers Robertson Davies, Margaret Atwood, and Alice Munro had been nominated for the prestigious Booker Prize. Playwright Michel Tremblay and screen stars Donald Sutherland and Kate Nelligan were widely popular.

To show another side of Canada, in 1988 our cultural counsellor Curtis Barlow created a three-week program with Liberty, the Regent Street fashion and fabric shop. Liberty focused their entire fall collection on a dozen Canadian designers such as Joyce Gunhouse and Judy Cornish of Comrags, Derek Price and Tess Roman of Price Roman, and Alfred Sung.

In 1990, we held *Canada in the City*, a two-week program in the Broadgate complex featuring Canadian music, dancers, and artists, including paintings by singer Joni Mitchell. I was also involved with Cirque du Soleil's first London show. The only site they could book was in Wimbledon, in southwest London. They wanted a more central location, so they turned to Reed Scowen, *délégué général du Québec*, who came to me. Together we called on the British Council, an organization involved in education and culture. They found better space near Waterloo Bridge. Six months later, Cirque du Soleil said they'd like Lady Diana to attend their next show, and we were able to help make that happen, too.[4]

As was the custom, during Evensong at Westminster Abbey on Canada Day in 1990, I read the New Testament lesson. Sitting in the chair designated by the coat of arms for the Canadian High Commissioner, I suddenly found myself overcome by the august surroundings. This was where kings and queens are crowned; greats from the past are buried here. My hands shook as I read from the first letter of St Paul to the Corinthians. Apparently I sounded fine, but it was a shock to suffer stage fright after a career of public speaking.

My duties at the Royal Edinburgh Military Tattoo made me less nervous. I wore my bowler hat for the ninety-minute tribute by military bands and the massed pipes and drums with Edinburgh Castle as a backdrop. All I had to do was stand and take the salute whenever the organizers played a spotlight on me.[5]

Some meetings were tougher to arrange than others. At one point, I was having trouble tracking down R.Y. Jennings, my adviser at

Cambridge. He was a fellow at Jesus College but spent much of his time in The Hague on the Court of Justice. Slipping into "Cambridgespeak," I said to my secretary, Marilyn Conley, "If you can't reach him at The Hague, call Jesus." She stared at me for a moment and then said, "I have some pretty good connections, but they're not *that* good."

A tourist can plan a holiday visit in order to attend one event, like the annual Chelsea Flower Show, but the advantage of a long-term stay was that we were able to see everything. Summer sporting events alone could fill a year-long calendar: Centre Court at Wimbledon, rowing at Henley, the Royal Enclosure at Ascot, and Epsom with Lord Fairhaven, the senior steward. I usually did poorly with the tote, certainly not well enough to quit my day job.

There was the Cup Final at Wembley Stadium and the England–India cricket match at Headingley in Leeds where I saw the rising young Indian superstar Sachin Tendulkar. I dropped the puck at a hockey game between Oxford and Cambridge. We saw wonderful West End theatre: Albert Finney in *Another Time*, Dustin Hoffman in *The Merchant of Venice*, and Peter O'Toole in *Jeffrey Bernard is Unwell*. There was opera at Covent Garden, recitals at Wigmore Hall, and symphonies at the Barbican, usually in attendance with politicians or executives. We once shared a box at Royal Albert Hall with Second World War songstress Vera Lynn, who became a frequenter of Grosvenor Square.

We also made an early morning visit to Billingsgate fish market to promote Canadian products. One of the fishmongers had followed his forebears but proudly told us that his son, Simon Newnes, had gone up to Oxford. We invited Simon to a dinner in June 1990 for Prince Edward. Also invited were Grant Wach, the captain of the Oxford Blues hockey team, and Sebastian Coe, an Olympic gold medalist who later sat in Parliament.

On average, I gave a speech every week. My main message at the time was that the Canada–US Free Trade Agreement was working well, but Canada remained very interested in trade with Britain and the European Union. But while we welcomed progress toward a single market, I said we worried about a Fortress Europe mentality where standards for plywood, lumber, and telecommunications could be drawn up in ways to shut us out. All you can do is hammer away, hoping that Canada's interests are taken into account.

I also reminded audiences that we sought to maintain investment flows. The UK was Canada's second-largest foreign investor with about $15 billion in holdings, and the third-largest source of portfolio investment, about $4 billion annually. Tourism was big business, too, with 500,000 UK visitors to Canada each year, the second-largest source after the US; 650,000 Canadian tourists visited the UK annually.

Ties between many Canadian and British groups were strong. Typical were Canadian lawyers and judges who regularly attended symposia with their British counterparts. One year, their usual venue was booked so I called Sir John Lyons, the master of my college at Cambridge, to see if Trinity Hall could offer space. He was happy to help, and the arrangement was renewed in subsequent years. In 1994, I was made an honorary fellow of Trinity Hall, a far cry from my days as a lowly graduate student, and a glorious title that remains one of my proudest connections with the UK.[6]

19

Maggie and the Royals

Viewed from Canada, the Royal Family may seem distant or, to some, even irrelevant. But I defy even the grouchiest anti-monarchist to live in London for a while without learning to respect the Royals. They work hard at their jobs. The Court Circular lists their daily duties in the newspapers at great length. Each of them regularly participates in numerous public events, including calls on mayors and munici-palities, ribbon-cuttings, hospital tours, award presentations, tea with luminaries, fundraising events, visits with veterans, and presiding at banquets.

At one time or another, we were in the presence of Her Majesty the Queen and the Duke of Edinburgh; Prince Charles and Lady Di; Princess Alexandra and her husband, Sir Angus Ogilvy; the Duke and Duchess of Gloucester; Prince Edward and Prince Andrew; and the Queen Mother. Of all the people, from many walks of life, that we met in the UK, the three I most admired were all women: the Queen, the Queen Mother, and Margaret Thatcher.

When we entertained The Queen and Prince Philip for dinner at the official residence at 3 Grosvenor Square, we also invited, among oth-ers, Deputy Prime Minister Sir Geoffrey Howe and his wife, Elspeth; Garry Weston, chairman of Associated British Foods; and Michael Ignatieff, then a columnist with the *Observer* and later leader of the Liberal Party of Canada. That occasion also included Paul Reichmann whose company, Olympia & York, had erected First Canadian Place in Toronto as well as the World Financial Center in New York and was in the throes of building Canary Wharf in London. The Palace let it be known that the Queen was most interested in meeting him.

The Queen also met all – and I mean *all* – members of our household. Before we went to London, we had a Hungarian Vizsla. Britain's strict rules against rabies meant all arriving dogs must be quarantined for six months. I didn't want to put Pashka through that agony, so we gave her to friends of Nikki. Adrian had promised Sonja a dog while we were living in London, so we acquired two black Labradors called Teal and Grosvenor.

Barry, our house manager and butler, wanted Mrs Mac – as he called Adrian – to put the dogs away during dinner. Adrian pointed out that the Queen hadn't hidden her corgis when we had lunch at Buckingham Palace, so our dogs attended. Teal slept throughout dinner, resting her head on the royal foot the whole time. Her Majesty didn't seem to mind in the least.

We would also see the Queen at such occasions as garden parties, the Annual Diplomatic Dinner, and Trooping the Colour. At five feet four inches, she was smaller than you might expect. Since I was tall, the Queen could easily spot me in a crowd. She would work her way toward me, put her hand on my arm, look up with those bright blue eyes, and ask about some matter of importance to Canada. For instance, during the 1990 Garden Party at Buckingham Palace, the Queen sought me out to talk about Oka after the Mohawks of Kanesatake erected a barricade to their land that led to a showdown with police and then the army. She knew every detail about that dramatic crisis.

There is a particular protocol to events such as the Annual Diplomatic Dinner, held at Buckingham Palace in November. The hundred or so diplomats and their spouses posted in London assemble well ahead of the Royals. The delay is of such duration that the invitation warns the ladies to wear comfortable shoes. You stand on one foot waiting for them to come and then stand on the other foot waiting for them to go because nobody can leave until they do.

Still, there was a certain frisson the first time we drove through the gates at Buckingham Palace, the Canadian flag fluttering on the hood of CAN 1, Adrian wearing an evening gown, I in white tie. On the second occasion, we knew the drill, and felt like old pros. When the invitation arrived during our third year on the mad carousel of diplomatic life, I must admit there was a niggling question, "Do we have to go to the palace *again*?" Of course we went, and enjoyed ourselves, except for the waiting-around part. By then, we were so well known to the palace staff that one of them threaded his way through the multitude with a cold martini on a silver tray for Adrian that everyone standing nearby eyed with envy because they just had the usual warm white wine.

But amidst all the grandeur of representing Canada, there hovered what I called "the Little England mentality." Someone at a dinner would mistake my accent for an American's. I'd correct them and then often listen to a dreary monologue about how Britain fought alone during the Second World War. I would remind them that by September 1940, the major part of two Canadian infantry divisions were stationed in England. I'd point out that Canada trained a significant number of pilots in the Royal Air Force, the Royal Canadian Air Force, and the Royal New Zealand Air Force. Britain also entrusted much of its gold bullion and marketable securities to the safety of the Sun Life vaults in Montreal.

But such one-on-one efforts would take forever to convince an entire populace. I believed that the reason Canada's war efforts were so little recognized was the lack of a war memorial in London to honour the almost 1 million Canadians who served with Great Britain during the First and Second World Wars. General Desmond Smith, a decorated soldier turned businessman who was married to Belle Shenkman, a social doyenne who promoted Canadian arts and commerce in London, decided to do something about the omission. He began the hard work of raising the necessary money and of convincing Whitehall.

One rainy morning in November 1990, Adrian and I set out to seek an appropriate site with Dès Smith and Conrad Black, who owned the *Telegraph* and had also undertaken to raise some of the necessary funds. We looked at possibilities on The Strand, near Admiralty Arch, Hyde Park Corner, and elsewhere. Nothing seemed suitable until our driver, Brian Griffith, said, "High Commissioner, what about Canada

Gate?" Brian's idea was inspired, and we quickly chose a spot behind Canada Gate, commissioned in 1911 to honour the death of Queen Victoria, and erected in the same gilded wrought iron as the gates across the road at Buckingham Palace.

The site was on Royal grounds, so it fell to me to seek the support of the Queen Mother and, through her, the Queen's advisers. I arrived at Clarence House, the Queen Mother's residence, at 10:30 a.m. on the appointed day. She came bouncing down the stairs and said, "That location will be just right. That decides it." There was a brief pause, then she added, "Well, that completes our business. Let's have a drink!" Staff immediately appeared bearing glasses of gin for a toast.

My other favourite vignettes involving the Queen Mother both occurred during a reception at our residence. This time it was our second black Lab, Grosvenor, who sought to be involved. As the Queen Mother came through the reception line, Grosvenor nuzzled his way between her and the rest of us. "My goodness, he wants attention," she said. "There's no ignoring him," I admitted. Declared one newspaper headline, "Black Prince Meets Queen Mother."

Later that same evening, I watched as the Queen Mother talked at length with Ernest "Smokey" Smith, the only Canadian private to be awarded the Victoria Cross in the Second World War, the highest honour for bravery. The two of them were the same height, about five feet, and he held her entranced, talking about the time in 1944 when he was with the Seaforth Highlanders and repulsed a counterattack by the Germans, thereby securing a bridgehead across the Savio River in northern Italy.

The Queen eventually unveiled Canada Memorial on June 3, 1994, long after we'd gone home. Designed by Quebec artist Pierre Granche, the red granite work features bronze maple leaves on an inclined surface over which water flows so the leaves look as if they are floating. In conjunction with the memorial, scholarships are awarded annually for UK citizens to study in Canada and Canadians to study in the UK. Among the park benches added later was one contributed by Adrian to honour her father, Captain Evatt Francis Merchant, who in November 1944 was killed in action in Holland while he was a Canloan officer to the British unit of the Queen's Own Cameron Highlanders.

Other matters were more controversial. While there were no out-standing bilaterals between Canada and the UK, there were two potential irritants. The first was apartheid in South Africa. While Canada and the United Kingdom were both against that nation's policy of racial segregation, Prime Minister Thatcher disagreed with Prime Minister Mulroney's belief in economic sanctions, saying sanctions would only cause more unemployment among blacks. In her view, the South African government would eventually do the right thing. She was correct. F.W. de Klerk, president of South Africa, gave a speech in London soon after he came to power in September 1989 that signalled the end of apartheid. In February 1990, at the opening of Parliament in Cape Town, de Klerk announced reforms that led to the freeing of the jailed Nelson Mandela, leader of the African National Congress.

The other potential problem was the planned purchase by Canada of up to twelve nuclear submarines. Shipyards in the UK and France had both made bids. After two years of consideration, the Mulroney government decided that Canada could not afford to spend up to $8 billion on submarines at a time of widespread cutbacks that included closing military bases.

I was dispatched to deliver the bad news to the secretary of state for defence, George Younger. I expected him to be disappointed or angry. But Younger said, with a twinkle in his eye, "I'm relieved. I was worried that you would have to explain to Mrs Thatcher that Canada had decided to buy the French submarine. That would have been no fun for you at all."

Britain is filled with history, beautiful vistas, and pomp and circumstance at every turn, but there was nothing more magnificent than Margaret Thatcher in full flight. I had seen how Pierre Trudeau could dominate any setting, and Margaret Thatcher was just as compelling. While Pierre had charisma and a certain shyness that made women want to either mother him or marry him, the Iron Lady seemed to pull everyone toward her as if by some magnetic force.

No one described Thatcher's uncompromising style better than she did. "A leader must lead, must lead firmly, have firm convictions, and see that those convictions are reflected in every piece of policy," she told the *Daily Express* after Nigel Lawson had resigned in 1989 as chancellor of the exchequer over policy differences. "How can I change Margaret Thatcher? I am what I am. Who are these people who change their policy with every passing wind, and trim every sail? They have never believed in anything in their lives."1

Thatcher had a close relationship with Mulroney. My coming to London as his appointee ensured an enthusiastic welcome. A fierce storm, the worst in three centuries, with wind speeds up to 180 kilometres per hour, swept through the south of England a year earlier, uprooting 15 million ancient oaks, plane trees, and conifers. To replace the lost trees, Pat MacAdam, press counsellor at the High Commission, organized a donation from the Canadian forestry industry of 35,000 broad-leafed trees such as maple and ash as well as 26 million evergreen seeds – one from each Canadian.

It was my good luck to arrive at the same time as the donation, a few samples of which were arranged on the Cabinet table for our visit to 10 Downing Street. I must say that the place looks better from without than within. While there are vestiges of its architectural heritage in aspects such as the eighteenth-century marble floor in the foyer, much of the place is a rabbit warren of rooms and higgledy-piggledy hallways.

As Pat later described our meeting, "The prime minister was in rare form. She had kicked off her high-heeled shoes. She was prancing around like one of Glace Bay's pit ponies brought out of the darkness and up to the surface when the miners took their annual vacation." After the brief ceremony, Thatcher decided we'd all have drinks. She looked at me and said, "You look like a Scotch and soda man." Another press officer who was with us, Terry Blocksidge, was "a Buck's Fizz man." Pat was "a real ale man" until he told her that he'd given up drinking a decade earlier. The rest of us graciously accepted her selection.2

Among Margaret Thatcher's many talents, in addition to knowing what she wanted and having the determination to secure it, was her ability to deal with political leaders. Having fought her way to the top in a profession dominated by men, she seemed to revel in her success in male company – not as their equal but as their better. Even her ever-present handbag was no mere accessory; she wore it like a weapon. Mulroney was astute enough to recognize her substantial ego, and he was skilful in maintaining a respectful role with her. She was inclined to lecture. He accepted the hectoring tone at no cost to any principles.

Toward the conclusion of our time in London, Thatcherism was also coming to an end. Senior members of the Conservative Party as well as many backbenchers had turned against her. We'd be at dinners where Cabinet ministers would speak openly and in disparaging terms about Thatcher. But no one wanted to bell the cat and tell The Iron Lady she had to go.

One night at a dinner in Holyrood Palace in Edinburgh, Adrian sat beside William Whitelaw, who had been Thatcher's closest adviser as home secretary and deputy prime minister. Willie, as he was widely known despite being a viscount, had by then resigned as leader of the Lords. His advice, so wise in the past, was now rarely offered. Willie said that Thatcher could not see the gathering storm. "Surely, Lord Whitelaw," said Adrian, "if *you* told her, she'd listen." "Not even me," he replied. "Only [her husband] Denis could get through and he won't tell her."

Such candour was something we enjoyed as Canadian representatives. I remembered with embarrassment the rather cavalier manner with which we Cabinet ministers treated the diplomatic corps in Ottawa. In Britain, ministers were friendly, freely took us into their confidence, and always trusted that those confidences would be kept. The bureaucrats at Whitehall, however, were just the opposite. There was no humiliation that the British public servant would not suffer to curry favour with the Americans and almost nothing they would do for Canada except under the most extreme pressure.

My views, which may seem harsh, were subsequently confirmed. Briefing documents prepared for Thatcher's visit to Canada in 1983 and released in 2013 by Britain's National Archives demonstrated the low esteem in which British officials held Canada. They thought Pierre possessed "unsound personal views" on the balance between Eastern and Western powers. As for Canadians as a whole, we were "inordinately insensitive," said the notes that described what they saw as weakening ties between the two countries.

Her own party members finally jettisoned Thatcher through a leadership review in 1990. Once she failed to win on the first ballot, she chose resignation over embarrassment on the next ballot, and the party picked John Major, Thatcher's chancellor of the exchequer. As Thatcher said, standing outside 10 Downing Street, "It's a funny old world."

If the rise to power of Ted Heath and Margaret Thatcher was evidence of the displacement of the upper class by the middle class, the arrival of John Major offered further proof of the breakdown of the gentry's historic leadership monopoly. Major came from humble origins; his father was a circus performer. Under Major, the Conservatives won a majority in the 1992 election, and were eventually beaten by Tony Blair and the Labour Party, but not before the Conservatives enjoyed eighteen years in office. Despite that ignominious end to her time at the top, Thatcher's place in history was assured by her strong views and the economic revival she brought about through the encouragement of free enterprise, privatization, and lower taxes.

Canadians were suffering through their own bout of disunity in the form of the Meech Lake debate, the constitutional accord cobbled together by Prime Minister Mulroney and the premiers. Pierre spoke against Meech at a Senate hearing because he feared it would lead to a sidelining of the West. Meech collapsed in June 1990 due to the opposition of Newfoundland and Manitoba.[3]

As one who was working abroad for my country, my concern about the direction of the national debate was probably greater than that of most Canadians because I felt helpless to do anything about it. Prime Minister Mulroney and the premiers tried again with the Charlottetown Accord in 1992. To me, Charlottetown made more sense than Meech. The three political parties and all the premiers supported Charlottetown, which then faced a national referendum. Again Pierre came forward to criticize the consensus, arguing that it meant the end of a unified Canada. The accord was defeated in a national referendum.

I could not help but wonder why Canadians could feel so at odds with one another. If Canada were divided into two or more separate states, the influence of each on the other members of the international community would be substantially reduced. Any fragmentation would mean something less than the whole.

During our time away, we made several trips home for such occasions as speaking to the Empire Club of Canada in Toronto, attending a symposium at Queen's University, or accepting an honorary doctorate from the University of New Brunswick. I felt particularly grateful for the latter: I received the same honorary degree that UNB had bestowed on my father forty years earlier. "Canada as we have known it is an inheritance that those of my generation received from our parents," I told the convocation, with constitutional matters in mind. "The members of this graduating class are entitled to look to my generation to pass on that inheritance unimpaired; not just the physical real estate with its remarkable natural endowments, but also the inheritance of a successful working community. You are entitled to demand of my generation that we should so manage national affairs that that inheritance will still be available to be passed on."[4]

When the time came to leave London in 1991, we were happy to have served, and happier still to be headed home. I didn't want the dogs to fly in the cargo hold of a plane, so in August we sailed from Southampton on the QE2 with our two dogs aboard on the top deck in sumptuous digs. As the great ship left her berth, Ron Berlet, minister, economic and commercial affairs at the High Commission, circled the vessel several times in a sailboat flying a Canadian flag so large it looked as if it might topple his boat. The sight created quite a stir among passengers at the railings and brought tears to our eyes.

Once we were settled again, I received a congratulatory letter from Prime Minister Mulroney. "As you have in the past, you served your fellow citizens with distinction, pride, and commitment in a delicate and demanding function," he wrote. "This, in no small way, has convinced me of the wisdom of continuing the long tradition of appointing dedicated, competent and non-partisan individuals to our High Commission in London!"

I was honoured to be a diplomat – although I can't say I ever got used to being called High Commissioner or Your Excellency – but any non-partisan cloak I briefly wore was quickly cast aside upon our arrival home. I began my political life working for the Liberal Party in the 1958 general election and a stalwart Liberal I remained.

20

Plugged In

Returning from London in 1991, I rejoined my former law firm again, and found it much transformed after three years. McCarthy & McCarthy had merged in 1990 with Clarkson Tétrault to create McCarthy Tétrault. As a result, the firm had 500 lawyers in seven Canadian cities plus Hong Kong and London. The change was not all for the better. After a while, I concluded that the firm did not really know how to use the expertise of former politicians and diplomats such as myself to everyone's best advantage.

In the US, folks can more easily move among many fields. There, such back-and-forth between government on the one hand and business, law firms, and think tanks on the other, offers benefits for individuals in particular and society in general. In Canada, we have a few business–government personnel exchanges, but for the most part, we keep people slotted in silos.

While the Macdonald Commission and my time as High Commissioner were enjoyable pursuits, in some ways such activities had a detrimental impact on my career. I never earned the kind of compensation I could have if I'd just aimed to increase my own net worth. Instead, I regularly interrupted my private sector life for public sector roles. I have no regrets about that, that's just what I did. More people should do the same and serve their country.

I believed that such appointments were good for McCarthys, too. Such roles raised the profile of the firm and brought in business as a result. But because I was regularly diverted from the full-time practice of law, some of the younger members at McCarthys – particularly the

litigators – were unhappy with what they saw as my insufficient financial contribution and did not prize the experience I brought. In 2002,
I left McCarthys, and through the good offices of Senior Adviser
David Atkins at Lang Michener, joined that firm, now called McMillan
after a merger.

After London, I rejoined three boards: Alberta Energy, Siemens, and
Boise Cascade. I also became a director at Sun Life Assurance Co. and
TransCanada PipeLines Ltd. On some boards, retirement at seventy
was mandatory. Others let you continue longer. As a result, at various
times over the years, I was a director for about two dozen companies
– not all at once, I hasten to say – from Aber Diamond Corp. to Vector
Wind Energy Inc.

For decades in Canada, only the elite filled seats on boards of
directors. CEOs appointed their friends, oversight was minimal, and
directors acted simply as rubber stamps. That finally began to change
following a 1993 report for the Toronto Stock Exchange called *Where
Were the Directors?* written by Peter Dey, a former chair of the Ontario
Securities Commission.

As a result, the Toronto and Montreal stock exchanges instigated a
set of best practices guidelines. There were an increasing number of
directors appointed who were independent of management and more
committees created to monitor specific areas such executive compensation and reports from the auditors. Directors at all companies
worked harder, poring over thick binders of information sent several
days in advance of meetings. Among other improvements, bank
boards shrank from a crowd of as many as sixty directors down to a
more effective fifteen.

By 1998, I was serving on eight boards, two of which I chaired,
Siemens and Celanese Canada Inc. Even though corporate governance
was improving, there were still those in the business community who
resisted. As recently as 2004, I gave a speech at a retreat of Lang
Michener partners entitled "The Board Meeting? Not a Social Event."[1]
As pressure for improvement continued, audit committees gained
new powers and would regularly meet the outside auditors without
management in attendance. Search firms were retained to find new
directors rather than pick from the small pool of people previously

known to the company. New directors took orientation programs and toured company locations to familiarize themselves with operations. Of course, none of these improvements meant that every company performed well or management didn't make mistakes, but director timidity diminished and the tone and tempo of board meetings was vastly improved.

As directors, we weren't involved in the day-to-day business. In general, directors are supposed to keep management's feet to the fire. In that regard, some boards required more effort than others. One such "tough love" assignment occurred after I was named a trustee of the Clean Power Income Fund. Others trustees named at the same time in 2001 were John Fox, of Washington, DC, managing director of Perseus, an investment banking company, and Don McCutchan, international policy adviser in the Toronto office of law firm Gowling Lafleur Henderson. In 2005, we were joined by Sean Conway, a former Ontario Liberal MPP, who was director of the Institute of Intergovernmental Relations at Queen's University.

Although we were called trustees, we functioned as directors of the fund established by Stephen Probyn, president and CEO of Clean Power Inc. Stephen was a visionary who sought nothing less than a global green revolution. His Clean Power Income Fund owned facilities in Canada and the US that generated power using wind, water, and biomass. He had been in politics, working as an adviser for Margaret Thatcher, Nova Scotia premier John Buchanan, and Pat Carney when she was minister of energy, mines and resources.

Stephen loved to do deals, some of which had the unfortunate tendency of saddling his companies with assets that didn't always produce sufficient profits. After several years of increasing tension caused by management bringing to the board for approval what I thought were bad deals, I became fed up and threatened to resign. Stephen said, in effect, "That's probably a good idea."

At that point, other trustees intervened. The negotiated outcome was the creation in August 2005 of a special committee of trustees, aided by outside counsel, to investigate value enhancement opportunities. We all greatly admired Stephen, but we had to act in the best interest of all shareholders. I was not on that committee, but I certainly approved its existence. John Fox chaired the committee that included Don McCutchan and Allen Jackson, chairman of the board of trustees.

The committee oversaw the sale of a portion of the company in 2006 to reduce debt and, in 2007, arranged for the acquisition of the remaining assets of Clean Power Income Fund by Macquarie Power & Infrastructure Income Fund. I cite this case because it demonstrates the amount of work and worry that goes into a responsible position such as trustee or director. Joining a board is a demanding role, as well it should be. You are acting on behalf of investors whose money is at risk. I took such roles seriously.[2]

My board work also kept me connected with politics, not always to helpful advantage. In 1988, Siemens applied to the federal government for – and was granted – relief from paying duty on all imported medical equipment and parts. Budgetary and legislative approvals, however, were delayed until 1995. During that period, Siemens continued to pay the duties, always assuming they would receive a rebate going back to the 1988 decision.

As Siemens chairman, I wrote to Paul Martin Jr on 3 September 1996 in his capacity as minister of finance, seeking to recover the $828,000 in duties paid that had been declared no longer collectible in 1988. I heard nothing for two months, so I wrote again on November 5, enclosing a copy of the earlier letter.

A conference call was arranged for November 27, during which an assistant deputy minister in Finance said the department would be taking no action on the matter. We were told that Siemens would eventually receive an official letter, but the answer was no, there would be no remission of duties, no explanation why, and no place to appeal the decision.

Paul is to be congratulated for his fiscal probity as finance minister. There's no question that his scrupulous budgets set the stage for Canada's sound economic performance right through the global meltdown of 2008–09. But I'd like to think that any taxpayer, whether corporate or individual, would have received fairer and more transparent treatment from my officials when I was finance minister than Siemens did under Paul Martin Jr.[3]

A major benefit from my role as a director on various companies was being plugged into a constant flow of information. An Alberta Energy Co. board meeting in London before I was High Commissioner featured a discussion about a pending acquisition as well as a series of briefings on the international oil market, the state-of-play in the North Sea, and opportunities and problems in the Caspian Sea – especially Azerbaijan and Iran. Because Alberta Energy had discovered a kimberlite pipe (a sign there might be diamonds) while drilling for oil and gas in Canada, we also had a presentation about the global diamond market and the role of De Beers, the dominant firm in the business.[4]

While in London, I took the opportunity to call on the European Bank for Reconstruction and Development (EBRD) in my capacity as chairman of the Atlantic Council of Canada. The Canadian government was helping finance post-graduate programs in Central and Eastern Europe, so this was an occasion for briefings by EBRD on these newly emerging countries. For an insatiably curious person like me, such sessions provided a deluge of constant learning.

In addition to my role at the Atlantic Council, at various times I chaired many other not-for-profit organizations, including the International Development Research Centre, Institute for Research on Public Policy, Canadian Council for Public-Private Partnerships, the Design Exchange, and the Institute for Corporate Directors. I also raised money for York University, Friends of Cambridge, United Way, the Canadian War Museum, and the Corporation of Massey Hall and Roy Thomson Hall, among others.

Adrian gives back to the community as a member of the Justices of the Peace Appointments Advisory Committee. She is a board member of Shakespeare Globe Centre of Canada; a director of the Canadian Battlefields Foundation; a past governor of the National Theatre School of Canada; and works with Dixon Hall Music School, a community program for underprivileged children in Toronto's Regent Park. The two of us co-chaired the advisory board of the Trudeau Centre for Peace and Conflict Studies at the University of Toronto for eight years. In 2008, we both received the Arbor Award given by U of T in recognition of personal service to the university.

I believe deeply that community service is an essential part of being a citizen. In my convocation speech in 2000, when I received an honorary doctorate from the University of Toronto, I urged graduates to become involved. "As Canadians, we have received accolades from the UN over the past several years for the quality of our community. If we have deserved that praise, and I believe we have, it is not just because of government policies and actions. It is because millions of Canadians have devoted time and concern to make this a better place. Theirs has been a devotion that no government could command, nor corporation buy. My invitation to you is to engage, each in your own way, in community service to continue that record."[5]

It never ceased to amaze me how many times in life I was just one telephone call away from the next exciting assignment. I received just such a call in November 1995 from Brenda Elliott, Ontario minister of environment and energy, to chair the Advisory Committee on Competition in Ontario's Electricity System. I saw this opportunity as every bit as important as the Royal Commission that led to free trade. I was delighted to accept. I knew how such committees functioned, had a professional interest in the topic, and applauded Ontario premier Mike Harris for making a bipartisan appointment to such a crucial study.

Our daunting mandate was this: Should Ontario alter how it dealt with electrical power, long a monopoly under provincial control, and open it up to competition with private-sector companies that could build, manage, and maintain facilities for a profit? The other committee members were Jan Carr, vice-president, transmission and distribution division of Acres International Ltd, a consulting engineering firm; Robert Gillespie, chairman and CEO of General Electric Canada, a manufacturer of electrical products; John Grant, former director and chief economist at investment bank Wood Gundy Inc.; Darcy McKeough, CEO of Union Gas Limited from 1979–86; Sylvia Sutherland, a two-term mayor of Peterborough and chair of the Municipal Electric Association's environmental advisory committee; and Dr Leonard Waverman, professor of economics and director, Centre for International Studies, at the University of Toronto.

Since 1906, when Adam Beck founded the electric power system in Ontario, the goal was to create and provide public power at cost. Any surplus funds would either pay for expansion of the system or bring about lower rates. An editorial in the *Globe and Mail* at the time of my appointment called Ontario Hydro "the worst of all possible utilities: public but not accountable ... regulated only by itself, able to amass multibillion-dollar liabilities guaranteed by taxpayers." There were "years of bloated bills, unaccountable and secretive management, colossal public costs and serious waste."[6] It was hard to disagree.

There were high hopes for our work. "Mr Macdonald has become man of the kilowatt hour. The second Macdonald commission will hopefully prove as momentous for an open, competitive continental electricity market as the first one was for continental free trade," said an op-ed piece in the *Wall Street Journal*. "By properly privatizing Ontario's electricity system, Mr Macdonald may well salvage the hemispheric market reform process that his first commission helped to launch a decade ago."[7]

To be clear, our committee was not asked, "How do we privatize?" The question was, "How would you introduce *competition* to Ontario's electricity system, whether the assets were publicly or privately owned?" We were given just five months to study Ontario Hydro, the largest electric utility in North America, with $9 billion in revenues and 3.8 million customers. We were assigned several high-calibre policy staff members from the Ministry of Energy and spent less than $500,000, a modest total that covered all costs, including personnel secondment, administration, per diem fees for committee members, and our travel expenses.

As a monopoly, Ontario Hydro dominated the market through many advantages not given to business. Ontario Hydro did not pay income, corporate, or property taxes, giving grants instead to municipalities that were substantially lower than the taxes levied on private-sector companies. Water rentals paid to the province by Hydro did not reflect fair market value. Worse, the government used Hydro to generate revenue by adding the cost of social programs to electricity charges even though there was no relationship between the two.

Despite such favourable conditions, Ontario Hydro had serious financial issues. In planning for the future, Hydro added substantially to its nuclear generating capacity only to find that the anticipated demand was not forthcoming. The result was a burdensome debt load;

the cost of servicing that debt sent electricity rates soaring. When we asked how certain conditions had come about, or how relationships had developed, too often there was no institutional knowledge. The culture of Ontario Hydro was deeply bureaucratic. Many employees went about their jobs without giving a thought to better, more innovative approaches.

Our committee held public hearings in six cities – Toronto, London, Kitchener, Sudbury, Thunder Bay, and Peterborough. We heard seventy-three presentations and met with fifty-three groups and experts. We also received 223 written submissions as well as almost 300 letters, telephone calls, and other comments. Most supported increased choice and flexibility in products and services. They also wanted efficient and accountable rate structures. We could see that a monopoly on energy transmission might make sense (one set of wires could serve many), but there was no similar advantage when it came to producing energy.

Our report, entitled *A Framework for Competition*, was delivered to Minister of Environment and Energy Elliott on June 7, 1996. We did not advocate replacing a public monopoly with a private monopoly because a truly competitive marketplace requires a number of sellers. Instead, we recommended competing market units for power generation as well as separate, independent entities for transmission. We believed that market discipline was a far stronger method of identifying the true cost of electricity, while making sure that the cost was reasonable and fair. In our view, prices should be set by producers and consumers in a climate of open and fair competition rather than behind closed doors at Ontario Hydro.

In all, we made more than fifty recommendations under a theme of moving toward a competitive system, first in wholesale operations, then in retail, by bringing together buyers and sellers in a common marketplace, welcoming private investment, and running things on a more businesslike basis with no advantage given to Ontario Hydro.

In 1998, two years after our report was submitted, the Harris government began to take action by splitting Ontario Hydro into five parts, including Ontario Power Generation, which got all the generation facilities, and Hydro One, which took over the high-voltage transmission grid. Government said it intended to privatize both, but there were new problems. Seven of the nineteen nuclear power stations in Ontario had to be shut down. Repairs and refurbishments cost billions of dollars and went on for years.

The planned privatization of Hydro One, announced by Premier Mike Harris in 2001, was cancelled by his successor, Ernie Eves, in 2003. The Dalton McGuinty government, elected later that year, did not want to sell hydro assets either. Instead, it closed coal-fired plants in favour of gas-fired facilities, tinkered with pricing by continuing the freeze begun by the previous government, and then later putting into place a ten per cent discount.

I thought for a time that gas-fired plants would help increase the supply of electricity, but the costly cancellation of two such facilities by the McGuinty government in 2011 shows that that particular solution remains troubled. Nor was their plan to encourage numerous privately owned generation facilities ever fully functional. McGuinty's successor as premier, Kathleen Wynne, has the potential of being a great leader, but the baggage of the past weighs heavily upon her.

I can only conclude that the political arm can neither manage the energy file nor modernize hydro facilities with alacrity. The recommendations we made in 1996 were right not only for the times but also for the future. In the end, the political will for thoughtful change in Ontario did not exist. Many of the problems our committee identified still exist. While I believe that governments gave up too quickly, I may have underestimated the difficulty of moving to a more competitive market. Usually, when there is good will on all sides, great goals can be achieved. That did not happen in this instance. Today, private-sector energy companies will only invest in Ontario if they are granted long-term government guarantees.

Public opinion also played a part in what happened. Few people wanted to see the heritage generators at Niagara Falls run by a corporation motivated by profit. Governments could claim they listened to the voters. But, to my mind, their mistake was in not explaining what wrongs the policy was intended to right and why competition in electricity was the best outcome. I willingly accept some of the responsibility. Maybe if I'd taken it upon myself to convince the public of the need for competition, then they, in turn, would have put pressure on the government. I spoke out for free trade, but I had support from the Mulroney government. I couldn't have achieved much momentum in electricity competition without the backing of Premier Mike Harris and his successor, Ernie Eves.

Whatever the policy issue, it is incumbent on the government to explain, persuade, and convince the electorate. If you don't believe in something sufficiently to make a case, how do you bring about change? Political leadership of whatever stripe demands vision and execution or you're nothing more than static figures atop a wedding cake of rosy dreams.

Reflections on a Life

No, I never became prime minister. I never wanted to be the head of government and didn't need the role to establish my sense of self-worth. Going from an Ashbury boy in the visitors' gallery watching parliamentary proceedings all the way to the front bench of Pierre Trudeau's government was grand ride enough for me.

As chairman of the Macdonald Commission, I wasted no time on partisan matters or the petty side of politics. I was able to change the very nature of our economy forever by overseeing thorough research, envisioning a strategy, and making the case for free trade. The respect for our work has grown with the passing years. "Not for nothing was it nicknamed the Royal Commission on Everything," wrote columnist Andrew Coyne in the *Globe and Mail* in 1995, ten years after the report was issued. "It was instantly recognized, for good or ill, as a revolution in the making. The extraordinary thing is that, by and large, and to an extent unmatched by many such exercises before and since, that revolutionary potential has been realized. If Mr Macdonald's plea that the report's recommendations be enacted as a package was not fulfilled, neither was the prediction of the president of the Canadian Labour Congress, Dennis McDermott, to the effect that the $20-million report was 'deader than a dodo bird.'"

Free trade was not the only policy idea that gained traction. "Go through the commission's many recommendations and it is astonishing how many have been enacted, attempted or at least have achieved broad acceptance. Indeed, it is possible to interpret the last 10 years as having been spent putting the Macdonald commission's report into effect. In all likelihood, so will most of the next 10. Whether in Liberal or Conservative guise, we are now governed by the Macdonald Party; our national ideology is Macdonaldism," said Coyne.

Coyne went on to list recommendations that had been carried out, often with bipartisan support: privatization of Crown Corporations; overhaul of regional development grants; the designation of public money for entire sectors rather than particular firms; deregulation of transportation and communications; scrapping the last remnants of the National Energy Program; limiting regulatory scrutiny of foreign takeovers only to larger deals; reduction in overfishing; changes to timber stumpage fees; and a simplified personal income tax system with a broad exemption for savings.

In Coyne's view, economics had become mainstream. "If politicians of whatever stripe are today more inclined to listen to economists – if the economists have taken over the asylum – that is in part because economists' ideas are less foreign-sounding to the public at large. That is the enduring legacy of the Macdonald commission's work."[1]

I am sad to say that of all the policies proposed by the Macdonald Commission, the one that received the least attention was an issue that mattered most to me: help for the least advantaged in our society. Despite some advances, there has been too little progress in improving the plight of the elderly, low-income families with children, and the working poor. This systemic problem was among my major concerns when I addressed the nominating meeting on that fateful night in September 1961 when I first ran in Rosedale. I could give that same speech today, there remains so much to be done.

The same could also be said about some other issues. For example, I believe that all Canadians must have access to the best possible education. That includes technical skills training as well as a grounding in science, mathematics, and the arts that will foster more effective adaptability to the multiple changes in the environment that young people will face during their working lives.

Above all, we need to improve labour relations between teachers and provincial governments. The quality of education must not be subject to the vicissitudes of contract talks or the ups and downs of the economy. I am deeply indebted to half a dozen exceptional teachers who had a significant influence on my life. That high quality of leadership in the classroom is fundamental to develop not only reasoning and comprehension in specific subjects but also to inspire students to fulfill themselves to the greatest extent possible.

Throughout my life, no one was tougher on me than I was on myself. Whether it was doubts about my career choice while at Osgoode Hall or worries about my accomplishments as a Cabinet minister, I always wanted to do better. No amount of praise was ever enough to slake my concern that I was doing enough for my country. This was not about my ego; it was about my contribution.

In 1990, after I had been posted to London as High Commissioner, I awoke in the middle of the night and sat disconsolately on the side of the bed until Adrian asked, "What's the matter?" "I've been a failure all my life," I replied. She chuckled and said, "Have you read your CV lately?" On the one hand, Adrian was right. I'd been a Cabinet minister, chaired a Royal Commission, helped raise four successful children, met world leaders, and had people right across Canada urge me to run for leader of the Liberal Party. On the other hand, that's how I felt in the darkened bedroom.

That time in London was the last such miserable moment in my life. I can now look back and better understand what was happening. I was never one of those in public life who thought others hung on my every word. Indeed, I was more likely to lean toward humility and self-deprecation. After all, I was the one who said I didn't have the royal jelly to be leader. Others were aghast at my honesty. To me, such a realistic self-assessment was the only possible approach to life and how to live it. Moreover, I probably suffered from a mild form of what Winston Churchill referred to as his "black dog," those times when you are simply overcome by a negativity that wells up unbidden from within, despite personal and professional success at every turn. I believe I was able to use those bleak moments to propel myself into activity and accomplishments that went far beyond what I otherwise would have been capable of.

I also came to know that I had deep roots from growing up in the home of my forester father. Because of those roots, I stood tall, feared no one, and could not be blown over by any storm, from Alberta or anywhere else. Just as the novels of Margaret Atwood explore life as a journey toward self-knowledge, I have followed a similar path in search of understanding my authentic self more fully. For every one of us, that's the final, and best, frontier.

It is also true that others can sometimes see you more clearly than you see yourself. According to one description of me in a 1977 article, "He has all the new virtues. He is determined, disciplined, lucid and, in terms of sheer, cold intellect, he is brilliant. Emotional crusades don't impress him." None of this went to my head even though, along with my Cabinet posts, I was also chief political minister for Ontario in the government of Pierre Trudeau. For all the power I was perceived to possess, I saw myself as little more than a complaint department for people like Ontario MPPs who had gripes with Ottawa. "Any unallocated bitch is my problem," I was quoted as saying in that same piece. "I bat in clean-up spot."[2]

Out of all my efforts as minister for Ontario, I am most proud of how I worked with others such as Toronto mayor David Crombie and Canadian National Railways CEO Bob Bandeen to change the face and function of the city. In October 2012, as I walked hand-in-hand with Adrian to the launch of a new book, *The Power of Why*, written by my stepdaughter Amanda Lang, I couldn't help but think about some of the triumphs in which I was involved and the legacy I left behind.

We had travelled by subway to Union Station, and then walked west on Front Street. Visible up Simcoe Street was Roy Thomson Hall, the home of the Toronto Symphony Orchestra (TSO) since 1982. That concert hall would never have been built where it is now had I not intervened. I was able to move the site a few blocks east of the original intended location so that construction could be expedited and thus provide the cultural anchor for an area that had been little more than rusting railway lines and rundown factories. One year I was guest conductor at the annual Christmas concert in Thomson Hall. In a nod to my time as minister of national defence, the TSO played the "Colonel Bogey March." My instructions were simple: stop when the orchestra stops. I hope no one noticed that my left foot was still thumping after their last note.

The book launch Adrian and I attended was held in the atrium of the Canadian Broadcasting Centre, originally slated to be built in various Toronto-area locations, including suburban Don Mills.[3] I was part of the push to have it right downtown on Front Street, thereby adding to the growing nucleus of cultural, office, residential-tower, and tourism sites just west of the downtown. Planning delays and construction meant the Centre didn't open until 1993, at which time it joined the soaring CN Tower across Front Street that was built on my watch and quickly became an iconic symbol for Toronto throughout the world.[4]

Further east, Mayor Crombie and I helped bring about the creation of 14,000 units of low-cost housing in the St Lawrence Market area, the largest such development in Canadian history. The livable elements of that residential project continue to be copied across Canada today. By the time construction was getting underway, I had announced my resignation from Parliament. A photograph taken at an event in November 1977 to acknowledge the start of work shows me with the mayor. The picture is amusing because not only is he still shorter than me even though he climbed onto a chair to deliver his remarks but also I'm near an EXIT sign, an accurate description of what was happening next in my political life.

I cannot look upon any of these landmarks without feeling a sense of pride for the role I played. As the epitaph in St Paul's Cathedral for architect Christopher Wren says, *Lector, si monumentum requiris, circumspice*, "Reader, if you seek his memorial, look around you."

Of honours, I have received a few. I was granted the Freedom of the City of London that, among other things, gives me the right to herd sheep over London Bridge, something that I have yet to do. I am a Companion in the Order of Canada, the highest civilian order in the country. As a Cabinet minister, I was sworn as a member of the Queen's Privy Council for Canada, a lifetime appointment. I am proudest of the title "Honourable" that is granted to all federal Cabinet ministers. As the Honourable Donald Stovel Macdonald, I have tried to live up to my core beliefs, my underlying values, and that high calling.

No award or title, however, has made me happier than my wife Adrian. We are the loves of each other's lives and have been since 1988. In 2002, we sold our Toronto home on Marlborough Avenue and moved full-time to what had been our weekend place in Uxbridge. We added three bedrooms and two bathrooms so that the farm could sleep twenty and become the focal point of visits from our extended family of ten children and the growing number of grandchildren.

The farm was an idyllic place to celebrate occasions from Christmas to christenings, but after almost a decade, the commute to work, visit friends, or attend evening events in Toronto became onerous. In 2011, we sold the farm and bought a townhouse near Yonge and St Clair in midtown Toronto. Adrian and I are delighted to be living in the heart of the city again and revel in travelling everywhere by subway.

From time to time people ask, if I could live my life over again, would I do the same things. If I were young again, I would happily seek a career in public life. Running for Parliament was the best and most important thing I did. All other aspects of my life flowed from that moment when, all other possibilities having been exhausted, John Clarry turned to me and asked, "Why don't you become the candidate?"

Canada has been very good to me. And I hope I have been good for Canada. As I think about Canada, my feelings don't lend themselves to a balance sheet or a mathematical proof. Instead it's all about identity and community. I have a visceral sense that, of all the places on earth, this is *my* country, and of all the peoples in the world, these are *my* people.

Our present prosperity and high standard of living is proof that most of the problems of the past have been overcome. In addition to achievements at home, we have also made massive contributions that include our armed forces in two World Wars, the Korean War, United Nations peacekeeping, and, more recently, Afghanistan, as well as the talents of those Canadians who have won international prominence in their fields of science, entertainment, business, and the arts. I believe we have the will and the wherewithal to overcome any obstacles that stand in our way. Our dreams have always been as big as this land.

I have but three regrets in life. While I feel privileged to have attended Harvard and Cambridge, maybe I would have been wiser to take one of those years instead at Laval or the University of Montreal where I could have studied in French and become bilingual. My second regret is the death of Ruth in the prime of her life, just as she was finally coming into her own. The third was the passing of my parents when I was still young and did not yet have any children. I would have liked them to see their grandchildren and let me show more appreciation for all that they did for me.

As time passes, I have generally become more able to show my emotions. Perhaps this is universal for men as they grow older, become less competitive, and become more caring. Or maybe it's just my own mortality that's on my mind. All I know is that when old friends die, I find myself overcome with sadness. Talking about my own father, gone for more than fifty years, can still bring tears to my eyes.

As card-carrying members of the Liberal Party, Adrian and I continue to care about the party's future. I campaigned door-to-door when my stepsons, Timothy and Andrew, ran for Parliament. Anyone who knows Adrian is well aware there is no more committed Liberal. As Issy Sharp, founder of Four Seasons, once said to her, "Your public service and involvement in politics is in your DNA."

Recent party leaders Stéphane Dion and Michael Ignatieff both had commendable personal characteristics, but the party machinery was dysfunctional, out of date, and unable to help them. Bob Rae served as a distinguished interim leader who gave to politics and his country far more than he ever received in return. Had he come to us earlier, he would have made a great prime minister.

After a very open voting process in April 2013, more than 100,000 Canadians voted by telephone or online when Justin Trudeau was chosen leader of the Liberal Party. I believe Justin has the people skills and policies to lead the Liberal Party with honesty and integrity. But a party is more than just a leader; there also need to be lots of believers and doers. An article published on January 26, 2012, noted that the Macdonald Commission "led us out of a historical cul-de-sac and revolutionized our economy. It is a feat we need to repeat today, so Macdonald's triumph deserves our attention," wrote Brian Lee Crowley, managing director of The Macdonald-Laurier Institute, an Ottawa think tank. "Where is this generation's Don Macdonald? And where is the prime minister who will put him to work?"⁵ I am confident that such people exist in the Liberal Party that is being reshaped even now.

Beyond that optimism, I make no predictions for the future. I was never very good at prognostication. During my first news conference as minister of energy, mines and resources in 1972, I said I was "certain" a pipeline would be built in the Mackenzie Valley to bring natural gas south from the Beaufort Sea. We're still waiting.

While a memoir such as this is, by definition, about the past and not the future, I do have five hopes for my country and my fifteen grandchildren for that better world I tried to build. First, I hope that Confederation remains intact and that Quebec does not separate.

Second, long-term investments must be made to improve the standard of living, skills, and employment opportunities for the First Peoples of Canada. They will have a particular role to play as the Northwest Passage becomes a major thoroughfare between the Atlantic and Pacific oceans. It is essential that Canada should be in total control of navigation and all related facilities. Those who dwell in the region must be given every support in the task of helping to protect and preserve our North, a wondrous place that I first saw as a law student working for the summer and in my many later visits.

Third, I hope that Canada remains a haven and a hope where individuals can achieve great goals and where immigrants are celebrated. We must continue to be a civil society of freedom and tolerance where all races, creeds, colours, and religions are respected. We have been lucky to be spared the kind of ethnic tension that roils elsewhere. We cannot leave it to luck. We must protect our freedoms.

Fourth, Canada must remain an independent nation, not part of some United States of North America. Nor should we allow our companies and our natural resources to be bought holus-bolus by forces from abroad. Foreign investment is welcome, but we who live here should control the essential elements of our society, both public and private. In recent years, we have suffered the loss of corporate control as well as the disappearance of too many head offices and their high-paying executive jobs. Governments must constantly be on guard to step in and block any foreign acquisition that is not in the national interest. I'd be far happier, for example, if all three of our major steel companies – Algoma, Stelco, and Dofasco – had remained in Canadian hands.

Fifth, while I agree there is a place for privatization and outsourcing, I also believe there remains a crucial role for government. The responsibility may well be reduced from days gone by, but grand goals do matter, and only a national government can realize our mutual dreams. There also remains much to do abroad. Canada has the position, the means, and, I would hope, the continuing inclination to play a leadership role in the world. We should not be content to leave the conduct of international relations to the Great Powers. Our aim should be to ensure that the interests of the developing countries are taken into account.

We build all our tomorrows on the shoulders of those who have gone before. I am even more positive today about Canada and our bountiful opportunities than when I was a young man of twenty-nine just starting out in politics. We may never achieve the idealistic status of Peaceable Kingdom, but we must never stop trying.

Acknowledgments

I have been writing this memoir for more years than it should have taken! The transcription was done by three invaluable people: Hennie Price, Pat Stuart, and Barbara Carmichael. I thank them for listening to my antiquated tapes. McMillans law firm, known as Lang Michener when first they kindly gave me an office, has been nothing but gracious and supportive. It was with pride in the firm that I carried their card.

With 350 pages of my ramblings in hand, Ron Graham put it into chronological and readable order. I thank him. Robert Lewis then came on board and began the process of archival research and writing with me. He was invaluable until his work took him elsewhere. At this point, friends decided I definitely needed a firm hand, and Patrick Gossage, Ramsay Derry, Peter Rehak, and Ethel Teitelbaum moved me forward in various and important ways. The most important was asking Rod McQueen to take on the final manuscript. Rod had been with Robert Stanfield when I was minister of national defence and had worked with us on the Royal Commission on the Economy. I knew his talents. Rod's charm, ability, patience, and writing skills have brought this book to fruition. Thanks are not enough.

Rod enlisted Chris Nolan, who scoured the collection at Library and Archives Canada seeking documents of interest, as did Rod himself with seventy boxes of papers I donated to the Clara Thomas Archives and Special Collections at York University. York's archivist, Michael Moir, made his facilities available and was very supportive. Family members, friends, and former colleagues provided recollections and anecdotes that were essential in the telling of my tale.

Linda McKnight, my agent at Westwood Creative Artists, was indefatigable in her quest for a publisher and found enthusiasm at McGill-Queen's University Press. At McGill-Queen's, Executive Director Philip Cercone led a professional and creative team that included Paloma Friedman, Ryan Van Huijstee, Filomena Falocco, Rob Mackie and Eleanor Gasparik.

But, most of all, I want to thank my wife Adrian. She has been a patient participant and guiding hand throughout this project. On many occasions, she remembered details about key events that I had long since forgotten and made the task fun at every turn. Moreover, she had thoughtful insights as well as suggestions for improved wording on every page.

Without her, there would be no book.

Donald S. Macdonald
March 2014

Notes

LAC refers to Library and Archives Canada, Donald S. Macdonald Fonds R11042. The finding aid is available online at http://data2.collectionscanada. ca/pdf/pdf001/p000000924.pdf.

York refers to York University Libraries, Clara Thomas Archives & Special Collections, Donald S. Macdonald Fonds F0598. The finding aid is available online at http://archives.library.yorku.ca/icaatom/index.php/donald-s-macdonald-fonds.

Cabinet minutes are part of the LAC collections and can be accessed online at www.collectionscanada.gc.ca/databases/conclusions/index-e.html.

Cabinet Conclusions are also on the LAC website at www.collectionscanada. gc.ca/databases/conclusions.

CHAPTER ONE
1 LAC, 1-1.
2 York, 001(4).
3 York, 002(10).

CHAPTER TWO
1 York, 001(1).
2 York, 001(2).

CHAPTER THREE
1 York, 001(6).

2 York, 003(6a).
3 York, 001(7).
4 York, 001(9).
5 York, 002(8).

CHAPTER FOUR

1 LAC, 49-27.
2 *Light Blue,* Michaelmas 1957, 71.
3 York, 002(6).
4 York, 004(6).

CHAPTER FIVE

1 York, 005(5).
2 LAC, 1-8; for a complete list of my publications, see York, 049(1).
3 LAC, 1-11.
4 York, 006(3).
5 York, 005(8).

CHAPTER SIX

1 York, 006(7).
2 York, 006(10).
3 York, 006(12).
4 York, 006(9).
5 York, 072(1).
6 York, 008(1).
7 *Hansard,* December 14, 1962, 2659.
8 John English, *The Worldly Years: The Life of Lester Pearson, Volume II: 1949–1972* (Toronto: Knopf Canada, 1992), 250–1.
9 York, 008(1).
10 LAC, 1-3, 10-12, 55-19.

CHAPTER SEVEN

1 York, 008(9).
2 York, 007(1).
3 York, 008(11).
4 Pierre Elliott Trudeau, *Memoirs* (Toronto: McClelland & Stewart, 1993), 84.

5 York, 008(4).
6 York, 008(4).

CHAPTER EIGHT

1 York, 009(2).
2 Pierre Elliott Trudeau, *Federalism and the French Canadians* (Toronto: Macmillan of Canada, 1968), 178–9.
3 English, *The Worldly Years*, 354–5.
4 Don Peacock, *Journey to Power: The Story of a Canadian Election* (Toronto: Ryerson Press, 1968), 197.
5 For more on their conversation, see Ramsay Cook, *The Teeth of Time: Remembering Pierre Elliott Trudeau* (Montreal & Kingston: McGill-Queen's University Press, 2006), 47ff.
6 York, 009(7).
7 LAC, 21-19.
8 York, 009(7).
9 LAC, 50-12.

CHAPTER NINE

1 LAC, 122-5.
2 LAC, 49-18; York 055(5).
3 J.L. Granatstein and Robert Bothwell, *Pirouette: Pierre Trudeau and Canadian Foreign Policy* (Toronto: University of Toronto Press, 1990), 22. The cousin referred to was Lieutenant General Richard C. Stovel, who was Canadian Forces military attaché in Washington, DC, 1971–74, and Deputy Commander-in-Chief at NORAD in Colorado Springs, 1974–76.
4 John English, *Just Watch Me: The Life of Pierre Trudeau, 1968–2000* (Toronto: Knopf Canada, 2009), 555.
5 Trudeau, *Memoirs*, 196.
6 Gordon Robertson, *Memoirs of a Very Civil Servant: Mackenzie King to Pierre Trudeau* (Toronto: University of Toronto Press, 2000), 259.

CHAPTER TEN

1 Winston Churchill, *Great Contemporaries* (London: Fontana Edition, 1959), 254.
2 *Vancouver Sun*, September 5, 1968.

3 LAC, 131-1.
4 Paul Wells's blog, *Maclean's*, May 10, 2005. Accessed at http://web.archive.
   org/web/20050525032311/www.macleans.ca/topstories/politics/article.
   jsp?content=20050523_105939_105939.
5 York, 008(12).
6 *Hansard*, July 24, 1969, 11616.
7 York, 007(6).
8 *Hansard*, December 8, 1969, 1709.

CHAPTER ELEVEN
1 *The Globe and Mail*, September 26, 1970, A3.
2 *The Toronto Star*, October 13, 1972.
3 LAC, CC, October 15, 1970.
4 LAC, 241-10.
5 *Hansard*, October 16, 1970, 198.
6 Accessed at www.cbc.ca/archives/categories/politics/civil-unrest/the-
   october-crisis-civil-liberties-suspended/just-watch-me.html.
7 York, 026(4).
8 York, 010(1).
9 Robert Bothwell, Ian Drummond, and John English, *Canada since 1945:
   Power, Politics, and Provincialism* (Toronto: University of Toronto Press,
   1989), 374.
10 Trudeau, *Memoirs*, 149.
11 York, 072(2).
12 *The Montreal Gazette*, August 26, 1971.

CHAPTER TWELVE
1 York, 026(4).
2 York, 015(3).
3 *The Toronto Star*, October 31, 1972.
4 York, 012(12).
5 LAC, 242-2.
6 LAC, 233-5.
7 LAC, 233-9.
8 LAC, 138-4.
9 York, 014(13).
10 York, 027(1).

11 York, 026(10).

12 York, 012(13).

13 I am grateful to the Glenbow Library and Archives and the Petroleum Industry Oral History Project for sharing transcripts of interviews with Premier Peter Lougheed, Bill Mooney, David Mitchell, and others.

14 LAC, 242-13.

15 York, 013(1).

CHAPTER THIRTEEN

1 York, 016(7).

2 Cabinet document 1257-73.

3 LAC, CC, July 24, 1975.

4 Trudeau, *Memoirs*, 195.

5 LAC, 290-5.

6 LAC, 288-19.

7 Speech in the House of Commons, June 14, 1977, LAC, 289-5.

8 *The Montreal Gazette*, February 4, 1976, 37.

9 York, 016(8).

10 York, 022(4).

11 Michel, then only thirteen months old, must have been elsewhere.

12 York, 015(13).

13 Report by Canadian Press, *Ottawa Journal*, April 1, 1977.

14 *Calgary Herald*, September 7, 1977.

15 York, 027(8).

16 *Dealing with Inflation and Unemployment in Canada* (Toronto: Royal Commission on the Economic Union and Development Prospects for Canada and University of Toronto Press, 1986), 91.

17 York, 028(8).

CHAPTER FOURTEEN

1 York, 010(10).

2 York, 034(17).

3 York, 023(2).

CHAPTER FIFTEEN

1 Mackasey was elected, served two years, then resigned to run federally in a by-election in Ottawa Centre in 1978, but lost. In 1980, he was elected MP in

the Ontario riding of Lincoln. Marchand lost his bid for a seat in the Quebec Legislature but was appointed to the Senate and became Speaker in 1980.

2 York, 072(6).

3 York, 032(8).

4 John A. Munro and Alex I. Inglis, eds., *Mike: The Memoirs of The Right Honourable Lester B. Pearson, Volume 3* (Toronto: University of Toronto Press, 1975), 27.

5 *The Financial Post*, December 1, 1979.

6 York, 072(8).

7 York, 032(8).

8 York, 032(10).

CHAPTER SIXTEEN

1 LAC, 310-15.

2 York, letter to Pierre Trudeau, April 9, 1973, 026(8).

3 LAC, 324-16.

4 York, 035(4), 039(5), 042(9).

5 LAC, 337-10.

6 LAC 331-4.

CHAPTER SEVENTEEN

1 Gregory J. Inwood, *Continentalizing Canada: The Politics and Legacy of the Macdonald Royal Commission* (Toronto: University of Toronto Press, 2005), 248.

2 *The Toronto Star*, May 31, 1977.

3 York, 019(9).

4 *The Globe and Mail*, November 19, 1984, 1.

5 Michael Hart, with Bill Dymond and Colin Robertson, *Decision at Midnight: Inside the Canada–US Free-Trade Negotiations* (Vancouver: UBC Press, 1994), 34.

6 Statement issued by Gérard Docquier, May 30, 1985.

7 Quoted in a speech by BCNI CEO Tom d'Aquino to The Men's Canadian Club of Calgary, February 19, 1986, 11.

8 York, 072(4).

9 LAC, 358-8.

10 David E.W. Laidler and William B.P. Robson, eds., *Prospects for Canada: Progress and Challenges 20 Years after the Macdonald Commission* (Toronto: C.D. Howe Institute, 2005), 9.

11 York, 041(8).

12 York, 046(9-25).

13 *The Globe and Mail*, October 4, 2012, B1.

14 *The Globe and Mail*, September 19, 2005, A16.

15 *Inside Policy*, October 2012, 19.

CHAPTER EIGHTEEN

1 Craig Brown, *A Generation of Excellence: A History of the Canadian Institute for Advanced Research* (Toronto: University of Toronto Press, 2007), 56.

2 York, 055(3).

3 *The Toronto Star*, December 4, 1988, D1.

4 York, 057(8).

5 York, 055(10).

6 York, 054(5).

CHAPTER NINETEEN

1 Cited in *The Independent*, November 29, 1989, 18.

2 *Ottawa Sun*, January 11, 2004, 6.

3 York, 039(4).

4 LAC, 367-7.

CHAPTER TWENTY

1 York, 072(7).

2 York, 051(1-4).

3 York, 050(11).

4 York, 036(6).

5 York, 054(11).

6 *The Globe and Mail*, January 31, 1996, A12.

7 *The Wall Street Journal*, March 15, 1996, Robert Blohm, A11.

CHAPTER TWENTY-ONE

1 Andrew Coyne, "A Decade of Macdonaldism," *The Globe and Mail*, September 9, 1995, D3.

2 *The Toronto Star*, September 6, 1977, A9.

3 LAC, 10-13.

4 York, 023(10).

5 *Winnipeg Free Press*, January 26, 2012, A10.

Bibliography

Azzi, Stephen. *Walter Gordon and the Rise of Canadian Nationalism.* Montreal & Kingston: McGill-Queen's University Press, 1999.

Bothwell, Robert, Ian Drummond, and John English. *Canada since 1945: Power, Politics, and Provincialism.* Toronto: University of Toronto Press, 1989.

Brown, Craig. *A Generation of Excellence: A History of the Canadian Institute for Advanced Research.* Toronto: University of Toronto Press, 2007.

Cahill, Jack. *John Turner: The Long Run.* Toronto: McClelland & Stewart, 1984.

Chénier-Cullen, Nicole. *I Found My Thrill on Parliament Hill: An Entertaining Look at the Storied Life of Trudeau Era Cabinet Minister, Bud Cullen.* Bloomington, Indiana: iUniverse, 2009.

Clarkson, Stephen. *The Big Red Machine: How the Liberal Party Dominates Canadian Politics.* Vancouver: UBC Press, 2005.

Cohen, Andrew, and J.L. Granatstein. *Trudeau's Shadow: The Life and Legacy of Pierre Elliott Trudeau.* Toronto: Random House, 1998.

Cook, Ramsay. *The Teeth of Time: Remembering Pierre Elliott Trudeau.* Montreal & Kingston: McGill-Queen's University Press, 2006.

Danson, Barney, with Curtis Fahey. *Not Bad for a Sergeant: The Memoirs of Barney Danson.* Toronto: Dundurn, 2002.

Davey, Keith. *The Rainmaker: A Passion for Politics.* Toronto: Stoddart, 1986.

Dilks, David. *The Great Dominion: Winston Churchill in Canada, 1900–1954.* Toronto: Thomas Allen, 2005.

English, John. *Just Watch Me: The Life of Pierre Trudeau, 1968–2000.* Toronto: Knopf Canada, 2009.

– *The Worldly Years: The Life of Lester Pearson, Volume II: 1949–1972.* Toronto: Knopf Canada, 1992.

German, Tony. *A Character of Its Own: Ashbury College, 1891–1991.* Carp, Ontario: Creative Bound Inc., 1991.

Gillespie, Alastair W., with Irene Sage. *Made in Canada: A Businessman's Adventures into Politics.* Montreal: Robin Brass Studio, 2009.

Goodman, Eddie. *Life of the Party: The Memoirs of Eddie Goodman.* Toronto: Key Porter, 1988.

Gordon, Walter L. *A Political Memoir.* Halifax: Formac Publishing Co. Ltd, 1983.

Granatstein, J.L. *Canada's Army: Waging War and Keeping the Peace.* Toronto: University of Toronto Press, 2002.

Granatstein, J.L., and Robert Bothwell. *Pirouette: Pierre Trudeau and Canadian Foreign Policy.* Toronto: University of Toronto Press, 1990.

Gwyn, Richard. *The Northern Magus: Pierre Trudeau and Canadians.* Toronto: McClelland & Stewart, 1980.

Hart, Michael, with Bill Dymond and Colin Robertson. *Decision at Midnight: Inside the Canada–US Free-Trade Negotiations.* Vancouver: UBC Press, 1994.

Hustak, Allan. *Peter Lougheed: A Biography.* Toronto: McClelland & Stewart, 1979.

Inwood, Gregory J. *Continentalizing Canada: The Politics and Legacy of the Macdonald Royal Commission.* Toronto: University of Toronto Press, 2005.

Jamieson, Don. *A World unto Itself: The Political Memoirs of Don Jamieson, Volume II.* St John's, NF: Breakwater, 1991.

Jenkins, Roy. *Churchill: A Biography.* New York: Farrar, Straus and Giroux, 2001.

Kierans, Eric, with Walter Stewart. *Remembering.* Toronto: Stoddart, 2001.

Laidler, David E.W., and William B.P. Robson, eds. *Prospects for Canada: Progress and Challenges 20 Years after the Macdonald Commission.* Toronto: C.D. Howe Institute, 2005.

Litt, Paul. *Elusive Destiny: The Political Vocation of John Napier Turner.* Vancouver: UBC Press, 2011.

MacLaren, Roy. *Commissions High: Canada in London, 1870–1971.* Montreal & Kingston: McGill-Queen's University Press, 2006.

– *The Fundamental Things Apply: A Memoir.* Montreal & Kingston: McGill-Queen's University Press, 2011.

– *Honourable Mentions: The Uncommon Diary of an M P*. Toronto: Deneau Publishers & Co. Ltd, 1986.

MacNeil, Robert. *Wordstruck: A Memoir*. New York: Viking, 1989.

Manthorpe, Jonathan. *The Power and the Tories: Ontario Politics – 1943 to the Present*. Toronto: Macmillan, 1974.

Martin, Paul. *A Very Public Life, Far From Home, Volume 1*. Toronto: Deneau, 1983.

– *A Very Public Life, So Many Worlds, Volume 2*. Toronto: Deneau, 1985.

McQueen, Rod. *Leap of Faith*. Toronto: Cowan & Company, 1985.

Moore, Christopher. *McCarthy Tétrault: Building Canada's Premier Law Firm*. Vancouver: Douglas & McIntyre, 2005.

Mulroney, Brian. *Memoirs: 1939–1993*. Toronto: McClelland & Stewart, 2007.

Munro, John A., and Alex I. Inglis, eds. *Mike: The Memoirs of The Right Honourable Lester B. Pearson, Volume 3*. Toronto: University of Toronto Press, 1975.

Newman, Peter C. *When the Gods Changed: The Death of Liberal Canada*. Toronto: Random House, 2011.

Oliver, Craig. *Oliver's Twist: The Life and Times of an Unapologetic Newshound*. Toronto: Viking Canada, 2011.

Peacock, Donald. *Journey to Power: The Story of a Canadian Election*. Toronto: Ryerson Press, 1968.

Place, I.C.M. *75 Years of Research in the Woods: A History of Petawawa Forest Experiment Station and Petawawa National Forestry Institute, 1918 to 1993*. Burnstown, Ontario: General Store Publishing House, 2002.

Radwanski, George. *Trudeau*. Toronto: Macmillan of Canada, 1978.

Ritchie, Charles. *Undiplomatic Diaries, 1937–1971*. Toronto: McClelland & Stewart, 2008.

Robertson, Gordon. *Memoirs of a Very Civil Servant: Mackenzie King to Pierre Trudeau*. Toronto: University of Toronto Press, 2000.

Sharp, Mitchell. *Which Reminds Me ... A Memoir*. Toronto: University of Toronto Press, 1994.

Smith, Denis. *Gentle Patriot: A Political Biography of Walter Gordon*. Edmonton: Hurtig Publishers, 1973.

Stursberg, Peter. *Lester Pearson and the American Dilemma*. Toronto: Doubleday Canada, 1980.

Torontonensis, Volume LIII. Toronto: The Students' Administrative Council, University of Toronto, 1951.

Trudeau, Pierre. *Federalism and the French Canadians.* Toronto: Macmillan of Canada, 1968.

– *Memoirs.* Toronto: McClelland & Stewart, 1993.

Index

Note: Page numbers in italics refer to illustrations.

Aber Diamond Corporation, 224
Advisory Committee on
     Competition in Ontario's
     Electricity System, 228–30
Afghanistan, 97, 238
Aird, John Black, 184
Alberta, 126, 127, 131, 133, 134
Alberta Energy, 135, 224, 227
Alexander, Lincoln, 112
Alexandra, Princess, granddaughter
     of George V, 214
Algoma Steel, 241
Amirault, Claire (step-grand-
     daughter), 207
Amirault, Jane (step-grand-
     daughter), 207
Amirault, Kate (step-grand-
     daughter), 207
Amirault, Paul (stepson-in-law), 207
Andras, Robert ("Bob"), 159
Andrew, Prince, Duke of York, 214
Anti-Inflation Board (AIB), 157
Appel, Bluma, 207

Appel, Bram, 207
Arafat, Yasser, 118
Arctic sovereignty, 122
Argentina, 168, 203
Argus Corporation, 185
Armstrong, Elgin, 114
Armstrong, Jack, 133, 134
Arnold, Matthew, 171
Asbestos Strike (1949), 74
Ashbury College, 6–7, 15–16, 17, 64,
     115
Ashdown, Paddy, 186
Asia-Pacific Economic Cooperation
     (APEC), 203
As It Happens (CBC radio program),
     140
Athabasca tar sands, 128, 132–4
Atlantic Council of Canada, 227
Atlantic Provinces Economic
     Council, 192
Atlantic Richfield Canada, 132, 134
Atlantic Sugar Refineries, 53
Atomic Energy of Canada, 15

Atwood, Margaret, 211, 235–6
Austin, Jacob ("Jack"), 93, 129, 166
Auto Pact, 71, 196, 201
Azerbaijan, 227

Baldwin, Ged (Gerald), 106–7
Ball, George W., 90
Bambi (film), 18
Bandeen, Robert ("Bob"), 236
Bank für Gemeinwirtschaft, 187
Bank of Nova Scotia, 53, 184
Barber, Clarence L., 190, 198
Barlow, Curtis, 211
Basford, Ron, 179
Beauchesne, Arthur, 108
Beck, Adam, 228
Bégin, Monique, 179
Bennett, R.B., 115
Benson, Edgar J., 64, 65, 79, 103, 114
Berg, Arnie, 23
Berger, Thomas R., 65
Berlet, Ron, 222
Berman, Harold J., 26
Bernier, Ivan, 190
Berton, Pierre, 83
The Big Store (film), 158
Bilderberg Group, 186–7
Birgitte, Duchess of Gloucester, 214
Bishop, Harding, 69
Bishop Strachan School, 56
Bissonnette, Lise, 186
Black, Conrad, 216
Black Watch (regiment), 96–7
Blair, Tony, 221
Blais, Jean-Jacques, 179
Blaxhill, F.H., 5
Blocksidge, Terry, 219

Boise Cascade Corporation, 185, 224
Bomarc missiles, 68, 123
Bombardier, 204
Borden, Sir Robert, 27, 201
Borg, Julian (step-grandson), 207
Borg, Vincent, 207
Bork, Robert, 26
Borrie, Robert, 118
Bothwell, Robert, 97–8, 121
Bouey, Gerald, 159
Bourassa, Robert, 117, 118
Boyd, Liona, 177
Brain, Arthur Donovan ("Buggy"),
    7, 16
Brandon College, 12
Brazil, 203
Breton, Albert, 190, 193–4
Brewin, Andrew, 65
Brezhnev, Leonid Il'ich, 164
Britain. *See* United Kingdom
British Columbia, 173
British Council, 211
British Museum, 33
Brown, Craig, 204
Bryant, Michael, 187
Buchanan, John, 225
Buckingham Palace, 215–16
Buckley, William F., Jr., 186
Bulganin, Nikolai Alexandrovich,
    165
Bundy, William ("Bill"), 186
Burke, Edmund, 111
Burney, Derek, 206
Burns, Arthur F., 162
Burns, John, 115, 116
Business Council on National Issues
    (BCNI), 199

Caccia, Charles, 180
Cadieux, Léo, 96, 97, 114
Cadieux, Marcel, 166
Cairns, Alan, 190
Calgary Herald (newspaper), 162
Calgary Olympics, 210
Callaghan, James, 160, 162
Callwood, June, 83
Cambridge University, 26, 29, 30,
    31–2, 33, 75, 227
Canada: bilingualism, 84–5, 176,
    200; constitution, 188, 221; dollar,
    63, 88, 159; economy, 154–5, 157,
    159, 163, 204, 226, 233; flag, 71; in
    G7, 174; and GATT, 33; global role,
    203; health care system, 63, 71; in
    the Korean War, 19, 238; and
    NATO, 17; oil production, 126–9,
    132–4, 171–2; peacekeeping mis-
    sions, 122–3, 238; in Second World
    War, 3, 6, 14, 238; stance on
    China's representation at UN, 77;
    in Suez Crisis, 30–1; trading his-
    tory, 195–6; and the United
    Nations, 11, 30–1, 238. *See also*
    elections; Macdonald
    Commission; *individual
    provinces*
Canada Forestry Act (1949), 34–5
Canada in the City (festival), 211
Canada Life Assurance Co., 53–4
Canada Memorial (UK), 216–17
Canada Pension Plan, 71
Canada since 1945 (Bothwell,
    Drummond, and English), 121
Canada–US Free Trade Agreement
    (FTA), 202, 204

Canadian Alliance for Trade and
    Job Opportunities, 201
Canadian Armed Forces, 115, 157,
    238
Canadian Auto Workers (CAW), 202
Canadian Bank of Commerce, 57
Canadian Battlefields Foundation,
    227
Canadian Charter of Rights and
    Freedoms, x, 84
Canadian Corporate Management,
    61
Canadian Council for Public-
    Private Partnerships, 227
Canadian Forces Northern Region,
    122
Canadian House of Commons
    (Stewart), 108
Canadian Institute for Advanced
    Research (CIFAR), 205
Canadian Labour Congress, 58, 158,
    233
Canadian Manufacturers
    Association, 199
Canadian Utilities, 209
Canadian War Museum, 227
Canary Wharf, 215
CANDU nuclear reactors, 167–8,
    168–9
Caouette, Réal, 72, 73, 91
Carleton University, 16, 17
Carney, Pat, 225
Carr, Jan, 228
Carrington, Peter Carington,
    6th Baron, 186
Carstairs, John, 207
Carstairs, Sharon, 207

Carter, Jimmy, 160
Carty, Christopher (son-in-law), 175
Carty, Lucas (grandson), 175
Catto, Henry, Jr., 208
CBC (Canadian Broadcasting
    Corporation), 200, 237
Celanese Canada, 224
Chalk River Laboratories, 15
Chandler, Marsha, 187
Charlebois, Noreen Mary Terese, 22
Charles, Prince of Wales, 186, 215
Charlottetown Accord, 221
Chile, 203
China, 77, 165–6, 168, 169–71, 203
A Choice for Canada (Gordon), 78
Chou En-lai, 49, 169–71
Chrétien, Jean, 79, 133, 153, 162, 163,
    176–7
Churchill, Winston, 10–11, 106, 235
Cirque du Soleil, 211
Cité Libre (journal), 76
Cities Service (Citgo), 132, 133
Clark, Joe, 176, 177, 181, 182
Clark, Stanley, 35
Clarkson, Gordon (law firm), 60–1
Clarkson Tétrault (law firm), 223
Clarry, John, 54, 57, 58, 238
Clean Power Income Fund, 225
Coe, Sebastian, 212
Cohen, Mickey, 93
Cold War, 68, 72, 98
Collins, A.F. ("Chip"), 133
Columbia River, 172–3
Commerzbank, 187
Committee for an Independent
    Canada, 90
Commonwealth of Nations, 29

The Confederate (newspaper), 5
Confederation of National Trade
    Unions, 74
Conley, Marilyn, 212
Conservative Party (UK), 169, 220,
    221
Conway, Sean, 225
Cook, Ramsay, 82, 86
Co-operative Commonwealth
    Federation (CCF), 58, 60
Cornell, Ward, 167
Cornish, Judy, 211
Côté, E.A., 117
Council of Canadians, 199
Coutts, Jim, 159, 161, 178, 179, 181
Cox, Archibald, 26
Coyne, Andrew, 233–4
Crawford, Purdy, 25
Creighton, Donald, 70
Criminal Code, 116, 119
Crispo, John, 202
Croll, David A., 72
Crombie, David, 176, 236, 237
Crosbie, John, 181
Cross, James, 114, 121, 122
Crowe, Marshall, 166
Crowley, Brian Lee, 239–40
Culver, David, 201
Czechoslovakia, 17, 72, 73–4

Daily Express (newspaper), 219
Daiter, Harvey, 40
Daniel, C. William ("Bill"), 133
Danson, Barney, 179, 185
D'Aquino, Thomas ("Tom"), 201
Davey, Dorothy, 207
Davey, Jim, 84

Davey, Keith, 59, 161, 179, 181, 207

Davies, Robertson, 211

Davis, Bill, 22, 126, 133, 134, 153

Davis, John ("Jack"), 65

De Beers, 227

Decision at Midnight (Hart, Dymond, and Robertson), 199

Defence in the 70s (white paper), 122

Defence Production Sharing Agreements, 196

de Klerk, F.W., 218

Dell, Edmund, 156

Delta Kappa Epsilon (Deke), 17–18, 20–1

Denmark, 170

Dent, Frederick B., 167

Design Exchange, 227

DesLauriers, William, *40*

Desmarais, Paul, Sr., 184–5, 186

Le Devoir (newspaper), 162

Dey, Peter, 224

Diana, Princess of Wales, 211, 214

Dickie, Bill, 133

Diefenbaker, John: in 1957 election, 35; in 1958 election, 57–8; in 1962 election, 64–5; personality, 99; pro-British outlook, 58; relationship with author, 66–7, 128, 159; relationship with Pearson, 68; on Trudeau's safari suit, 81

Dillon, Dick, 133

Dino, L., 191

Dion, Stéphane, 239

Disraeli, Benjamin, 171

Dixon Hall Music School, 227

Docquier, Gérard, 190, 198, 199

Dofasco, 241

Dominion Bank, 53

Dominion Forest Service, 5, 17

Donaldson, Gordon, 76

Donat, Robert, 15

Douglas, Tommy, 72, 91, 112, 118

Douglas-Home, Alec, 187

Dow Chemical Canada, 192

Drew, George, 58

Drouin, Marie-Josée, 186

Drummond, Ian, 121

Drury, Charles Mills ("Bud"), 64, 81, 114, 176

Duplessis, Maurice LeNoblet, 74

Dymond, Bill, 199

Eden, Anthony, 30

Edinborough, Arnold, 87

Edward, Prince, Earl of Wessex, 212, 214

Egypt, 29–30, 127

Eigg, 4

elections: 1911, 201; 1958, 57–8; 1962, 64; 1963, 64, 68–9; 1965, 64, 69, 74, 78; 1968, 64, 90–1; 1972, 126; 1974, 131, 154; 1978, 176; 1980, 181–2; 1984, 189; 1988, 202

Elizabeth, Queen, consort of George VI (Queen Mother), *146*, 214, 217

Elizabeth II, Queen of Great Britain, *148*, 210, 214, 215

Elliott, Brenda, 228, 230

energy crisis, 125–32

An Energy Policy for Canada (green paper), 127

English, John, 85, 98, 121

Environment Canada, 192

European Bank for Reconstruction and Development (EBRD), 227
European Union, 160
Evans, John Robert, 176
Eves, Ernie, 231, 232
Expo 67, 81

Fairbanks, Douglas, 209
Falconbridge, John Delatre, 32
Al Fatah, 118
Faulkner, Hugh, 20, 107
Federalism and the French Canadians (Trudeau), 84
Financial Post (newspaper), 179, 200
First Baptist Church, 12–13, 67
First Nations, 240
Fisher, Douglas Mason ("Doug"), 75
Fisher, Harold, 35–6
Fitzmaurice, Sir Gerald, 33
Flanagan, Frank, 209
Fleming, Donald, 62
Ford, Gerald, 139, 172–4
Foreign Investment Review Agency (FIRA), 196–7
Fotheringham, Allan, 69
Fox, Bob (nephew), 55
Fox, David (nephew), 55
Fox, Ed (brother-in-law), 17, 34, 55
Fox, Harold, 54
Fox, Jim (nephew), 55
Fox, John, 225
A Framework for Competition (Ontario energy commission), 230
France, 30, 170, 174, 195, 218
Francis, Frank, 26, 27
Fraser, Blair, 8

Frayne, Trent, 83
Frazee, Rowland, 199
free trade: author's change of heart on, 196–8; effects on Canadian economy, 204, 233; international agreements on, 202–3; Mulroney's support for, 201, 232; opposition to, 198, 199, 202; previous prime ministers and, 195; Trudeau's opposition to, ix, 202
Freud, Sigmund, 178
Freund, Paul A., 26
Front de Libération du Québec (FLQ), 114, 115, 116, 117–18, 122
Frum, Barbara, 83, 140
Fuller, Lon L., 26, 156
Fulton, Davie, 82

G7, 174, 210
Gandhi, Indira, 48
Gaudreault, Amédée, 66
The Gazette (newspaper), 158
General Agreement on Tariffs and Trade (GATT), 33, 195, 203
A Generation of Excellence (Brown), 205
Germany, 174, 196
Getty, Don, 127, 129, 132–3, 135
Gibson, Gordon, 84, 207
Gibson, Kilby, 207
Gignac, Jacques, 131
Gillespie, Alastair, 9, 179, 207
Gillespie, Robert, 228
Globe and Mail (newspaper), 115, 162, 198, 203, 229, 233–4
Gloucester, Duke of. See Richard, Prince, Duke of Gloucester

Gloucester Street Convent, 6
Godsoe, J. Gerald ("Gerry"), 190
Goodman, Benny, 20
Goodman, Harry, 20
Gorbet, Fred, 93
Gordon, Walter L.: chair of Royal
    Commission, 189; inclusion in
    Pearson's 1966 Cabinet, 79; as
    Liberal candidate in 1962 elec-
    tion, 59; relationship with author,
    43, 60, 78–9, 105, 154, 196; resigna-
    tion as finance minister, 78–9;
    retirement from politics, 90
Goudge, Stephen T. ("Steve"), 62–3,
    182
Gouzenko, Igor, 13
Gowling, MacTavish, Osborne and
    Henderson (law firm), 22
Gowling Lafleur Henderson (law
    firm), 225
Goyer, Jean-Pierre, 84
Granatstein, J.L. ("Jack"), 97–8, 121
Granche, Pierre, 217
Grant, John, 228
Gray, Herb, 64, 155
Gray, John, 162
Great Canadian Oil Sands (GCOS),
    133
Greene, Joe, 88
Greenland, 170
Griffin, Anthony, 186
Griffith, Brian, 209, 216–17
Gulf Oil Canada, 129, 132, 133
Gunhouse, Joyce, 211
Gzowski, Peter, 83

Hamilton, Alvin, 127

Hamilton, Elizabeth (Dowager
    Duchess of Hamilton and
    Brandon), 210
Hamilton, William McLean, 190
Hampton, Lionel, 20
Haney, Reginald, 40
Harriman, Averell, 197
Harris, Mike, 228, 231, 232
Harrison, Jim, 9
Hart, Michael, 199
Harvard Business School, 57
Harvard Law School, 24, 25–6
Harvard University, 75, 76
Hayden, Salter, 53, 54, 59
Healey, Denis, 156
Heath, Edward, 167–9
Heeney, Arnold, 93
Hellyer, Paul, 79, 83, 88, 89, 98, 115
Henry, Charles, 60
Henty, G.A., 8
Hersey, John, 7
Hewitt, Adrian ("Bud"), 22
Highland Clearances, 4
Hill, Don, 27
Hitler, Adolf, 3, 15, 17
Home of the Hirsel, Alec Douglas-
    Home, Baron, 187
Honey, Russell, 84
Hong Kong, 222
Hood, Bill, 93, 159
Hopper, Wilbert Hill ("Bill"), 93,
    129
Hoveyda, Amir-Abbas, 172
Howard, Paul, 4
Howe, Elspeth, 214
Howe, Sir Geoffrey, 214
Hunter, Elsie, 7

Hurst, John, 18
Hurtig, Mel, 199
Hutchison, Barbara ("Bobbie"), 56
Hutchison, George (father-in-law), 56, 65, 119
Hutchison, Lillian (mother-in-law), 56, 119, 158
Hutchison, Ruth (wife): ambivalence about party leadership bid, 182; death, 205, 239; family background and personality, 56–7; illness, 99, 154, 204; in 1974 election campaign, 137; pictured with family, 142; work for CIFAR, 205
Hydro One, 230–1

Ignatieff, Michael, 214, 239
Ilsley, James Lorimer, 13
Imperial Oil, 132, 133
Income Tax Act, 113
India, 168
Inside Policy (journal), 204
Institute for Corporate Directors, 227
Institute for Research on Public Policy, 227
Institut Le Rosey, 171
International Court of Justice, 13, 33, 55, 212
International Development Research Centre, 227
International Monetary Fund, 160
Inwood, Gregory J., 196
Iran, 131, 171–2, 227
Israel, 30, 127, 203
Italy, 174

Jackman, Hal, 27, 68–9, 150
Jackson, Allen, 226
Jackson, E. Sydney, 184
Jackson, Meghan (granddaughter), 175
Jackson, Ned (son-in-law), 175
Jackson, Sarah (granddaughter), 174
James, Henry, 29
Jamieson, Donald Campbell, 97, 100, 114
Japan, 174
Jennings, Peter, 186
Jennings, Robert Yewdall, 29, 55, 211–12
Johnson, Daniel, 85
Johnson, Harry Gordon, 197
Johnson, Lyndon B., 71
Johnson, William, 198
Johnston, Don, 207
Judge, Thomas Lee, 173
Just Watch Me (English), 98

Karsh, Yousuf, 10–11
Keenleyside, Hugh, 93
Kellock, Roy Lindsay, 13
Kelly, Leonard Patrick ("Red"), 62
Kerr, Henry, 40
Keynes, John Maynard, 203
Kierans, Eric, 88, 98
King, William Lyon Mackenzie, 10, 22, 58, 61, 195–6
Kirby, Michael J.L., 180, 188
Kissinger, Henry, 166, 186
Knowles, Stanley, 107, 109, 111, 112, 118–19
Koocanusa, Lake, 173
Korean War, 19, 238

Kosygin, Alexei Nikolayevich, 164–6
Kremlin, 72

Labour Party (UK), 221
Laing, Arthur, 84, 114
Lalonde, Marc, 82, 83, 92, 100, 116, 130, 179
La Macaza, QC, 123
LaMarsh, Judy, 79
Lamontagne, Gilles, 186
Lamoureux, Lucien, 64
Lang, Adrian (stepdaughter), 120, 151, 207
Lang, Adrian Merchant (wife): commitment to Liberal Party, 239; community service, 227; conversation with Whitelaw on Thatcher, 220; dedication in memory of father, 217; earlier marriage, 120, 205–6; at launch of The Power of Why, 236–7; in London, 145–6, 149, 169, 210, 215, 216; maternal grandfather, 16; name, 208; during October Crisis, 120; pictured with family, 151; at Pierre Trudeau's funeral, x; relationship with author, 206–7, 209, 235, 238; religious denomination, 17
Lang, Amanda (stepdaughter), 120, 151, 207, 236
Lang, Andrew (stepson), 151, 207, 239
Lang, Elisabeth (stepdaughter), 151, 207
Lang, Gregory (stepson), 151, 207
Lang, Maria (stepdaughter), 151, 207

Lang, Otto, 120, 179, 206
Lang, Timothy (stepson), 151, 207, 239
Lang Michener (law firm), 224
The Lang & O'Leary Exchange (CBC program), 207
Laporte, Pierre, 115, 117, 121, 122
Laskin, Bora, 103
Laubman, Donald C. (Major General), 124
Lauk, Gary, 173
Laurier, Sir Wilfrid, 58, 83, 201
Lauterpacht, Sir Hersch, 33
Lavasseur, Pierre, 84
Lawrence, Barney, 17
Lawson, Nigel, 186, 219
LeBlanc, Dominic, 101
LeBlanc, Roméo, 101, 179
Léger, Annette, 132
Leitch, Merv, 133
Lesage, Jean, 35
Lévesque, René, 83, 122, 159, 162
Lewis, David, 65
Lewis, Stephen, 153
Libby Dam, 139, 172
Liberal Party of Canada: attempt to unify English and French Canada, 85; author's affinity with, 58; compared with NDP, 67; continentalist outlook, 61; future, 101, 239; in the 1962 election, 64–5; in the 1968 election, 91; in the 1972 election, 126; in the 1974 election, 131; in the 1978 and 1979 elections, 176; in the 1980 election, 181; in the 1984 elections, 189; opposition to free trade, 202; period of renewal, 74

Liberty (department store), 211

Light Blue (magazine), 32

Lightning Fastener Company, 54

Lipstein, Kurt, 32

Lockhart, Owen, 24–5

Lockhart & Trusler (law firm), 24

Lom, Herbert, 15

London, 214–15, 216–17, 223, 237

London School of Economics, 33, 76

Loss, Louis, 26

Lougheed, Peter: campaigning for free trade, 201; at government negotiations on tar sands, 133, 134, 135, *138*; relationship with author, 125, 134, 135, 158; stance on oil prices, 126

Lower, A.R.M., 23

Lynch, Charles, 110, 123

Lynn, Vera, 212

Lyons, Sir John, 213

MacAdam, Patrick ("Pat"), 219

McAfee, Jerry, 133

McCarthy & McCarthy (law firm): author and, 24, 35, 175, 179, 185, 187; management and clientele, 53–4; merger with Clarkson Tétrault, 223; size and reach, 185, 223

McCarthy Tétrault (law firm), 223–4

McCutchan, Don, 225, 226

McDermott, Dennis, 233

Macdonald, Althea (daughter), 64, *142, 151*, 175

Macdonald, Angus (grandfather), *37*

Macdonald, Angus (grandson), 175

Macdonald, Barbara Leigh (daughter), 63–4, *142, 151*, 175

Macdonald, Bill (lawyer), 181

Macdonald, Bill (uncle), *37*

McDonald, David, 122

Macdonald, Donald Angus (father): birth, 5, *37*; career, 6, 12, 14, 106; death, 34–5; education, 5, 16; as a father, 14, 15, 21, 176, 239; honorary degree, 222; wartime career, 5, *38*

MacDonald, Donald C., 60, 162

Macdonald, Donald Stovel: ancestral background, 4; baptism and near-drowning, 13; chairmanship of non-profit organizations, 227; chairmanship of Ontario energy commission, 228–30; childhood, 5–6, 8, 14–15, *39*; children and grandchildren, 63–4, 174, 207; corporate directorships, 135, 184–6, 224–7; education, 6–7, 9, 16–19, 21, 24–6, 29, 32–4; French-language ability, 83, 182, 239; great size, 9, 31, 98, 110, 210, 215, 237; as High Commissioner to U K, 145–9, 169, 206–7, 208–22; honorary degrees and fellowships, 21–2, *150*, 213, 222, 227–8; as House leader, 105–13; legal training and career, 22, 24–5, *40*, 53–4; marriages, 57, 206–7; as member of parliament, 62–71, 72–4; as minister of defence, 6, *45, 47, 97*, 114–24, 125, 236; as minister of energy, mines and resources, 125–35, *138–9*, 172–4, 187–8, 201, 240; as minister of finance, 154–8, 159–60, 163, 201; as minister without portfolio, 92–5,

96, 102–4; musical tastes, 20; nickname, 18–19; party leadership bid, 160–1, 177–83, 188; pets, *145*, 215, 217; prizes and awards, 23, 26–7, 130, 227, 237; residences, 7–8, 23, 56, 77–8, 175–6, 207, 238; retirement from politics, 160–3; satirical songs about, 130, 159; sporting prowess, 9, 19, 31–2, *41*, 54–5; at the United Nations, 75–6; views on NATO, 97–8, 115. *See also* Macdonald Commission

Macdonald, Hugh ("Sam") (uncle), 9–10, *37*

Macdonald, Ian, 130

Macdonald, Janet (sister), 6, 17, *39*, 55, 168

McDonald, John B., 54

Macdonald, Minnie (grandmother), *37*

Macdonald, Nikki (daughter), 64, 81, *142*, *151*, 159, 175, 205

Macdonald, Nona, 21

Macdonald, Salim ("Sam") (grandson), 175

Macdonald, Sir John A., 58, 70, 92, 195, 208

Macdonald, Sonja (daughter), 64, *142*, *151*, 159, 175–6, 208

MacDonald clan, 4

Macdonald Commission: cost, 200; members, *143*, 190; mission, 55, 189–90; Pierre Trudeau and, ix, 188; public hearings, 191–3; reception and implementation, 200–3; report and recommendations, 193–4, 195–200; retrospective

assessments, 203, 233–4, 239–40. *See also* free trade

McDonnell, James Smith, 186

McDonnell Douglas, 185–86

MacEachen, Allan, 88, 96, 113, 174, 181, 186

McGee, Ken, 23

McGillivray, Don, 158

McGill University, 56, 128

MacGregor, Kenneth R., 184

McGuinty, Dalton, 231

McIlraith, George, 114

Mackasey, Bryce, 66, 79, 155, 176, 249n1

McKeough, Darcy, 133, *138*, 167, 201, 228

MacLaren, Roy, 31, 180

Maclean's (magazine), 8, 69, 70, 75, 90, 108

MacLeod clan, 4

McLuhan, Marshall, 81

McMillan (law firm), 224

McMillan, Binch (law firm), 179

MacMillan, Margaret, 186

McMurtry, Denton, 58

McMurtry, Ria, 208

McMurtry, Roy, 208

McNair, Arnold Duncan, 1st Baron, 33

MacNeil, Robert (Robin), 8, 78

The MacNeil/Lehrer NewsHour (PBS program), 8

Macpherson, Duncan, *51*, *144*

MacPherson, H.P. (Reverend), 16

Macquarie Power & Infrastructure Income Fund, 226

MacTavish, Duncan, 22

Magna International, 204

Maitland, Alan, *140*

Major, John, 221

Mandela, Nelson, 218

Manitoba, 221

Mann, F.A., 33

Mansfield, Mike, 173

Manufacturers Life Insurance (Manulife), 184, 185

Marchand, Jean: entry into politics, 74; during October Crisis, 114, 116; and party leadership, 77, 80; resignation from federal politics, 176, 249–50n1; views on NATO, 98

Martin, Paul, Jr, 101, 207, 226

Martin, Paul, Sr: initiative to UN on China, 77; meeting with Alexei Kosygin, 165, 166; party leadership campaign, 83, 88, 89; relationship with author, 75, 81, 89; style in Cabinet, 96

Marx Brothers, 158–9

Massey Hall, 227

Matthews, Beverley, 53, 59

Meech Lake Accord, 221

Memoirs (Trudeau), 99, 122, 155

Merchant, Adrian. *See* Lang, Adrian Merchant (wife)

Merchant, Evatt Francis (Captain), 217

Mercosur, 203

Messer, John Rissler ("Jack"), 190, 198

Michener, Roland, 62

Mining Association of Canada, 192

Mitchell, David E., 135, 179

Mitchell, Joni, 211

Mohammad Reza Pahlavi, Shah of Iran, *50*, 171–2

Mondale, Walter F., 162

Montreal Star (newspaper), 75

Montreal Stock Exchange, 119, 224

Mooney, William J. ("Bill"), 132–3

Moreau, Maurice, 83

Morse, Wayne L., 173

Mulholland, William, 186

Mulroney, Brian: and Meech Lake Accord, 221; relationship with author, *149*, 222; relationship with Thatcher, 218, 219, 220; support for Macdonald Commission, 195, 201

Mulroney, Mila, *149*

Munro, Alice, 211

Munro, John, 89

Mustard, Fraser, 205

Mutual Life Assurance, 184

Nasser, Gamal Abdel, 30

National Archives (UK), 220

National Defence Act, 115

National Gallery of Canada, 209

National Liberal Federation, 22

National Press Club, 130

National Theatre School of Canada, 227

Nelligan, Kate, 211

New Brunswick, 167

New Democratic Party (NDP): in the 1962 election, 65; in the 1968 election, 91; in the 1972 election, 126; in the 1974 election, 131; compared with Liberal Party, 67; formation, 58; opposition to free trade, 202

Newfoundland and Labrador, 221
Newman, Peter C., 90, 107
Newnes, Simon, 212
Nicholson, Aideen, 180
Nixon, Richard M., 26, *46*, 156, 158, 166–7
Nixon, Robert, 153
North American Free Trade Agreement (NAFTA), 203, 204
North Atlantic Treaty Organization (NATO), 17, 97–8, 115, 120–1, 122, 184
North Bay, ON, 123
Northwest Passage, 240
Nozzolillo, Louie, 23
Nymark, Alan, 190

O.A. Brodin (ship), 27
October Crisis (1970), *44*, 93, 114–24
Ogilvy, Sir Angus, 214
oil prices, 126, 127, 128–9, 131, 132, 172
Oka Crisis, 215
O'Leary, Gratton, 8
Olson, Horace Andrew ("Bud"), 72, 101
Olympia & York, 214–15
O'Neill, Thomas, 57, 59, 62
Ontario, 126, 133, 134, 167, 228–32, 236
Ontario Advisory Committee, 102
Ontario for Trudeau Committee, 84, 85
Ontario Hydro, 229–31
Ontario Leaders Foundation, 178
Ontario Liberal Party, 27, 153, 231
Ontario Power Generation, 230
OPEC (Organization of Petroleum Exporting Countries), 128, 131, 172

Order of Canada, 71
Osgoode Hall Law School, 19, 22, 24, 32, *40*, 75
Ottawa, 65–6
Ottawa Journal (newspaper), 8
Ottawa Kiwanis Club, 128
Ottawa Normal Model School, 6
Ottawa Valley, 126
Ouellet, André, 176
Our Lady of Perpetual Help Catholic Church, 70
Oxford University, 31–2

Pai Hsiang-kuo, 169
Pakistan, 168
Palme, Olof, 186
Panarctic Oils, 125
Paproski, Steven, 158
parliamentary reform, 105–13
Parliamentary Rules and Forms of the House of Commons of Canada (Beauchesne), 108
Parti Québécois (PQ), 83, 122, 159
Pearson, Lester B.: international outlook, 58; and 1968 leadership campaign, 87–8; on party leadership, 179; personality, 99–100; relationship with author, 64, 80, 81, 203; relationship with Diefenbaker, 68; in Suez Crisis, 30–1; unification of English and French Canada, 84–5; and United States, 71; and Walter Gordon, 79
Pelletier, Gérard, 74, 89, 98, 101–2
Pennell, Larry, 79
People's Republic of China. *See* China

Pépin, Jean-Luc, 120, 157
Petawawa Forest Experiment
    Station, 14
Petawawa Military Reserve, 14
Peters, Angela Cantwell, 190
Peterson, David, 8, 202
Petro-Canada, 129, 201
Philip, Prince, Duke of Edinburgh,
    214
Picard, Laurent, 190
Pickersgill, John Whitney ("Jack"),
    10, 60, 109
Pickford, Mary, 209
Pickup, John Wellington, 24
Pictou, NS, 4
Pirouette (Granatstein and
    Bothwell), 97–8
Pitfield, Michael, 159, 190
Pitt, William (the Younger), 15
Plumptre, Beryl, 157
Porter, Douglas, 204
Potts, Joe, 88–9, 179, 180
Power Corporation, 184–5
The Power of Why (Lang), 207, 236
Powis, Alfred, 186
La Presse (newspaper), 74, 122
Price, Derek, 211.
Prichard, Rob, *150*, 180, 182, 187
Priorities and Planning Committee,
    94, 98
Probyn, Stephen, 225–6
Progressive Conservative Party:
    Beverley Matthews and, 53;
    Drew's leadership, 58; in the 1962
    election, 64–5; in the 1963 elec-
    tion, 68–9; in the 1968 election,
    91; in the 1972 election, 126; in the
1974 election, 131; in the 1978 and
    1979 elections, 176; in the 1984
    election, 189; Stanfield's leader-
    ship, 79, 91, 107, 109, 154
Prud'homme, Marcel, 118–19

Quebec: Alberta and, 126; Asbestos
    Strike, 74; Civil Code, 156; entre-
    preneurial culture, 191–2; 1976
    election, 159; nuclear power in,
    167; October Crisis, *44*, 93, 114–
    24; Quiet Revolution, 35; separat-
    ism in, 74, 117, 159, 240
Queen Elizabeth 2 (ship), 222
Queen's Own Cameron
    Highlanders (regiment), 28, 217
Queen's Privy Council, 105, 237
Question Period (CTV program), 160
Quiggan, George Robert
    (Reverend), 13

Radcliffe College, 57
Rae, Bob, 8, 239
Rae, John, 8
Ralfe, Tim, 119
Ralliement des Créditistes, 72, 91
Ralston, James Layton, 13
Ransome, Arthur, 8
Rapides-des-Joachim, 14–15
Rasminsky, Louis, 88
Read, John Erskine, 13, 195
Reagan, Ronald, 197, 201
Reichmann, Paul, 214
Reid, Tim, 86
Reisman, Heather, 207
Reisman, Simon, 201
Report on Business (journal), 130

Richard, Prince, Duke of
Gloucester, 214
Richardson, Elliot, 26
Richardson, James, 176
Riddell, W. Craig, 163
Riding Mountain National Park, 12
Ritchie, Cedric E., 184, 185
Robert, J.J. Michel, 190
Roberts, John, 110–11, 186
Roberts, Leslie, 75
Robertson, Colin, 199
Robertson, Dalton, 200
Robertson, Gordon, 78, 93, 102, 128
Robertson, Norman, 93
Robinette, John J., 54, 102
Robinson, Kathryn, 180, 182
Robson, William B.P. ("Bill"), 200–1
Rockcliffe Public School, 55–6
Rockefeller, David, 186
Roman, Stephen B., 187
Roman, Tess, 211
Romania, 168
Roosevelt, Franklin D., 61
Rosedale (riding), 27, 57–60, 62, 126,
176, 182
Rosedale Liberal Association, 57, 58
Rotstein, Abraham, 90
Rowell, Newton Wesley, 27
Royal Air Force, 5, 216
Royal Canadian Air Force, 4, 216
Royal Canadian Army Corps, 57
Royal Canadian Military Institute,
168
Royal Canadian Mounted Police
(RCMP), 70, 117, 119, 122, 157
Royal Commission on Bilingualism
and Biculturalism, 200

Royal Commission on Corporate
Concentration, 185
Royal Commission on the
Economic Union and
Development Prospects for
Canada. See Macdonald
Commission
Royal Edinburgh Military Tattoo,
211
Royal Flying Corps, 5
Royal New Zealand Air Force, 216
Roy Thomson Hall, 227
Ruckelshaus, William, 26
Ruth, Nancy, 27
Rutter, Frank, 173

Sacre Coeur Catholic Church, 69
Safarian, A. Edward, 189
St Laurent, Louis, 10, 35, 58
St Luke's United Church, 69
St Peter's Anglican Church, 69
Saint Pierre and Miquelon, 170
Salomon Brothers, 187
Saskatchewan, 131
Saturday Night (magazine), 87
Saudi Arabia, 131, 172
Scales, Larry, 23
Schick, Werner B., 187
Schmidt, Helmut, 47, 124, 160, 162,
174, 186
Schwartz, Gerry, 207
Scotiabank, 53, 184
Scotland, 4, 28
Scott, Austin Wakeman, 26
Scott, David, 8
Scott, Ian, 8, 181
Scottish National War Memorial, 28

Scowen, Reed, 211
Seaforth Highlanders (regiment), 217
Seaman, Daryl, 190
Segal, Hugh, 187
Sellers, Bob, 133
Shaker, Paul (son-in-law), 175
Shaker, Salim ("Sam") Macdonald (grandson), 175
Shakespeare Globe Centre of Canada, 227
Sharp, Isadore ("Issy"), 239
Sharp, Mitchell: in 1962 election, 62; in Cabinet, 79, 87, 100–1, 166; on Nixon's tan, 167; during October Crisis, 114, 118; stance on NATO, 97
Shaw, Artie, 20
Shell Canada, 129, 133–4, 185
Shenkman, Belle, 216
Shoyama, Thomas ("Tommy"), 93, 133, 154, 158, 161, 190
Shultz, George Pratt, 160
Sibley, Leonard, 7
Siemens Electric, 185, 224, 226
Simon, William, 130
Simpson, B. Napier, 175
Skelton, O.D., 93
Smallwood, Joey, 88
Smart, Angus, 4
Smith, David Chadwick, 190
Smith, Desmond (General), 216
Smith, Ernest ("Smokey"), 146, 217
Smith, Harold, 167
Smith, Stuart Lyon, 178
Social Credit Party, 65, 101
Sofía, Queen of Spain, 186

Le Soleil de Québec (newspaper), 66
Soros, George, 186
South Africa, 218
South Korea, 168, 203
Soviet Union: author's visit to, 72–3; in the Cold War, 68; Gouzenko Affair, 13; membership in WTO, 203; Protocol of Consultations with, 97; in Suez Crisis, 29; take-over of Czechoslovakia, 17
SS Princess Helene, 10
Stacey, Barry, 209, 215
stagflation, 131, 156
Stalin, Joseph, 164–5
Stanbury, Robert, 22, 83
Stanfield, Robert: attacked over parliamentary reform, 111, 112; election to party leadership, 79; failure to defeat government, 87–8; in 1968 election, 91; in 1972 election, 126; in 1974 election, 154; and Quebec, 85, 118
Starr, Michael, 72
Statten, Taylor, II, 174
Stelco, 241
Stevens, Geoffrey, 162
Stevens, Sinclair McKnight, 22
Stewart, Ian, 161
Stewart, James, 75
Stewart, John, 108
Stirling, Grote, 115
Stollery, Peter, 180
Stone, Arthur, 25
Stovel, Chester (maternal grandfather), 6, 168
Stovel, Harry (uncle), 3
Stovel, Lloyd (uncle), 3

Stovel, Marjorie (mother), 4–5, 6, 12, 15, *39*, 56
Strong, Maurice, 129
Suez Crisis, 29–31
Sung, Alfred, 211
Sun Life Assurance, 224
Supreme Court of Canada, 103, 157
Sutherland, Donald, 211
Sutherland, Sylvia, 228
Sweden, 193
Swiss Bank Corporation, 187
Sykes, Rod, 120
Syncrude Canada, 132, 133–4, 201
Syria, 127

Taiwan, 77, 165–6
Tang, Nancy, 169–70
Tang Ke, 169
tar sands, 128, 132–4
Taylor, Ashley (stepson-in-law), 207
Taylor, Gavin (step-grandson), 207
Taylor, Victoria (step-grand-daughter), 207
Teitelbaum, Ethel, 82–3
Teitelbaum, Mashel, 82
Telegram (newspaper), 60, 75, 162
10 Downing Street, 168, 219
Tesher, Ellie, 210
Thatcher, Denis, 220
Thatcher, Margaret, *147*, 169, 214, 218–21, 225
Thomson, Shirley, 209
Timbrell, Dennis, 133
Time (magazine), 65
Today (NBC program), 130
Toronto, 210, 236, 237
Toronto-Dominion Bank, 204

Toronto Flying Club, 61
Toronto Star (newspaper), 60, 67, 116, 210
Toronto Stock Exchange, 224
Toy, Sam, 21
TransCanada PipeLines, 54, 224
Tremblay, Michel, 211
Trepanier, John O., 35
Tresilian, Robert, 54
Trinity College (University of Toronto), 17, 21–2
Trinity Hall, Cambridge, 26, 29, 213
Trudeau, Justin, x, 101, 159, 239
Trudeau, Margaret, 99, *137*
Trudeau, Pierre Elliott: on author's character, 98–9, 155; British view of, 220; energy policy, 128–9; and John Turner, 153–4; leadership style, 93, 94, 95–6, 99–100, 161–2; Liberal leadership campaign, *42*, 82–9; 1968 election, 90–1; 1974 election, 131, *137*; 1980 election, 181–2; and the October Crisis, 114, 116, 117, 119, 122; opposition to free trade, ix, 202; opposition to Meech Lake, 221; patriation of constitution, 188; personality, x, 76–7, 80–1, 86, 91; relationship with author, ix, 76, *141*, 154, 161–2, 176–8; resignation as party leader, 178
Trudeau, Sacha, 159
Trudeau Centre for Peace and Conflict Studies, 227
True North (exhibition), *148*
Truman, Harry S., 197
Trushak, Terry, 133

Turner, John: in Cabinet, 79, 89, 116; and Liberal leadership, 88, 177, 181; as minister of finance, 153, 155, 166; in 1962 election, 64, 65; opposition to free trade, 202; as prime minister, 189; relationship with author, 101, 178–9

Union Bank of Switzerland, 187
Union Carbide Corporation, 53
United Kingdom: end of empire, 29, 31; in G7, 174; 1974 election, 167, 169; relationship with Canada, 195, 210–11, 213, 216, 218, 220; in Suez Crisis, 30
United Nations: author's speeches to, 75–6, 97; and China, 77, 165; drafting of charter, 11; and GATT, 33; peacekeeping missions, 30–1, 122–3, 238
United States: Atlantic coast, 170; economy, 156, 171; in G7, 174; imports of Canadian oil, 128, 130, 139; relations with United Kingdom, 210, 220; in Suez Crisis, 30; support for Taiwan, 77, 165; trade relations with Canada, 195–6; Vietnam War, 71; Watergate, 26, 167
United Way, 227
University of London, 33
University of New Brunswick, 5, 16–17, 222
University of Ottawa, 83
University of Paris, 76
University of Toronto, 17–18, 75, 227

University of Toronto Law School, 187
University of Victoria, 175
University of Western Ontario, 57
Upper Canada College, 9
Urquhart, Eileen, 23

Vance, Cyrus, 184
Vancouver Olympics, 97
Vancouver Sun (newspaper), 173
Vector Wind Energy, 224
Venezuela, 131
Vietnam, 71, 73

Wach, Grant, 212
Wadds, Jean Casselman, 143, 190
Walker, David James, 58–9, 60, 64, 167
Walker, James, 54
Wallace, Catherine Theresa, 190
Wall Street Journal (newspaper), 162, 229
War Measures Act, x, 116, 117, 118, 119
Warren, Jack Hamilton ("Jake"), 167, 169, 173
Watergate, 26, 167
Waterloo, Battle of, 4
Waverman, Leonard, 228
Wellington, Arthur Wellesley, Duke of, 4
Wells, Paul, 108
Western Guard, 70
West Germany, 174, 196
Westminster, Gerald Grosvenor, 6th Duke of, 208
Westminster Abbey, 211

Weston, Garry, 214

Whelan, Eugene F., 64, 100

Where Were the Directors? (Dey), 224

Whitaker, Bud, 19

White House, 166

Whitelaw, William Whitelaw, 1st Viscount, 220

Wilde, Oscar, 113

Wills, Terry, 159

Wilson, Harold, 169

Wilson, Teddy, 20

Winnipeg General Strike (1919), 118

Winters, Robert, 79, 83, 88, 89

Wishart, David, 180

Wonnacott, Paul, 197

Wonnacott, Ronald J., 197

World Trade Organization, 33, 203

World War I, 168, 216, 238

World War II, 3, 6, 14, 164–5, 216, 217, 238

Wren, Christopher, 237

Wright, Richard ("Tuscar"), 7

Wynne, Kathleen, 231

Yamani, Ahmed Zaki, 25–6, 131, 172

Yanover, Jerry, 108

Yes Minister (BBC program), 93

Yom Kippur War, 127, 131

York University, 175, 227

Young, John Humphrey, 197

Younger, George, 218

The Young Mr Pitt (film), 15

Yukon, 23

Zhou Enlai, 49, 169–71